The Chakras in
Shamanic Practice

Eighth Chakra
White Light • Expansion • 70+ Years
Radiance • Expansion vs. Limiting Attachment

Seventh Chakra
Violet • Loving Each Other • 55–70 Years
Spiritual Connection • Mastery vs. Distraction

Sixth Chakra
Indigo • Helping Each Other • 40–55 Years
Clear Sight, Intuition • Integrity vs. Despair

Fifth Chakra
Blue/Turquoise • Ether, Arutam
25–40 Years
Expression, Power to Manifest
Generativity vs. Stagnation

Fourth Chakra
Green • Air • 18–25 Years
Compassion, Forgiveness
Intimacy vs. Isolation

Third Chakra
Yellow • Fire • 12–18 Years
Will, Identity, Commitment
Identity vs. Confusion

Second Chakra
Orange • Water • 6–12 Years
Creativity, Emotion, Sensuality
Industry vs. Inferiority

First Chakra
Red • Earth • 0–6 Years
Trust, Groundedness
Trust vs. Mistrust

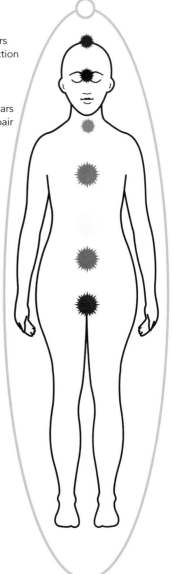

The Chakras and the Energy Body

The Chakras in Shamanic Practice

Eight Stages of Healing and Transformation

SUSAN J. WRIGHT

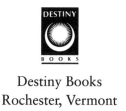

Destiny Books
Rochester, Vermont

Destiny Books
One Park Street
Rochester, Vermont 05767
www.DestinyBooks.com

Destiny Books is a division of Inner Traditions International

Note to the reader: *This book is intended as an informational guide. The techniques and exercises described herein are not meant to be a substitute for professional medical or mental health care or treatment. They should not be used to treat a serious condition without prior consultation with a qualified health care professional.*

Library of Congress Cataloging-in-Publication Data

Wright, Susan J. (Susan Jane), 1960–
  The chakras in shamanic practice : eight stages of healing and transformation / Susan J. Wright.
    p. cm.
  Includes bibliographical references and index.
  ISBN-13: 978-1-59477-184-2
  ISBN-10: 1-59477-184-7
  1. Chakras—Miscellanea. 2. Shamanism—Miscellanea. 3. Mental healing. I. Title.
  BF1442.C53W75 2007
  131—dc22

                                                              2007011667

Printed and bound in the United States by Lake Book Manufacturing

10 9 8 7 6 5 4 3 2 1

Illustrations by Doreen Grozinger
Photography by Sham Seelenfreund

Text design by Virginia Scott Bowman and layout by Priscilla Baker
This book was typeset in Sabon

To send correspondence to the author of this book, mail a first-class letter to the author c/o Inner Traditions • Bear & Company, One Park Street, Rochester, VT 05767, and we will forward the communication.

To my mother, Jane Alice, who set me free to be my authentic self, and to my daughter, Kelly Claire, who has captured my heart for eternity

Contents

Foreword

Late at night, the surf thundered against the Florida beach. As I struggled out of the water I thought I heard the sound of drumming. Peering toward the dark land, seeing nothing, I concluded that it was an illusion, the breakers echoing off sand dunes and distant buildings.

It was the next-to-last night together for our group of about sixty men and women who had spent the past three days in a workshop dedicated to transforming the world into a better place. We had just shared a powerful ceremony, connecting with the earth of the beach, the fire in the stars, the air from the wind, the water of the ocean, and what the Shuar of the Amazon call "Arutam," the Quechua of the Andes, "Ushai" and the Tibetans, "Ether." This Fifth Element is known by indigenous cultures around the world as a force that enables us to change our individual consciousness and, in doing so, the world. Many of us had ended the ceremony by plunging into the Atlantic.

I stood on the beach for a moment breathing in the salty air and admiring the moon that was rising phantomlike from the waves, nearly full, an orange beacon that seemed to pull me out into the universe, like a physical confirmation of the shamanic belief that we are all one, there is no separation. I thought of a similar night when Don Esteban Tamayo, the great Otavalan shaman from the high Andes of Ecuador, had seen the moon's reflection on the ocean for the first time in his life. "*El camino del Yachak,*" He exclaimed. "The shaman's path."

The drumming grew louder. There was no longer any doubt in my mind that it was not the surf. I turned away from the moon and followed the light it cast up the beach, toward that sound. My eyes adjusted; a shadow materialized. Moving. Dancing. Slowly at first, then quickening with the rhythm of the drum. Faster and faster, bending, swirling, gyrating in the moonlight—flying along the shaman's path.

I took several steps toward this apparition, wondering if I had somehow emerged from the ocean into another dimension, another time or place, and knowing at the same time that I had not. I was on this beach, bathed by the wind and the moon, experiencing the magic of a special moment.

As I approached, the outline of the drummer seated on the sand joined that of the dancer. Several other shadowy figures clustered around them. Someone came up and nudged me. "Susan Wright's dancing the elements," a woman's voice purred. "Isn't she incredible?"

I had known Susan as a therapist and devotee of shamanism and shapeshifting, a student of mine and a beautiful, compassionate soul who reached out to heal and comfort those in need; but this was a side of her I had never seen before. I stood on the beach that night, transfixed, as she danced the elements in the light of the moon, accompanied by the surf and the drum.

Afterward I walked her back to the hotel where the workshop participants were staying. "It's my passion," she said with that contagious smile of hers. "Dancing is shapeshifting and healing. It doesn't matter how old you are or what physical condition you're in, you can always dance in one way or another."

The next morning, at my invitation, Susan led all of us at the workshop through the Dance of the Chakras. She was right; she taught us moves that were easy for everyone. Not only was it invigorating and fun; it was also extremely powerful, transformational work.

Since then Susan and I have cofacilitated several workshops. For me, it is always an ecstatic experience. Her creations epitomize the true meaning of *magic*. They take us to new levels of consciousness, empowering us to accomplish goals we previously only imagined, to realize our deepest dreams.

I am so pleased that Susan Wright now is sharing herself and her magic with a wider audience, through this wonderful book.

Read, learn, enjoy—and shapeshift yourself and the world.

JOHN PERKINS

John Perkins is *The New York Times* bestselling author of *Confessions of an Economic Hit Man, Shapeshifting, The World Is As You Dream It, Psychonavigation, The Stress-Free Habit,* and *Spirit of the Shuar.*

Acknowledgments

I'd like to express my sincere appreciation to all who supported the process of this book at Inner Traditions; especially Jon Graham, who encouraged me to go as deep as I dared to find my truest voice, and Vickie Trihy, who used her creative expertise to deftly arrange the emergent intricate songs of my spirit. I am thrilled that many people will now read the music of this book and sing their own songs of beauty.

Thank you to John Perkins for your enthusiastic responses to the earliest seeds of this book and your masterful feedback and tireless encouragement. This is my tree, John!

Thank you to all my teachers, students, clients, and friends for the opportunity to keep learning, refining my skills, growing, and enjoying.

The sacred circle of living goddesses that surround me fill my heart with poetry. I am deeply grateful for all their support. Thank you Rebecca Kane, Leigh Reeves, Sara Rubin, Lynne Berrett, Robin Kupietz, Cathy Sweet, Shelley Volk, Andrea Cannistraci, Rhona Wexler, Andrea Ossip, Geri Pelliccio, Marion LoGuidice, Roberta Omin, and Kelly Jamieson. I am also nourished by the memories of those living afar, including Renie, Cat, Wendy, Mary, Bee, Naomi, Shirley, Andrea,

Rivka, Lauren, Steve, Susan, Liana, Seleka, and Hermene, and the dead, including Betty, Frank, Margaret, Spoof, Evgen, and Patrice.

Thank you to my strong and sweet brother, Kevin, for surviving childhood with me and expressing interest in this book, and to Francis, my daughter's consistent and devoted father. And thank you to Eric for your patience, Scott for your loyalty, and especially my dear Mark, for your amazing expandable heart.

Thank you, Pachamama, for life itself, and thank you to the substance and spirit of the trees that hold these many words.

Introduction
Evolution of a Shaman

I often tell people that after my devastating childhood, I had to rebuild myself from toothpicks and gum, matchsticks and tape, because what was left was so fragmented and fragile. I frequently felt as though I was building a model without any kit or plan. I worked hard at it, with diligence, consistency, and passion, and am now essentially whole. Because of this fragmentation and conscious reconstruction I have been blessed with practical knowledge about healing that generalizes to other people. As a shaman I can support people only in making connections I have already made for myself; I can safely take people only places I have already gone.

This book presents a process for healing that has been many years in the making. It is rooted in the teachings of the shamans from indigenous cultures, but also integrates wisdom drawn from diverse cultures and spiritual orientations. While its underlying concepts of developmental crisis are drawn from Western psychology, the tasks we will use to address and heal these challenges are derived from the earth-centered practice of shamanism. These ancient practices and ceremonies effectively address the unhealed wounds we all hold in our histories that keep us from moving forward as individuals and as a humane culture.

As a shaman, when I teach I always engage my students in an experiential activity before I begin to directly discuss the topic of the class. This allows the concepts to emerge from an organic, heart-centered place, rather than the narrow, limited realm of linear logic. In this book I may offer this experience through a suggested task, or by bringing you along on the retelling of part of my own journey. In keeping with that heart-centered approach, before I explain how this book works and the developmental concepts it reflects, I would like to share the story of how I became a shaman.

I tell my story of transformation and healing to help you envision how your own life can be transformed. We can't change the original wounds we suffer, but we can profoundly change our relationship to them. One way to do this is by embracing the spiritual, transformational aspects of our stories.

THE CALL TO SPIRIT

Shamans are called by spirit. Since the business of the shaman or medicine person is healing and therefore integrity, very often spirit calls a shaman by breaking the person they once were into pieces in some way. As the straw man in *The Wizard of Oz* discovers in his frightening encounter with the possessed monkeylike creatures, sometimes it is only possible for us to learn what we are made of after we have been torn apart by some inner or outer force, our insides strewn around on the ground.

My "straw man" time came when I was twenty-two years old.

I had already spent five years in psychotherapy to address the fallout, on every level of my being, from having a schizophrenic father, a bipolar, alcoholic stepfather who abused me physically and sexually, and a perpetually adolescent mother. To preserve my sanity, I had moved out of my parents' home at sixteen years old. Within the next several years I became a licensed massage therapist and was beginning to make a modest, reliable living. In my external life I was just beginning to create the security and stability for myself that no one had ever provided for me.

Unfortunately, at this time my paternal grandmother was diagnosed with terminal liver cancer. Though I didn't see her often, my grandmother Betty was still an anchor for me, a reminder that somebody relatively sane and grounded cared about my well-being. She never could allow herself to see into the specifics of my untenable situation, but she clearly loved me. I used to see her every Sunday until well into my teens.

While my grandmother's body was wasting away, my own was shrinking, almost as if we were having parallel deaths. My five-foot seven-and-a-half inch body had reduced from a hundred and forty-two pounds to one hundred and seven. I knew I was not anorexic because I was very concerned about this weight loss and I knew I was getting too thin. I was just not able to do anything to stop it.

As my paternal grandmother was moving farther away from ordinary reality, dying in a hospice, I was compulsively engaged in what I now call the drama of the mirror. In addition to watching my body shed an entire quarter of its former self, I was also observing a devastating process of newly acquired adult acne. For many people acne might only be a slight embarrassment of sorts, but because of the years of sexual and physical abuse in my childhood I had learned to rely on my face and body to facilitate the only power I ever believed I really had . . . seduction.

I had started to model for a children's fashion magazine when I was five, around the time my stepfather started to abuse me. I began to understand I was a pretty girl and that there was a power associated with that. As I got older and needed love, my ability to seduce got me attention, affection, and sometimes a close relationship. I was trying to make up for not having received any of these things from my mother at any age.

I understand now there were many forces within me and connected to me that were more powerful than the appearance of my body and face, but I didn't yet understand that at twenty-two. My appearance was what felt powerful to me then, because of the dynamic of how it was exploited, and the pathological emphasis it is given in general in the culture at large.

So I agonized in front of the mirror for hours a day, watching what I imagined to be my power slip away, wanting to be dead without it. I was mortified by my apparent vanity, yet powerless over it. I did try the ineffective pharmaceutical pills and potions prescribed by a dermatologist and a strict macrobiotic diet. I struggled, with the help of my therapist, to get on about the business of my life and the things I loved, including yoga, t'ai chi, reading, writing, and learning more about healing. I could show up for my appointments with clients, and sometimes pursue these activities for hours, but then I would end up back in the mirror, stuck, locked into the hopeless struggle for reassurance and some new sense of myself that could work better and feel better than my old self. I realized how hard it was for me to look at myself and breathe at the same time (other than the very shallow breath necessary for survival).

I was in the mirror, locked between the shadows and the light, blaming myself for the acne, the weight loss, and my grandmother's death because I had to believe I had some control, and brutal self-blame was better than no control at all. I was terrified, as I was by the abuse at seven or eight, that everything would just keep getting worse . . . the acne, the scars, the weight loss . . . and I would be damaged beyond repair, dirty beyond redemption. I had no idea of where to go or how to live with the gaping wounds left from two decades of abuse. As I stared at my hopeless reflection, I thought perhaps I wasn't capable of healing because I had been so damaged by my childhood.

I had grown up believing that my hunger for a crumb of affection from my mother had somehow drawn my stepfather's hands and mouth to me at six and seven, where energetically they stuck, his sticky shame commanded by his arrogance to convince me it was mine. I could never forget that first hug—the initial relief of discovering that any human being could be affectionate toward me. I recalled with a fresh sense of shock and betrayal how I had been comforted at one moment by strong arms, then twisted, emotionally abducted into some dark place, made to share this shame that always disgusted me, accompanied by sounds that even a six-year-old knew had nothing to do with affection, and his slimy, open mouth. My present shame merged with the shame of the past.

On one level I felt as though my situation was all my fault—my grandmother's illness, my inability to attend to her, my weight loss, and the acne emerging from the depth of the shame within me, effacing my fledgling self-esteem. The emotional weed of shame flourishes in the fertile soil of a child's destroyed ability to believe in her inherent right to exist. But I had begun to understand in therapy that all children are born with a right to exist, and I began to entertain the idea that the guilt and shame I had been holding and was now releasing was perhaps not mine at all. I began to sense there were energies in my being that needed to be released and transformed. One part of me was stuck in the mirror, but another was reaching out.

At this juncture, Michael Harner, pioneering anthropologist and author of *The Way of the Shaman,* came into my life briefly. He was teaching a workshop with the same title, sharing with passion and sincerity some of what he'd learned from indigenous people.

I had not heard of shamanism before. I knew Native American tribes had medicine people and my imagination had been captured by their way of life, especially when, as a teenager, I visited my maternal grandmother in New Mexico where she lived near Geronimo Springs. The philosophy of living in balance with Mother Earth seemed like it made perfect sense to me (though at that age I could not imagine a world where the toilets didn't flush).

In his workshop, Michael Harner spoke about ordinary and nonordinary reality as these terms apply in the world of the shaman. As I understood it, ordinary reality is the level of reality where we negotiate for our concrete needs and wants, utilizing concrete means. For example, we can negotiate our need or want for food by gathering, hunting, farming, or shopping at the grocery store. It is the reality the ego is most connected to. Ordinary reality is also a linear place where events move in sequence and time moves from past to present to future. Since we must meet our practical needs, our healthy ego and ordinary reality are both important.

Equally important in shamanism, however, is nonordinary reality—the level of reality where we negotiate our spiritual life. Here our emotions flow, hearts open, and the higher mind attunes itself to the dynamic energies, images, beings, and spirits flowing out from the expansive wholeness of the universe. In nonordinary reality, time may move in any pattern so we may simultaneously heal the past, present, and future. This is the reality our spirit is the most connected to.

This concept was a very interesting exploration of reality for me, having grown up with the unreality of my parents' mental illnesses. The idea of having visions and other sensory imaginings was very scary to me, having been exposed to my father's auditory hallucinations my whole life. But hearing Michael speak about visions and journeys as part of nonordinary reality in his matter-of-fact, grounded, almost academic way, made it seem quite safe, natural, and practical. He was very supportive in the workshop and noticed that I seemed to have a talent for this process. I deeply appreciated being seen and being taught to use this gift in a safe way.

I was very grateful for all the psychotherapy I'd received by this time in my life and continued it for another twenty years. It provided enormous support in healing my fractured ego. But I came to know that I needed the vastness and richness and power of nonordinary reality as well to heal my extensive wounding. There was something in my soul that knew it had followed the way of the shaman many times in the past.

Just hearing about nonordinary reality opened up the whole universe for me. As I was walking on the beach near my home not long after the workshop, I almost strolled by a man sitting on a large boulder. Instead, I was magnetically drawn to his broad, kind features as I heard him say in a deep, soothing voice: "Finally." It was clear to me right away that he was a presence from nonordinary reality and not of physical substance; but what struck me was how ordinary it actually felt to encounter him, how matter-of-fact he was about greeting me. He told me he was my spirit guide, and he had been waiting for me to notice him for a very long time. Maybe at times I had—he looked very familiar to me.

A deep peace that I hadn't felt since I was very little came into my being when I heard his voice and its sound vibrated in my body. I experienced a sense of safety that I had never felt before. The gentle power of his presence enveloped me and has held me ever since. This guide is with me to this day and has been a tremendous support to me in my consciousness for over twenty years, shapeshifting between his human and animal forms.

Guiding Eagle told me that he had been my father in a previous life, and that we were a family of medicine people. I journeyed with him to the mesas of the desert near the Rio Grande where my grandparents and mother lived in the 1980s. We traveled back to more than a century before the Elephant Butte Dam and the man-made lake occupied so many acres of desert. In this journey I shapeshifted into the desert herself, before she was submerged beneath the pooling water from the river. I could feel the movements of the sacred rattlesnakes through my spine, my hands the embodiment of sacred tarantulas, the yielding of the earth, and the expansiveness of the sky. This was the first of many lessons I would receive from Guiding Eagle about the strengths that lived inside me and all the nurturing and love in the universe.

My spirit guide explained that I had been tested by the trials in this life, and that my persistence on the journey to shed the veils of illusion and addiction had been an initiation for me into shamanism. As I had been a massage therapist for a couple of years the idea of becoming a healer was not new to me. But shamanism encompassed so many dimensions, so many unknowns, and was therefore both exciting and comforting beyond anything I had ever known.

I so liked the idea of redemption. I was beginning to understand that my struggling and pain could transform into a positive wisdom and become an initiation into this healing world of shamanic power and knowledge. I was learning how to leave the unreality of disconnection from spirit and how to be present with others in my newly found connections. It gave me the greatest comfort to know that transcendence could happen at this personal level yet also have meaning for some greater good. I thought that perhaps this was what Malcolm X might have felt like, finding Allah in jail.

Somehow shamanism and its honoring of nonordinary reality as an actual, legitimate world made the deep places I had to go inside to heal a little less scary. To continue my healing became an exercise in the power of integrity and an opportunity to go to healing places I could one day lead other people through. I could do all this with Guiding Eagle holding my hand. I had never had a father before in the ways that I needed one. Shamanism gave me a hope I had never known before, a world of endless creative possibility while being spiritually connected to support and protection.

Within six months after the workshop with Michael Harner, so much had rebalanced in my being. I nourished my relationship with my spirit guide and watched my terror recede. I gained back some of the lost weight, and the acne diminished. I started a Gestalt psychotherapy training program and courses to complete my college degree. I was becoming more grounded, paradoxically, while spending time and conscious energy in nonordinary reality.

I began to move forward with my adult life in a way I previously couldn't, free from many addictions and destructive behaviors that had created so much misery for me in my very young adulthood. Never having been athletic because my body was not a safe place for me to be in my childhood, through immersing myself in the study of yoga and t'ai chi, I began to develop a relationship with my body that included compassion and a balance of sensual, feminine power and focused, masculine strength.

Through my relationship with my spirit guide, I finally had a parental relationship with someone who really saw and knew my spirit. This allowed me to truly go forward with my life, and to understand the process of healing, which I was beginning to realize was in fact my mission. Guiding Eagle was and is always available to me when I need him, with warmth, tenderness, knowledgeable support, and spiritual insights.

His presence allowed me to embark on the most important journey of my life—to fully explore and understand the process of how we heal as human beings. It took me twenty years to completely grasp and articulate this process. I learned its many intricacies and subtleties by applying this healing model first to myself and then in my clinical practice. This is the effective process I share in this book.

▼

I believe that when we tell our stories from a deep place we lead others on a journey to honor their own story. I do not share my story for sensational purposes or to shame or punish anyone. There is more than enough gratuitous violence in our culture, and we do not heal by blaming or punishing others. I have already healed my childhood wounds to a great extent through the techniques in this book.

Through knowledge of our own wounds we learn to acknowledge the wounds of others with compassion. We create a respectful dance of connection. I can't change what happened in my childhood, but I can use my story of protection, empowerment, and spiritual connection to weave a layer of healing energy through the tasks in this book.

EGO STATES AND ENERGY

In the course of my shamanic meditations and yoga studies, it became clear to me that healing has both a developmental and an energetic component. Distinct stages of development correspond to our chronological ages and the capacity of our nervous systems at those times to process events, information, relationships, complexity, and trauma. As I addressed my own childhood wounds with the help of my guides and a therapist, I recognized that the impact of traumatic events or situations is influenced greatly by the age of the individual at the time of the trauma.

After years of studying with powerful shamans and energy healers, I began to understand that the ego states of all our developmental stages exist in us simultaneously, in the form of energy. There is essentially one major developmental stage embodied in each energy center, or chakra, of the body. This idea led me to envision how powerful it could be to lead people through a sequential journey to address all of these stages of development and their possible wounds. I could see how various shamanic tasks could be very effective in healing the wounds associated with certain stages of development. In fact, in indigenous cultures certain tasks are required of people at appropriate life stages, to build power and balance. I discovered that by addressing all of these stages of development a person—even one who has suffered traumatic experiences—could grow into a profound, resilient integrity.

The process that you will engage in by completing the tasks in this book involves moving through the chakras sequentially, from the first to the eighth chakra. Each chapter addresses one chakra, examining the developmental challenges it embodies. For example, the first chapter addresses the first chakra (located at the base of the spine), which holds the energy of our ego state from birth through age six, the stage when we develop trust in others and ourselves. The chapter then explains and explores the shamanic tasks that help people heal the sometimes painful, paralyzing, and energy-draining issues that can grow out of less than successful resolution of this critical phase.

DEVELOPMENTAL THEORY AND THE CHAKRAS

The developmental component of this process is based in part on a melding of several influential psychological theories I have found valid and useful for my own healing as well as that of my clients, including Gestalt therapy and Erik Erikson's theory of developmental crisis. The Gestalt model I studied incorporated an aspect of "transactional analysis" that focuses on the three ego states within a person—the inner child, adult, and parent—and the interplay between these ego states. In Gestalt therapy we explore and try to heal the conflicts within the individual between the inner child and inner parent, often making use of psychodrama techniques. This approach helped me to understand firsthand the dynamics of the ego states within us, interacting among themselves and with the world.

After years of practice and study I came to believe there are more ego states than just the three. We have children and adults of many ages inside us, and these ages organize themselves loosely around the eight chakras and their corresponding developmental stages. Because a chakra is a wheel of energy, it energetically holds the issues of its developmental stage. In my healing practice and my own healing journey, I have found that developmental psychologist Erik Erikson's model of ego development and developmental crisis fits quite accurately with the ego states energetically contained within each chakra.

According to Erikson, each period or stage of a person's life calls for different tasks to be explored and completed as the person grows physically, emotionally, mentally, socially, and spiritually. Erikson referred to these stages as crises. In *Identity, Youth and Crisis* he explains, "Each stage becomes a crisis because incipient growth and awareness in a new part . . . together with a shift in instinctual energy . . . also cause a specific vulnerability in that part . . . crisis is used here in a developmental sense to connote not a threat of catastrophe, but a turning point. . . ." We resolve the crisis when we are able to successfully channel the emergent energy and awareness and achieve growth. However, if our environment is unsupportive and/or we suffer a psychic trauma during this phase, the crisis is not fully resolved and we are less prepared for the next developmental challenge.

In this book, Erickson's theory of developmental crises serves as a loose guideline for understanding the needs and challenges of the various ego states contained within our energy bodies as we progress through the life cycle.* The process that you will engage in to address these crises, however, will emphasize shamanic tasks and chakra work rather than Western psychology. Tasks to resolve these crises may include shamanic journeys or meditation, physical exercises, reflections, journaling, ceremony, and breathing techniques.

---

*While the crises for the first six chakras are derived from Erikson's model, those I attribute to the seventh and eight chakras are my own extrapolation.

Erickson believed all the developmental crises could be resolved at any time if the environment provided what was required. Therefore, all these crises are always resolving themselves within us. Each of us has all of these ages and stages within us, simultaneously making demands and providing perspective, insight, and wisdom. So use this book to keep growing at every stage, throughout your life cycle.

HEALING THE HUMAN FAMILY

The process you will experience in this book facilitates consciousness, giving you more power to choose the forms your energy takes as you develop more strength to manifest your dreams. This expanded consciousness and self-growth will enable you not only to realize your personal dreams but also your hopes for the greater good.

Very often our energy patterns can get stuck in old habits. By that I mean our energy will follow the beliefs we ingested whole from our families or our culture. Many of our societal problems come from beliefs most people have not been willing to question. Whether a belief is healthy or functional depends not only on whether it supports and balances us as individuals but also on its implications for the rest of the planet. Does the belief create safety and connection to Mother Earth? Does it support creativity, balanced emotional flow, healthy sexuality? Does it facilitate passion, energy, and the appropriate use of will and commitment? Does it balance the masculine and feminine energies? Is it wise? Is it spiritually connected? For how many of our cultural beliefs would these criteria be met?

It is important to hold the American Dream up to the light of these questions. All of us who live here in this country have held or have been held by some version of this dream. Those ancestors who came here of their own free will were seeking religious, political, or some other type of freedom of expression, and the opportunity to provide more economic security for loved ones. Somehow this straightforward, non-exploitive dream became, as one shaman keenly observed, a fantasy of the world as "playground for rich gringos." We need to trace this back both collectively and as individuals, so we can be conscious about how we started to allow our needs and wants to be met at the expense of others on such a grand scale.

Life provides us all with opportunities to refuse to swallow whole what we have been fed. We can study what does not feel right and begin to break it down. We can ask, how much of what we have been fed is truly digestible and how much is poisonous? We can find the baby and release the dirty bathwater. Then we have the chance to transform at both the personal and the institutional level. The greater the levels of consciousness we have achieved, the greater and more truly powerful the shapeshifts will be.

At this time in the evolution of humanity, we need to heal and change in alignment with Mother Earth, our sacred environment, so we can continue to exist as a species. In addition to having arrested development individually, we have collective arrested development as humanity. Tragically, we have already caused the demise or imbalance of many ecosystems, species of plants and animals, and groups of our fellow humans.

I believe this will shift as more individuals heal and we become more open to understanding the impact we make on the whole. Once an individual comes into healing and integrity, she or he has a profound understanding of how we can live together in mutual respect and have a powerful and positive impact on the world at large. Perhaps with consciousness and compassion we can use our joint energies to enhance the collective experience of humanity. We can live in balance with Mother Earth, the heavens, the divine feminine and the divine masculine, and all beings and spirits everywhere. My sincerest wish is that this book will be a help to you on your journey to heal yourself and to support all beings and spirits as they dance in exquisite balance with all other beings and spirits.

1

The Earth Is Our Mother

A Journey to Trust

The opportunity to be consciously present for the birth of my daughter was the pinnacle of my existence. It required me to journey to the deepest place in my soul. I finally got to know myself fully as the goddess, at last dispelling the impact of all the limiting images and concepts of womanhood that modern Western culture had imposed on me. I could at last integrate my healing sexuality with something magnificent and powerful. Learning that the vagina was not only a moist, yielding opening of ecstasy but also a birth canal with amazingly powerful muscles to successfully push a baby into a new universe was a gift to my previously fragmented female psyche.

The body does an intricate, paradoxical dance, a counterpoint of stretching and contracting, to bring the baby from the womb cave to the air for the baby's next stage of development. I spent the most intense part of labor—transition, when the cervix or mouth of the womb opens most rapidly—in the shower. As the water splashed my body, the moans came from deep within the earth, through my belly, vibrating out through my throat, echoing off the walls to fill my ears. As all the birth passages opened, I became ready to let go of my baby in one way so I could embrace her in another. In conception, pregnancy, birth, and child nurturing, a woman works hand in hand with Spirit and Mother Earth.

▼

This book invites you to give birth to yourself anew and to heal the psychic wounds from the past that require your loving attention. Your map for that journey to healing will be the chart of the chakras and the energy body (fig. 1.1). Chakras are wheels of energy associated with specific

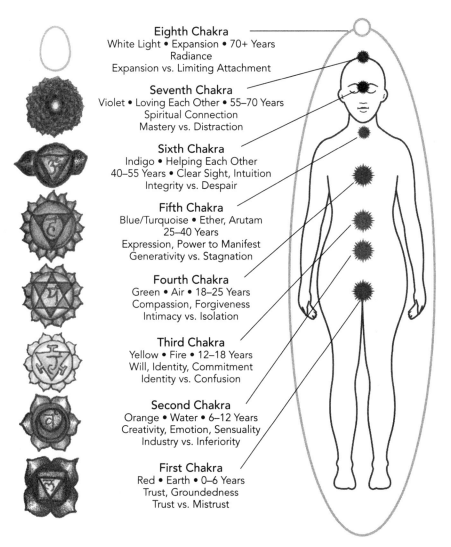

Eighth Chakra
White Light • Expansion • 70+ Years
Radiance
Expansion vs. Limiting Attachment

Seventh Chakra
Violet • Loving Each Other • 55–70 Years
Spiritual Connection
Mastery vs. Distraction

Sixth Chakra
Indigo • Helping Each Other
40–55 Years • Clear Sight, Intuition
Integrity vs. Despair

Fifth Chakra
Blue/Turquoise • Ether, Arutam
25–40 Years
Expression, Power to Manifest
Generativity vs. Stagnation

Fourth Chakra
Green • Air • 18–25 Years
Compassion, Forgiveness
Intimacy vs. Isolation

Third Chakra
Yellow • Fire • 12–18 Years
Will, Identity, Commitment
Identity vs. Confusion

Second Chakra
Orange • Water • 6–12 Years
Creativity, Emotion, Sensuality
Industry vs. Inferiority

First Chakra
Red • Earth • 0–6 Years
Trust, Groundedness
Trust vs. Mistrust

Fig. 1.1. The Chakras and the Energy Body

locations in the body. The collective energy generated by the chakras as they spin surrounds us for about three feet or more past our physical body. This radiant envelope of energy is called the energy body.

Traditionally, each of the chakras is associated with a specific color, an element or essential dynamic energy, and a spiritual strength. In addition to showing the location of the chakras in the energy body, figure 1.1 also lists commonly acknowledged attributes of each chakra, along with some new attributes that I have discovered in my practice. Lastly, the chart displays the specific developmental ages and crises that I have found to be embodied by each of the chakras. The significance of all of these properties of the chakras will become clear as you work through the chapters.

We connect energetically to Mother Earth through the first chakra, which spins around the tailbone and pelvic floor (see fig 1.2). We feel the connection of our body to hers through this first chakra. This bond with Mother Earth is the foundation of our relationship with the divine feminine. This center is also associated with the element of earth, the relative solidness of our physical reality.

This first chakra energetically holds the issues of the first developmental stages, from birth to age six. This period encompasses the first three crises of development identified by Eric Erickson. These crises occur in all children, and they are all related to trust—first of others, and then of self.

The first crisis, trust versus mistrust, occurs between birth and age one. It is about the baby developing trust in relationship to its environment. If its parents are safe, loving, and nurturing, the baby will successfully resolve this crisis. If not, there is trauma and wounding, and this crisis will have to be resolved in some way later on in the life cycle.

The second developmental crisis is autonomy versus shame and doubt. This crisis occurs in children ages two through five. At this stage, we start to learn about healthy separation and autonomy as we go out and explore the world a bit on our own, periodically coming back to warm, loving affirmations and affection. If a child is not permitted to go and explore, is abandoned to an extreme degree, or made to feel fearful or shameful about his or her desire to explore the environment, there may be a lack of resolution of this developmental crisis.

The final developmental crisis embodied in this chakra is initiative versus guilt. This is a direct outgrowth of the previous crisis and occurs between the ages of four and six. If a child has a healthy sense of self, she

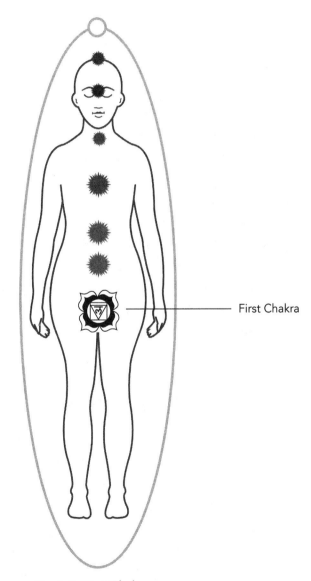

Color: Red

Element: Earth

Developmental Age:
0–6 years

Spiritual Strength:
Trust, Groundedness

Developmental Crisis:
Trust versus Mistrust

First Chakra

Fig. 1.2. First Chakra

or he will be able to initiate activities, expressing creativity and embracing responsibility, and ideally will be appreciated for these actions. If the child is punished for independent activity, she or he will experience guilt.

Self-trust is developed through appropriate mirroring. Healthy mirroring happens when a parent sees a child's feelings and responses to life and, in a respectful way, lets the child know that those feelings and responses are real and understandable. Mirroring is seeing with the eyes of the heart and having compassion for the experience of another, and it validates the child's inner life and view of reality.

To balance and heal the first chakra at the base of the energy body, we need to address several issues, including trust of others and ourselves, our relationship to our bodies and nature, and our connection to the divine feminine. Our spirits are released to walk on Mother Earth's body through the flesh of our biological mothers and the sacred miraculous journey of birth. Therefore, to begin our journey to trust it is important to heal our birth experience or trauma and to connect to the process of birth as the new beginning of each moment. It is also important to reconnect with this developmental stage by invoking our earliest memories and our connections to our caregivers. By assessing what life may have felt like for us then, how difficult (or not) it may have been for us to trust, we can gain insight into how to use the exercises in this chapter to expand our ability to trust ourselves and others.

RECONNECTING TO OUR EARLIEST MEMORIES

The womb experience is perhaps the most common experience we have as human beings. Regardless of our mother's environment or experience, some aspects of the womb experience are universal: its sacred darkness, soothing fluid, the peaceful, steady rhythm of the mother's heartbeat, and the warmth of her body temperature. The womb is truly of sacred design. It is a place where a mother's limitations interfere the least with her child feeling loved and developing in a healthy way. This is the place where our needs get met before we even know we have them.

Ancient cultures found that recapitulating this predominantly positive experience was profoundly healing and strengthening. Many cultures still practice rituals that evoke this experience, often in womblike structures such as the kivas of the Pueblo and Hopi people. Certain types of meditation and Eastern spiritual practice mimic the physical or sensory experience of the womb—for example, focusing on the heartbeat in Child pose in yoga (sitting back on the heels while leaning forward, belly resting on or between the knees). The flotation or sensory-deprivation tanks of the 1970s and '80s also re-created the womb experience. If we could all reconnect with a sense that we have everything we need because it comes from a sacred source, there would never be any reason to do violence to one another or to Mother Earth.

The birth of my daughter brought me into intimate connection with the power of the womb, and of Mother Earth, to instill trust in every child and to heal trust issues for those who experience trauma. After moving through the later part of my first trimester of pregnancy, when I felt like throwing up all the time, I really enjoyed being pregnant. My body was revealing itself to be capable of something quite the opposite of being confined or diminished. It was thankfully and miraculously expanding with new life and energy. Paradoxically, as my body expanded out into the world and my external energy journeyed out into the cosmos bearing new dreams of the future, my focus went inward to my generative core and then down into the center of the creative life force energy of Mother Earth.

I enjoyed holding and stroking the enormous hard, fleshy globe of my belly, which contained the miracle of life. The globes of my breasts grew and swelled, ready to produce food to nourish my baby when it was time to emerge. As the earth turned on its axis with each passing day, I was spiraling more deeply into the sacred garden, coming to know the warm, lush, profound place of blood and light.

I sensed what it might be like for my baby in my belly. Did she feel held and loved? Was there enough room? Was she trying to get more comfortable when she moved, or just trying out some part of her that had developed more fully? At night when I lay down to try to sleep, was she doing some ancient sacred dance only babies in the womb know? Who was she?

I can still sense my daughter, snug in her pristine amniotic sac, moving out of my womb. There was such pressure as she moved into and through the vaginal canal. So much focused, intensive pushing was required for the water that cradled her to gush out and for her head to at last emerge. I remember the strong, slippery caress of her shoulders, and the relief as she at last swam through and out of me, the smallest of dolphins, into the air. Her sweet cries told me I had given birth at last. I was exhausted and elated, holding my precious baby, having never seen a human quite so new before.

In the womb, a baby's needs get met before she or he has to ask. This is a vital part of the first developmental crisis because, unless there was drug abuse or some other very invasive action, we all have an experience in our bodies and being that trust was safe and possible.

The first task in this chapter will allow you to journey back to the womb and re-create or perhaps reinvent what you experienced in this crucial transition. You may want to ask your parents or other caregivers, if they are living, what they remember or know about your birth, such as whether it was vaginal or cesarean, natural or drug-supported, at home or at a birthing center or hospital, instrument-assisted or not. Based on some of these details and what you know about your birth parents, you may be able to imagine what your birth must have felt like for you.

My mother's experience of my birth was very different from my experience of my daughter's. My mother, enveloped in drug-induced "twilight" sleep, does not remember any details of my birth. As was typical of 1960, my father was not in the room. Birth had become a medical procedure with anesthesia, drugs, and instruments. At age twenty-three my mother was the disempowered goddess and my father the oblivious god. How sad that they were not really present to witness this true miracle and be affirmed in their glorious part in the mystery of the creation of life.

If they had been, this would have created a different beginning for me.

You may need healing for your birth trauma, or you may not. In either case it can be very nurturing to acknowledge the spiritual aspect of this blessed event. This next task can help to heal birth trauma and assist you as you honor the sacred beginning of your life.

If your experience of your mother was not so positive, this might be hard for you to do. At one point in my therapy, I imagined myself peacefully sleeping inside a closed tulip. It was a soft and gentle place. A traumatized client of mine used to curl up in bed next to a stuffed bear that made womb sounds when you turned a knob, including the heartbeat echoing through the amniotic fluid. I have also worked with people who have imagined very comfortable caves. This task can support you in being held with love as you are born anew into this moment.

Don't worry if this task is difficult to do. It may take a few tries to be completely present with the process so it can be healing. Later tasks may also provide you with the understanding and spiritual protection necessary to make a journey to the womb feel safer and more possible. Just do the best you can as you move through the tasks and the overall journey of this book.

⬥ Task One: A Journey to the Womb

See if you can imagine yourself in a womblike space. If your experience of your mother was basically positive, you may want to go right back to her womb. It is best not to be strictly biologically accurate about this, but artistic. Sculpt a holographic womb in your imagination with all your senses. Imagine the soothing warm fluid, the protection from over-stimulation, the vibration of the heartbeat. Know that you have everything that you need right now in this moment. All that you need is being provided for you. You can completely relax.

Sometimes it's best to re-create the experience in the physical environment. Curling up under a soft blanket in a relatively dark, warm room can work well, as can a warm bath in a warm room with an inflatable pillow.

If you don't like closed spaces, there is no reason why your womb can't be spacious. Feel free to create your womb, internally and externally, in a way that will make you feel nurtured and provided for.

After five to twenty minutes, when you are ready to emerge from the womb, allow yourself a gentle process of birth. Are there movements or sounds that you need or want to make? With gentleness and kindness, as you open your eyes, notice what nurtures you in your outer environment. This could be anything, including plants, the light through the windows, your pets, candles, art on your walls, a sacred altar, music, your meditation cushion, or a picture of your friends. Give thanks for all that nurtures you as you are welcomed back to ordinary reality. If there doesn't seem to be quite enough to nurture you, know that the process of this book will lead you in the direction of self-care and will help you create more of these types of connections. You may want to have a drink of water, juice, or tea.

Journal about how you felt during this process and perhaps how the journey compared to what you know about your original womb and birth experience.

Our next task will take us back to revisit our earliest memories. My earliest memories include my father, Frank, taking my brother and me to the Hayden Planetarium in New York City. Sometimes my father's educational excursions were not at all fruitful for me, as they bored me and gave me a headache, but the planetarium held powerful knowledge for my young soul. This is where I first sensed the wholeness of Mother Earth and her exquisite round shape, the globe.

Looking at our solar system, I understood that she was round like the other planets, orbiting around the warmth of the sun. I understood the cycles of night and day as she spun on her own axis. I understood how a year passed as she journeyed around the sun, causing the seasons to unfold into each other. There was a comfort in how we, humanity, were part of this exquisite dance of planets, satellites, stars, meteors, and space, moving in patterns that created cycles. The improvisations of randomness and chaos were modified by celestial choreography.

I could somehow sense that on this huge sphere of unimaginable proportions, everyone and everything was equal, because it was a big ball and not a ladder or a pyramid. I knew that the dirt and grass from my grandparents' yards were somewhere on the globe in a city called Yonkers. And that there were many other cities all around the vast roundness of the world where other little girls lived with land around them. I sensed the power, diversity, and wholeness of Mother Earth and her people and creatures. I sensed the magic of an Earth-connected life. Knowing about Mother Earth's richness and connection to the whole universe deepened my connection to her every time I saw rocks and trees. I imagined myself holding the globe in my arms, as if I were a goddess who could protect her, as she held me.

Other memories of my parents are bittersweet. My father sometimes took us to coin shows. He and my brother collected silver quarters and other currency. Money meant nothing to me in this preschool, kindergarten time of my life, but I held on to the precious coin of my father's love. This wasn't simple. Heads: he's smiling that "you are my precious sweetheart" smile, eyes swimming in love, floating in the skin around them. Tails: his brow is squeezed, face red, as he rages against the voices only he hears that taunt him. He curses them, "those damned idiots, boobs!" and his mother cries out to "Jesus, Mary, and Joseph!" as if she knew the holy family personally. She implores him repeatedly to "Stop it!" as if he actually could.

My mother was a beautiful, impatient butterfly, the soft brown wings of her hair often disappearing into a cocoon of cigarette smoke. She always seemed to be flying away to New York City to bars and parties, to the Hamptons, Fire Island, and work, without ever really seeing the flower of my heart. There was never any way to entice my mother with my sweetness, so I watched her in loneliness, longingly, feeling unworthy of her attention. My hunger for her was always intense, and when I couldn't bear it anymore I escaped to my imagination and connection to Mother Earth.

We are all nurtured by both maternal and paternal energy. It is important to explore how and where you connected to both, and how you internalized this connection. This next experience is an opportunity to explore what your life was like as a young child and how trustworthy your environment really was. As this task is a type of journey to your past, be gentle and go slowly with yourself if your childhood was painful. By all means, find a therapist or shaman if that level of support is required.

❖ Task Two: Remembering Your Earliest Life

I invite you to remember your parents and other caregivers as they were when you were at this young developmental stage and to journal about your general and specific experiences with them. Ask yourself, "How did they support me in developing trust in others and myself? In what ways did they make this difficult?"

Invoke your memories of infancy, the toddler years, and young childhood. You may have many colorful, wonderful memories that flood back as soon as you think of your caregivers at this time. On the other hand, I have worked with many clients who have few or no memories from this developmental stage. This is often because there wasn't adequate safety in the environment. If these memories do not come easily, there may be stories about you as a child that you've heard at family gatherings. What do these say about you and the dynamics in your family?

It helps some people to find pictures of themselves and their families at this developmental stage. Sit, surround yourself with these images, sensing their nuances, and breathe. How did you interact with your family in these pictures? Sense what it must have been like for you. To invoke all the senses in service of memory, it is helpful for some to listen to music that was played or popular when they were growing up, travel to their childhood homes, or taste their childhood foods. Did you have important caregivers other than your parents, exposure to an influential religion, or a chance to connect to Mother Earth? Find the riches and the challenges.

Imagine yourself—as a baby being held or nursing, when you first ate solid food, walked, talked, played, went to preschool and kindergarten. Allow the multisensory images of your childhood to appear, unfold, and blend as you record them in a journal, along with your enhanced understanding of what life was like for you as a young child.

CONNECTING WITH MOTHER EARTH

I have learned from experience that we cannot heal without the *kundalini,* or divine feminine energy, that radiates up from the rich magnetic core of Mother Earth. We channel her divine feminine energy, also called *yin* energy, through our first chakra. There are many important tasks that can help us strengthen and heal our first chakras.

From her side of the relationship, Mother Earth has always been and continues to be consciously loving. The pull of gravity is her ongoing embrace. It keeps us from flying off into space in our physical bodies. She loves us and holds us close, on her beautiful landscape. She feeds us. All our shelter, clothing, medicine, transportation vehicles, and other material goods, even those made of "synthetics," come from her originally. Mother Earth is lovely, abundant, and generous, and though we often forget, we are made, and continue to be remade every day, in her magnificent image through the substance of our ever-renewing cells. She is vast and has room in her consciousness for us all. Since she is always lovingly present and a marvelous provider, connecting to Mother Earth allows us the opportunity to heal many of our remaining issues around trust.

By connecting to Mother Earth, we fulfill ourselves in a very deep way. We see life in balance and we learn to trust in the natural process of life, including our own vulnerable and often difficult to embrace human process. If we embrace Mother Earth in our hearts, we can start to feel deeply taken care of and safe, so our greed disperses. Our greed heals because there is nothing we can have that is more profound than this connection to Mother Earth's consciousness. If we heal greed, the human race as a whole will heal, because we will no longer need to exploit each other, other creatures, or the environment. We must heal greed, otherwise our unmitigated avarice will make our mother uninhabitable for human life. If everyone on the planet did this next task, in a very short period of time all our affairs at every level would be conducted very differently.

As both my parents made trust a challenging issue, as a young child I was drawn to connect with Mother Earth. My mother's favorite stories from my infancy and toddlerhood were about me falling asleep on Mother Earth or eating dirt. I can still feel the persistent grit of sand in my teeth. I'm sure I was looking for a safe connection, and children at this age connect through their mouths. Perhaps because of the chaos and losses I was experiencing, I was drawn directly to Mother Earth for comfort when I was a year old.

At the time, my mother was dealing with my father's mental illness in its severest manifestation—which, after he threatened to kill us all, resulted in her having to commit him to a hospital. This left her preoccupied, frightened, impoverished, and not available for too much more than my most basic physical needs. Shortly after my father's hospitalization, they divorced. Before I was two, we moved in with my mother's mother, Margie. I have vivid memories of the land around my grandmother's house. I recall my love of the trees, especially my friend the crab apple tree, who would hold me in her limbs. She was the perfect size for me, with low branches I could easily climb and be enveloped in. The tiny, inedible crab apples seemed magical to me, like the choice food of fairies. Here, the mint grew wild and the soft grass smelled fresh. My grandmother felt like Mother Earth to me. She was sweet and unpretentious and she was the steward of the land.

Without my grandmother and her land, I could not tell you with certainty that I would be here today. The land, the trees, and my grandmother were and are magnificent spirit guides who lived and continue to live in me. They saw my value and basic life-force energy. They were powerful mirrors at a developmental stage when mirrors are crucial. Since I lived with Margie until I was just about six, I received some very powerful support for my ego strength in this stage of development.

If you don't do anything else in this book, please do this vital task. It will activate your first chakra and connect you to Mother Earth.

❖ Task Three: Massaging the Earth with Your Feet

Every day, take a walk on Mother Earth, acknowledging her sacredness. Even if you walk on the pavement or must wheel yourself on the floor inside your apartment because of a physical limitation, she is always underneath and all around. Sense this as you move, feeling the grass, dirt, sand, layers of rock, water, and magma deep beneath you.

Walk for a while if you can. But even if it is just five minutes, do it with your whole self. Return your consciousness to Mother Earth again and again. Feel your feet massaging her. Feel her massaging your feet. Feel her love for you in all the delights she expresses for your senses. Feel your love for her. Allow yourself to be moved by her beauty, and by your own.

At some point, it may be important for you to find a sacred outdoor place to go to every day, once a week, or during each moon cycle. You may even decide to make a pilgrimage to a more distant sacred place on a less frequent basis. The repetition of visiting the same place on a regular basis will facilitate an intimacy and trust, deepening this sacred relationship to Mother Earth.

If you found this last exercise hard to do, there may be blocks in your energy field or a hardness around your heart. Often, our hearts can become hardened because they have been broken or otherwise wounded. We also tend to push these difficult experiences out of our consciousness so we can get on with the mechanics of our lives. Take time to cleanse and soothe yourself with this next task as you deepen your sense of safe connection to the earth energy, bringing trust back into your heart, body, and being.

This cleansing works not only on our physical bodies but also on our energy bodies. Our being does not stop at our skin but extends out energetically into the space around our body. This energy field can be described as the aura that surrounds us, radiating out from us through the spinning of not just the first but all the chakras.

✦ Task Four: Cleansing and Healing with Kundalini Energy

During your daily walk, pause and stand on Mother Earth. You can do this task sitting down if necessary.

1. Brush your hands down your body or energy field from the crown of your head to the tips of your toes. You may actually touch your body with your hands and fingertips, or sweep through your energy field inches from the body, or use a combination of both techniques. Your hands may move quickly or slowly. Begin to release clutter and tensions, acute and chronic. Sweep down to Mother Earth and release to her this congested energy. You may need to stamp your feet or make sounds to release this toxic excess. Do the front of your body, and then reach around to the back of your body as best you can, making contact with as much of your body and energy field as possible.

   There will be areas where you feel density in your energy field. As you become sensitive to this, it will feel as though there is a thickness in these areas; perhaps it will be harder to move your hands through these places. These thickened areas are places of stress, tension, or trauma. Very often, the upper shoulder area is very congested and needs to be cleared. Spend time brushing the tension off this shoulder area. Pay special attention to clutter around the mind and tension around the heart. Shake your hands and release all the tensions to Mother Earth. You may shake your whole body to release. Mother Earth likes to receive our density, our heavy emotional states. She transforms the energy into power.

2. After a brief pause in which you acknowledge that you have let go of as much as you can for right now, draw Kundalini energy up from

Mother Earth. Scoop energy up from Mother Earth as though you were drawing water with your hands from a pure mountain stream, breathing, drinking it in, and blessing yourself as you become refreshed, pouring it all over yourself. Feel yourself fill with fresh energy. Where did you notice tension, trauma, or stress in the last step? Bring the rich healing energy up from the depth of Mother Earth to where you need it. Fill yourself.

3. Take another moment to feel. Has the connection to Mother Earth opened a bit more? Drink it in. Be deeply nourished in your energy.

4. Give thanks. It's important to express appreciation to all beings, spirits, and forces who provide spiritual support for us on our journey.

After establishing your walking practice of connecting to Mother Earth, you can ask her for a sacred object, or *huaca*. My favorite earth huaca is a rock from a sacred canyon in San Carlos, Mexico, close to my mother's house. There are worlds inside this rock, which comes from the ancestral home of the Yaqui indigenous people of Mexico. There are foggy, beautiful crystals at its center that pull me into its depth. I can begin to fathom the deep reaches of Mother Earth as my consciousness lovingly penetrates her rich complexity. I find the stillness and profound power at her core. Other layers of the rock seem to be petrified clay, sand, and wood from the desert, and stone from the mountains that emerged from the under-earth world. The water from the canyon seems to move between the crystals. There is a roundness in this stone that suggests the roundness of the whole earth. It resonates the echo of the canyon as I cradle it in my hands.

Your earth huaca can go in your medicine bag, which will be the sacred container for your sacred objects and other healing allies. You can carry this bag with you for energetic support and protection. Perhaps at some point you may use some of its contents to support others in their healing. During your use of this book, a bag may present itself to you for this purpose.

❧ Task Five: Finding a Sacred Earth Object

Walk in a place that is powerful and beautiful to you. Know that your intention for this task is to invite your earth huaca to come to you. It should be something that reminds you of and holds the power of the element earth.

Your sacred object will invite your attention. When you believe it has made contact with you, ask this sacred object if it is indeed yours. If it is, pick it up and hold it with reverence. Though it may feel silly at first, begin to dialogue with it. Open the lines of communication. Ask it if it has a message for you about your spiritual journey. Listen for the answer. New insights regarding your journey and its challenges may come to you as you hold and receive the wisdom from your earth huaca. You may begin to feel you are in the company of a spiritual ally.

Thank your earth huaca for its presence in your life, and thank Spirit for bringing it to you.

Staying connected consciously to nature is, sadly, apparently contrary to modern Western culture. It is very difficult within our male-dominated mind-set and power structures to admit our utter dependency on her, our Mother Earth, even though we cannot maintain our physical existence without her. In our fear of dependence, we have focused rather exclusively on God, the almighty father. We have deified the *yang* (the masculine life force from heaven) at the expense of the yin (feminine life force from the earth), believing we have to sacrifice our sacred animal nature to be spiritual beings and have success in the afterlife. Unfamiliar with the spiritual relevance, richness, and truth of our animal nature, we find its sensuality and passion to be frightening. As we learn to connect with the first chakra, the body, kundalini or yin energy, Mother Earth, and the divine feminine, we become more trusting of the wholeness of ourselves.

ACKNOWLEDGING AND HONORING
THE DIVINE FEMININE

According to traditional Western patriarchal religion, God, the father almighty, gave man dominion over all things. In this practice of dominion, people have been slaughtered and resources plundered. The yang aspect of God cannot be experienced with the usual five senses, the way the divine feminine and Earth can. Therefore, to many people, God has tragically become an abstraction. This abstraction has been manipulated so that it supports not just positive ideas, such as the brotherhood of man, but also negative, exploitive ideas such as colonialism and huge profiteering oil corporations. As I look around the world, I see the difficulties with this exclusively male God aptly demonstrated by the oppression of peoples and the destruction of the Earth's beauty and life-sustaining ability.

We need to embrace our real dependency and our sense of Mother Earth as a parent who loves us dearly. In our acknowledgment of this dependence, we are able to receive her blessing. There will be no humiliation in the acknowledgment of this. This is important to note, as we live in a culture that humiliates men about their normal dependency needs. For a healthy sense of trust to develop we need to learn to honor the ways in which we truly are dependent so we can heal this developmental stage and learn to meet our needs from trustworthy sources in the most direct way possible.

I don't endorse abolishing God the father from our consciousness, but rather adding God the mother—connection with a powerful, divine feminine presence. Without acknowledging the sacredness of Mother Earth, there can be no balance for us in this life. To save ourselves as a species, we must give her the respect a good mother deserves. We cannot conquer or "own" Mother Earth, except at the most superficial level. It takes maturity to acknowledge that over which we do not have power. Integrating the divine feminine and divine masculine requires a maturity that does not seem to be readily available in our culture at this time. But this work can help to develop it.

In my youngest years, there was almost nothing available in the culture to support my conscious connection to the divine feminine. I sensed the sacredness of my connection to the earth and I especially enjoyed the occasional walk in the woods with my father and finding pristine areas, however small, that had the appearance of being untouched by the ravages of humanity.

There was only a hint of the divine feminine in the Catholic Church of my childhood. As young as age three, I remember standing, sitting, and kneeling in church every Sunday morning next to my father and brother before we went to my grandmother Betty's for dinner. There was nothing in the church service that spoke to my or anyone else's feminine divinity. But, at some point in my early childhood, Betty taught me the prayer, Hail Mary, and gave me my first set of rosary beads. Now, this was exciting. The rosary beads formed a sacred circle of prayer, and the prayer that was said most often in the rosary was to the mother of God. "Hail Mary full of grace, the Lord is with thee. Blessed art thou among women, and blessed is the fruit of thy womb, Jesus. Holy Mary, mother of God, pray for us sinners, now and at the hour of our death. Amen." I rolled the round beads of the rosary between my thumb and index finger, squeezing as I prayed to the divine mother.

This seemed like a sacred secret. Up until this point, though I knew that Mary gave birth to Jesus, I hadn't been told she was the mother of God. I so liked the idea that God had a mother. It made God seem more human for one thing. And since I knew women's bellies swelled when they were pregnant, I liked the idea of Mary's belly being full of God. I also loved the idea of Jesus being the fruit; perhaps then Mary was the tree.

I just knew there had to be more to this Mary than the equanimity that exuded from every image I saw of the skinny lady in the droopy, but elegant robes. The Jesus-as-fruit image made her magical and powerful. I thought of her as the crab apple tree that created the food for the fairies in my grandmother's yard. I imagined her, pregnant with God, belly as large as a melon, cradling this globe in her robes—the creator of the creator. Perhaps I, too, could be a tree and one day bear fruit; not just a baby, but exotic spiritual fruit. There was something promising for me in this. To this day, I keep my original rosary beads in a deerskin medicine bag.

The way I have embraced shamanic practice is an honoring of the divine feminine and of myself as a woman. I have planted myself here, in the county of my birth, unearthed all the old demons of my family and culture and made peace with them, learning profound nuances about healing in my thoroughness. I have found this to be quite a different style from the male shamanic teachers, colleagues, and friends whom I discuss in this book, with their marvelous adventures to indigenous lands and powerful, expansive mystical experiences. I feel that my powerful capacities as a woman support me in expanding out from where I stand to embrace many ideas in the big womb of my consciousness. And my feminine capacity to go very deep, like Mother Earth herself, allows me to integrate them into the process described in this book.

In the next task we will journey to connect to the power of the divine feminine around and within us and receive the support it provides us on our healing journey.

✦ Task Six: Connecting to the Divine Feminine

Have your journal handy as you reflect about your connection to the divine feminine. We've already begun to explore a connection to Mother Earth in this chapter. Are there any other images that come to mind as you think about the divine feminine? Indigenous cultures connect with many faces of Mother Earth as the divine feminine. The Cherokee speak about Selu, the Corn Mother, and the Sisterhood of the Thirteen Clan Mothers, related to the cycles of the moon. The Shuar speak of Nunqui who spirals up from Mother Earth, and the Quechua speak of Pachamama (Mother Earth, Mother Universe). Cultures and religions around the world have expressed her presence in many forms including Tara, Kwan Yin, Mary, Gaia, Kali, Isis, and Venus.

How do you see her? As a goddess, saint, prophet, animal, angel, or other deity? Is your connection to her weak or strong? Do you see her vividly and feel energized by your connection or does she feel vague and distant? Can you talk to her, pray to her, or ask for guidance and support? Does she feel accessible to you in this way? Do you experience the divine feminine as a part of you? What do you feel, as a woman or as a man, about your connection to her?

Is there anything in your cultural or religious background that supports you in this connection? Is there anything in your personal history or cultural environment that might block this connection? It is a true act of power to look past the sexism in our culture to find the divine feminine.

Through bravely questioning and exploring this connection to the divine feminine you are strengthening it. As you have pondered and perhaps answered these questions, do you have a sense of other ways you can develop and strengthen your unique relationship to the divine feminine? Do you need to go back to the religious practices of your childhood, observing them with a fresh eye to see if the divine feminine is anywhere to be found? Would you enjoy going to a museum to see how images of the divine feminine have been depicted in different cultures through the millennia? Does it help you to have a statue or picture of her? Or are there simple everyday things you do that connect you to the divine feminine, like walking outside, gardening, preparing food, or doing yoga? Journal or otherwise reflect and create to explore these questions. Tell the story of your growing connection to the divine feminine.

CONNECTING TO THE BODY

In this chapter, we will nourish our connection with the earth on every level. In earlier tasks, we walked on Mother Earth and connected to her energy for spiritual healing. We will now do some exercises to feel the earth inside our physical bodies and beings. All that we are physically comes from Mother Earth. We are created and sustained by her. She is part of us as we are part of her. Through ancient movement practice, it is possible to cultivate a sense of connection to the earth within us and to feel a great trust in the Earth, in our bodies, and in ourselves.

The first chakra is the chakra of the body. As children, we are naturally connected to our bodies. We experience the gestalt, or wholeness, of ourselves. At some point in our education, we learn to separate ourselves and to identify primarily with the mind. Moving to connect with the earth and the body is about reconnecting with reality. Our spirit, who we really are, expresses itself through the amazing universe of the body. From this connection arises true knowledge. Neither the body nor the earth ever lies.

Sometimes the body is the most difficult level of self for people to embrace with their consciousness. Very often, it is because self-hate is acted out on the body. Many forces in our society, including the corporate media, urge us to either glorify the body in its culturally accepted "perfected" form, or to dispose of it, trashing it with self-loathing. In my preteen and teenage years, I began to feel very uncomfortable with my body. My clothes didn't seem to fit right as I awkwardly dragged myself through the days. I separated my body from my consciousness and started to reject it, barely able to look at myself from the neck down. I simply hadn't experienced enough love to keep all the pieces of myself together.

My relationship to my body was not about compassion, but about the festering hatred my stepfather leaked out onto me. By the time I was thirteen, I decided I was fat. I spent the next four or five years dieting, losing and gaining weight, while judging myself unmercifully in the frozen flatness of the mirror. I felt uncomfortable in my own skin. I was addicted to holding some perfected TV image of myself that could never be achieved, especially with my more voluptuous body type.

We need to move into relationship with the body as we have done with the earth. In early childhood, as we learn to move our bodies with greater coordination and direct them to interact with what we need and want, we attempt to assert our healthy autonomy and develop necessary initiative. As adults now engaged in a healing process focused on resolving these developmental crises, we are in a position to become supportive parents to ourselves—learning to be our own mirrors regarding physical exploration, adventure, competence, and pleasure.

It is best to embrace the body through conscious walking, yoga, t'ai chi, or forms of dance that create consciousness rather than impose rigid movement structures and injurious demands. Reflecting that principle, there are five different physical exercises within this next task. The first two exercises are from the ancient art of belly dance. Belly dance dates back many thousands of years and is a sacred dance of Mother Earth and the elements. The other exercises come from the ancient art and science of yoga, which originated in India thousands of years ago. I experience yoga as an earth-connected system of exercise. Many of its postures or body sculptures have nature-connected names, such as the Mountain and the Cobra poses.

◆ Task Seven: Moving with the Earth

Drawing Up Earth Energy

Stand in a relaxed manner with your feet about hip-width apart. Have your feet parallel, toes pointing directly forward. Allow the ankles and knees to be soft and unlocked. See if you can stack your rib cage on top of your pelvic bowl, and without slumping, let the flesh of the belly rest back into the bowl of the pelvis. This will keep your lower back safe from strain. Lift your heart.

Now, simply rock from foot to foot. Make sure your knees are not locked. Sway through the spine as you rock. This begins to move the synovial fluid in the joints of the body. This gentle rocking motion will draw the kundalini energy—magnetic, creative life-force energy—up from Mother Earth. There is an acupuncture point just underneath the center of the ball of the foot called "bubbling spring." As you rock, yin energy from Mother Earth will stream up through this point, and into the temple of your body. You can feel your solidness, your substance, as you sway, connected to the solidness and substance of Mother Earth. Release your fears as you feel supported.

To end, allow yourself to sway less and come to balance in the center, weight equally distributed on both feet.

Spiraling with Kundalini

Still standing with your feet hip-width apart, begin to gently make a circle with your tailbone and sitz bones (the base of the spine and the base of the pelvis). Move as though these bones were tracing a circle on Mother Earth. Massage your hips with this circle, enjoying the sensation. The hips are designed to circle. Allow this movement to massage your ankles and knees gently as you do this exercise. The kundalini energy spirals up from Mother Earth into the body through the first chakra, the legs, hips, and the base of the spine and pelvis. Swirl the kundalini energy in the sacred bowl of the pelvis and let it continue to move up through the spine.

When it feels right, change direction for a while. The kundalini spirals in both directions, just like the double helix in the DNA molecule. To end, allow yourself to spiral gently to the center, coming into stillness.

The Mountain

Mountain pose forms the basis for all the standing yoga poses. Standing with your feet a little more than hip-width apart, feel how your base extends down into Mother Earth through layers of soil, water, rock, and lava. Leave your hands at your sides and feel the crown of your head as the peak of the mountain. As in the previous exercises, it is important to stack the rib cage on top of the pelvic bowl and let the flesh of the lower belly gently press back to support the lumbar spine. Lengthen through your spine and neck.

You may also bring your arms above your head, elbows straight, palms together, with relaxed shoulders (fig. 1.3). Feel your peak reach toward the sky, pressing up through your fingertips. You may want to say to yourself, "Breathing in, I feel myself as the mountain. Breathing out, I know that I am solid."

Fig. 1.3

When you are ready, gently release the arms down, sweeping them to the sides, sweeping away any tensions or clutter in your energy field. Relax and feel the expansiveness of the mountain.

The Cobra

For Cobra pose, you need to come down to the earth and lie on your belly. Feel Mother Earth underneath you. Serpents are very much earth creatures. When you breathe in, feel your belly press down into Mother Earth, and when you breathe out, feel that pressure release. Take several breaths, starting to gently press the navel toward the spine, and the sacrum (the large triangular bone at the base of the spine) toward the sky, as you exhale, contracting the abdomen, perhaps lifting it off the earth slightly. This will help to support the lower back.

Gently bring your forehead to the earth as you surrender all thought. Slightly contract your gluteal muscles, also to protect your lower back. Bring your hands under your shoulders, palms facing down and forearms off the ground. Keep your arms in, pressing them gently against the rib cage (fig. 1.4, p. 40). Then, lift your head, shoulders, and breastbone slightly off the earth by pressing your shoulder blades and the back of your head up toward the sky, without using any arm strength. Repeat several times.

Now, retaining your core support (belly engaged and lifted off the earth, sacrum floating up toward the sky), press up, using your arms, lifting from the sacrum and the shoulder blades, coming into full cobra pose (fig. 1.5, p. 40). Feel yourself as the serpent, the powerful guardian of the earth. Make sure your shoulders drop down away from your ears, elbows bent. Breathe. Let your breath strengthen your core, your spine, your center. If this pose bothers your back at any point, release it and relax. If you are comfortable here, you may look over one shoulder, and then the other (fig. 1.6, p. 40). You may then release into the next exercise.

Fig. 1.4

Fig. 1.5

Fig. 1.6

Fig. 1.7

Child Pose

From cobra pose, use your arms and abdominal muscles to press your sitz bones (base of pelvis) back toward your heels to come into Child pose (fig. 1.7). Relax and allow your back to open. Let your breath massage your belly. If you need to, you can make room between your legs for your belly.

Know that you are a child of Mother Earth. You are made in her beautiful, magnificent image. Feel your own power in connection to her.

When you have finished Child pose, press yourself up, sit, or lie down and continue to feel your connection to Mother Earth.

In our culture, we tend to either deny the body and its desires and needs, or to overindulge them. Our bodies have become objects rather than vehicles for sacred, nourishing connection. We demand some type of arbitrary perfection from our bodies. Eve Ensler explores the insidiousness of this from every angle in her play *The Good Body*. The opening monologue ends with these lines: "What I can't believe is that someone like me, a radical feminist for nearly thirty years, could spend this much time thinking about my stomach. It has become my tormentor, my dis-tracter; it's my most serious committed relationship." The previous exer-cises and the following task can support you in trusting and honoring the body again.

❈ Task Eight: Bathing the Body in the Heart's Compassion

For this task, you may walk, stand, sit, or lie down. Check in with your body and all the sensations you are feeling. Notice warmth, coolness, tingling, numbness, comfort, discomfort, and any other sensations. Let yourself enjoy the symphony of sensation. Journey to your magnificent organ systems. Just be with your body the way a loving parent would be with a child. Sense the wonder of yourself.

If there is distress or pain, see if you can soften around it. Invite your heart to hold and embrace your body with love. If you have a symptom in a part of your body or feel judgmental or rejecting toward it, try to think about what it does. For example, if your feet hurt, focus on the conscious realization that the feet walk. They move you forward in life. Perhaps your feet need to be honored for all that they do for you every day. Maybe they need to be nurtured and loved.

Dialogue with your body. Do what feels right for you to balance your body. Really talk to it, and listen when it talks to you. Feel your body fully embraced by the compassion in your heart. See it glowing in the light of love. Try to do this task at least once every day.

CREATING A CORE OF SAFETY AND HEALING

From your work in this chapter you should get a general sense of your trust issues and the trust issues of our culture—how they were created and how they may be healed. One way to heal is to journey to nonordinary reality to bring back healing for this ordinary reality. In shamanic language, this is frequently called a "retrieval." In fact, a shaman may be defined as one who does this retrieval work. Because many of us did not have enough emotional, and perhaps physical, safety in childhood, it is important to start our healing adventures in nonordinary reality by connecting to a sacred place. This can be a place you've been in ordinary reality or one you only see when you travel in nonordinary reality.

The sacred place is a healing and nurturing place of deep connection to nature and wisdom. It will cultivate the safety, nurturing, and constancy that are the prerequisites for resolving our early trust issues in the first chakra and the ego state of the infant to six-year-old. Journeying to your sacred place can provide a step forward into consciousness and healing. By doing this exercise, we get to heal this youngest part of ourselves as we move into greater trust and a sense of safe connection. The sacred place will also be an important starting point for future journeys.

❖ Task Nine: Finding Your Sacred Place

You may choose to do this task using a shamanic drumming tape, having someone drum for you, lying outside surrounded by nature sounds, playing relaxing music, or in silence.

We'll begin by lying down on the floor or Mother Earth. (Please modify as needed for your comfort.) Relax your physical body. Breathe in relaxation, breathe out tension. Feel yourself getting heavier and heavier, sinking down into the earth on which you lie. Feel yourself held by the loving embrace of Mother Earth, fully supported, as you completely relax your legs, arms, torso, shoulders, neck, and head, releasing them to the pull of gravity.

Now, allow yourself to journey. Go—in your consciousness, your spiritual imagination—to your sacred healing place. Trust your spirit to take you to this special place in nature; perhaps you have been there before, perhaps not. It may be like watching a movie at first, and then being in the movie. See the forms and colors of your sacred place. Take them in deeply through your eyes to your nervous system. Perhaps you will also hear your sacred place through the songs of running water, birds, or the breeze. Take in the sacred natural music of this place.

Smell its fragrances. You can receive healing from this sacred place especially deeply through your sense of smell and its ancient, primitive connection to your nervous system and soul. Feel this place on your skin. Take in its textures, temperatures, and the movement and caresses of the air. Feel yourself completely present in the journey. Feel the nurturing spirits of any animal or plant life as well as the elements and the natural forms that embody them. You may want to ask your sacred place if it has a message for you. Or you may have a specific question that you are pondering. Ask sincerely from your heart, and allow your sacred place to answer. This answer may happen by something shifting or changing in your sacred place. You will be left to ponder the significance of this change. Or something in your sacred place may speak or communicate in a symbolic or sensual way, such as in dance or song. It may be a spirit, animal, tree, stream, rock, blade of grass, or other object. If it was a symbolic communication, sit with the sensuality of it and process it, allowing its meaning to reveal itself to you. Feel nurtured by this communication.

When you are ready, thank your sacred place and helping spirits. Carry this communication from Spirit back with you from nonordinary reality to ordinary reality. Record your experience in a journal. Over time, you may intuit how this communication can support you on the journey of your life.

Develop a profound trust in your sacred place as you travel to it for a few minutes each day. It will help you shift any wounding you may have around trust issues. You may have ongoing communication with any of the spirits from your sacred place. Feel how they are always there to support you.

If you are struggling with these tasks, it is extremely important to look for a trained therapist to support you in the process. I believe therapy is important for traumatized, fragile people. I believe that the work I did in my Gestalt therapeutic process made the connection with my spirit guides possible. Before therapy, I could barely remember what nurturing was, and I had rarely been protected. It wouldn't have even occurred to me to look for, or honor, these energies.

This leads us to our next task, the major task of this chakra: power animal or spirit guide retrieval. If the first chakra is not healthy, we cannot receive the kundalini energy that supports our life. If your trust was violated during this first developmental period, and the wounds have not been healed, you may still allow your trust to be violated, or you might violate other people's trust. You may also avoid situations that would be beneficial for your growth, but that require more trust than you can give.

Power animals are vital for the protection of this first chakra, and they facilitate our ability to trust in a responsible manner. By retrieving a power animal, you can protect this vital center as you prepare to release yourself from the old dramas. Power animals hold a place of profound significance in shamanic traditions. They provide us with the support and mirroring we need, allowing us to successfully resolve this crucial crisis.

The eagle is a very central power animal in the universe of my first chakra. My connection with Guiding Eagle, my first recognizable spirit guide, was life altering. He has since introduced me to his wife, Eagle Woman, who was my mother in a previous life. At my first meeting with Guiding Eagle and at many other times, I cried in the arms and wings of my beloved eagle parents, feeling held, comforted, nurtured, and inspired. My eagle parents held me in all the emotional ways I needed, for all the young places inside me.

About six years ago, shamans John Perkins and Llyn Roberts-Herrick led me in a powerful ceremony in which I was born again to my eagle parents in this life. Everyone at this workshop was invited to be born through a long birth canal of love and profound welcoming created by a double line of gentle, compassionate people. They touched me with care as I moved through them, like the cells of the vagina caressing the baby on its journey to the air. We chanted to the divine mother. In this ceremony, I felt held and encouraged by my eagle parents and born into their loving arms. I cried for at least an hour, finally fully at home with them in this life. My guides informed me that this birth would allow me to be more available for shamanic work in my community and the world community.

⊰❈⊱ Task Ten: Connecting with a Power Animal

Prepare for this journey by relaxing, preferably on Mother Earth, and going to the sacred place you found in task nine. Always connect to your sacred place fully, with all your senses.

You may find your power animal within your sacred place, or another animal, being, or force of nature could lead you to find your animal in a place beyond your sacred place. You may see your power animal several times during your journey. This is one way to know that this animal is your power animal. It is important to ask an animal that appears to you during this journey if it is your power animal. Wait for confirmation that does not seem ambiguous.

Your power animal may "speak" in movement, song, gesture, or other nonverbal expressions. Allow yourself to just feel these expressions until you have a sense of what they may mean and their relevance to your life.

If you have left your sacred place to meet your power animal, return there together. Dance or play with your power animal in your sacred place. Ask your power animal if it has a message for you. There may be a question you need to ask it. Have a conversation. Open up the flow of energy between you. Thank it for coming to you, and thank Spirit for bringing it to you.

Return to ordinary reality from your sacred place, feeling your power animal inside you or around you. Dance or move with your power animal. Allow yourself to become this animal as you dance and move to honor it. You may also make sounds like your power animal or sing its song. Feel this connection sensually in your body, deep in your cells. Know that this animal or spirit guide will probably become your new best friend or a vital member of your inner family. At times your guide may act as a healthy, loving inner parent—supporting your respectful, autonomous exploration of the world and encouraging you to take initiative to implement your budding ideas.

Record this journey in your journal. Record all your feelings and sensations, and any conversations with your power animal. Spend time with your power animal each day. You may do this in nonordinary reality when you journey to your sacred place. Or perhaps you will sense your power animal flying, walking, or crawling with you in ordinary reality, somewhere around or within your energy body. Feel the protection and love of this sacred companionship.

After journeying to nonordinary reality, always ground yourself by returning to the energy of Mother Earth, feeling enriched by your travels. When you have gathered some kundalini for yourself, consider sharing it with your loved ones. Your connection to a sacred place, your power animal, and Mother Earth may have empowered you to support others in their healing, the focus of our next and final task in this chapter.

You have gathered supports to resolve your own developmental crisis regarding trust, and now you can be a trustworthy, loving support to others seeking to connect with a safe person, healing energy from Mother Earth, and their own physical body. Gentle touch is a wonderful way for us all to heal issues around early nurturing and it feels great. Extending the healing energy you've gathered in this chapter through this next task expresses your flourishing sense of autonomy and ability to take initiative.

I use bodywork of this type as an integral part of my shamanic practice. Before you start this practice, ask that the energy be used only for the highest good of all concerned, in the service of health and balance.

Look at the chakra chart to see where the major energy centers are located in the body (fig. 1.1, p. 15). Your focus in this task will be to balance them—inviting them to be comfortably energized. Understand that chakras are wheels of light or vortexes of energy. You will be using Mother Earth's energy, the sacred kundalini that you have connected with in the earlier tasks, to energize or charge your own energy field, chakra by chakra, and then the energy field of the person you are working with. In this task we use our bodies and hearts as the instruments of healing, and the music that we play is divine.

❧ Task Eleven: Hands-on Healing with Kundalini Energy

Connect with your power animal or spirit guide, asking for support, guidance, inspiration, and protection. Have your partner lie on a massage table, a bed, or the floor and relax as you prepare for your healing work with her or him.

Stand at your partner's feet. First, reach down to draw the energy up from Mother Earth into yourself as we did in task four. Draw energy up with your hands and/or through your feet. You can rock from foot to foot or stand in relative stillness to facilitate this process. Draw the rich magnetic energy up through each of your chakras through the midline of your body, using your consciousness and breath. It may feel a bit like sucking the energy up through a straw through your legs and center of your torso as you inhale. Feel the energy or imagine a light enhancing the flow and radiance of each chakra. You may feel a warmth or sense that the chakra is spinning as the healing energy enters and balances the chakra, or perhaps you will feel a comfortable fullness or contentment in an area of the body where a chakra is located. It is fine to follow the chart until you are familiar with the location of each chakra.

When you have moved up through all the chakras in order, infusing them with energy, you will reach the crown of your head. Let the energy move out above your head and gather there. Feel beautiful white light from the heavens rain around your body like a glorious fountain. Sense your whole aura, your energy body in its entirety, for three feet completely around you. Enjoy experiencing the luminous wholeness of yourself.

Now, approach your partner. Continue to connect with the kundalini energy from the earth and the divine masculine light energy from the heavens. You will now energize and cleanse your partner's chakras with energy, one at a time, beginning at the first chakra. To start, move from the place where you have been standing at your partner's feet and position your hands in the vicinity of your partner's first chakra. Placing one hand on each of the hip joints, palms on top of the torso and fingers reaching around the sides, works best. You can also work a bit above the body, sensing the energy. (This works well for the first chakra, given its proximity to private areas of the body.)

If you sense density or thickness in your partner's energy field, you can clear out the chakra using sweeping, scrubbing, or other cleaning motions above the body. This sensing and cleansing motion is just like what you did in task four, but now you are doing this to another person. Use your consciousness and breath, but also your hands with appropriate touch that is comfortable for both of you. This should be an enjoyable, healing dance for both of you, with you doing most of the moving.

You may continue with the subsequent chakras in order, working in direct contact with your partner's physical body, and also in the energy field around the body. Simply place your hands in the vicinity of each chakra and channel the kundalini energy that you continue to draw up from Mother Earth, or you can make sweeping motions around the body, releasing what is no longer needed down into Mother Earth as you did in task four. Start to sense what is required. After you have energized and cleansed all the chakras, allow the light from the sun and stars to flow through your body, arms, and hands to the person you are working on, imagining this partner illuminated, loved, and healed.

Feel the flow of these sacred, sensual energies from the earth and the heavens. Enjoy them. You will know your partner has received healing from this task when you note increased warmth or coolness, pulsing, a sense of clarity or lightness in the energy, or that your partner is breathing more deeply, to name a few possibilities. When you sense that the energy vibration of her or his chakras has been raised, continue the dance of your hands as you powerfully sweep down through your partner's whole energy field, from the top of the head to the base of the torso, to balance it and smooth it out. Sweep down the legs to hold your partner's feet to ground her or him, deepening connection to Mother Earth for both of you. Thank Mother Earth and your power animal and your partner for providing you with an opportunity to dance with this energy in the service of healing.

Reflect on this chapter and honor the ways in which you have explored and healed issues related to birth, your body, connection to Mother Earth and feminine spirit, and trust. Appreciate the efforts you have made on your own behalf. Feel how you are beginning to be able to sense and use your healing energies, supported by the element of earth and by your spirit guides.

2

Woman of the Waves

A Journey to Emotional Freedom

A part of me will always be standing in the bow of my family's sailboat, one hand on the forestay, bare feet planted firmly on the deck, riding the swells, the ups and downs of the waters of Long Island Sound. The strong winds blow my long brown hair as the waves move my spine. I am alone with the elements in the bow of the boat, meeting them directly, fearlessly. I can handle them, however they may manifest themselves. They are my allies, the water, wind, and sun.

This was my meeting with Spirit. Trapped in my parent's house in winter, I dreamed of spring, summer, and fall when I would stand in just this place and be touched deeply, moved freely, and cleansed. I knew there was a message from the elements for me, from the depths of the sea, the light of the sun, and the whispering wisdom the wind carries from all corners of the earth, "You are the woman of the waves. You will ride out the storm with courage. You will plot and follow the course of your soul."

▼

In chapter 1 we explored the first chakra and Erickson's first three stages of development regarding building trust in others and self. The second chakra embodies the next stage of developmental crisis in his paradigm—industry vs. inferiority. The word *industry* is derived from the Latin word meaning "to build." This verb conveys the magnitude of skills and "self" it is the child's task to develop and master at this time.

Children learn so much about themselves and the world between the ages of six and twelve, the developmental stage embodied in this second chakra. They continue to explore the world, going off to school and other activities, playing with friends, and then coming back to their families. With adequate support, children at this stage get to know some of the nuances regarding how they feel about what is going on within and around them. They begin to recognize what they would like to create or express in response to these dynamics and events. They learn more about what they are drawn to and repelled by, what they need and want and what they don't. If they are supported, they will learn to take action to achieve according to their interests, curiosities, and passions.

The second chakra is located in the lower belly, in the sacred bowl of the pelvis where it connects to the sacrum (the triangular bone at the base of the spine) (fig. 2.1). As it spins it energizes our procreative reproductive organs as well as our vital spiritual dynamic of creativity. It is the emotional center of the body.

Since our culture is challenged around supporting children's emotional and creative expression, from a shamanic perspective there is much to be healed in this chakra. For that reason, this chapter will focus on connecting to our emotions and our creativity.

The second chakra is profoundly connected to the element of water. Water governs the "flows" of the body including the pelvic lymphatic fluid, the movement of urine through the kidneys and bladder, and the menstrual flow. Connecting to the movement of water in the body connects us to the movement of water in nature. Indigenous cultures and shamans embrace the healing power of water. The sacred energy of fluidity can support us as we feel our emotions and create from a deep place. You will see that some of the tasks in this chapter bring us into connection with the healing power of this second chakra element.

Toward the end of this developmental stage, children move into prepuberty, and some into puberty. Secondary sex characteristics often appear along with the rapid development of the reproductive organs. It is vital that children plant the seeds now for developing a positive sense

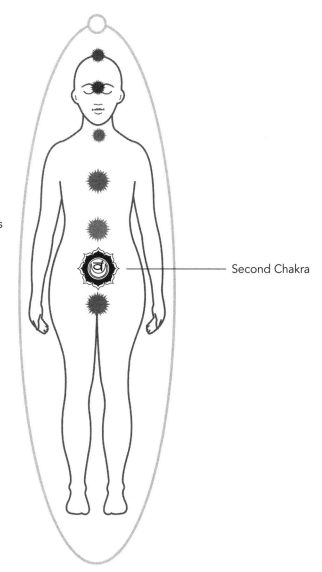

Color: Orange

Element: Water

Developmental Age:
6–12 years

Spiritual Strength:
Creativity, Emotion,
Sensuality

**Developmental
Crisis:** Industry versus
Inferiority

Second Chakra

Fig. 2.1. Second Chakra

of their sexuality. Healthy sexuality and a sense of wholeness and integrity must be achieved and maintained for self-esteem to grow strong and to minimize feelings of inferiority. So this chapter includes tasks for healing unresolved issues concerning sexual wholeness linked to this vital phase of development.

In shamanic terms I might also describe this developmental crisis as creativity versus sacrifice, which echoes Erickson's industry vs. inferiority but adds a vital spiritual component. Creativity is industry infused with the possibility of spiritual expansiveness; it allows for learning and expression beyond the often stifling status quo of our culture. Sacrifice, in the form of abandoning parts of ourselves that we think will be, or are being, judged unacceptable, is a dynamic that ultimately creates a sense of inferiority. So, in contrast to the often heartless, fragmented evaluations of self engendered by our society, it falls within the shamanic ideal to embrace all parts of ourselves and provide them with what they need to heal into self-esteem. To that end, this chapter concludes with the shamanic task of soul retrieval, providing an opportunity to gather back any pieces of ourselves that may remained locked in childhood traumas.

CONNECTING TO EMOTION

The second chakra is the emotional center of the body. Emotions are a vital source of enjoyment, depth, and richness in life, and they can spur us into healthy motion. Emotions move us toward and away from people and things, and they move us to create, to change, and grow. It is crucial to become knowledgeable about our emotions and connect to them, to have an open, accepting relationship with these energies. For example, if we did not allow ourselves to experience the emotion of anger, we would never know when to make boundaries with others and their abusive behaviors.

Dr. Nancy Boyd Webb, my professor of social work at Fordham University, tells children that feelings are something we feel in our bodies. She often gives the children she works with a blank outline of a body and asks them to fill in their emotions with color. This is an important self-knowledge exercise for children in a culture where we separate people from their emotions. How wonderful to be brought back into contact with your emotions in childhood, rather than adulthood, when rewiring the nervous system is so much more difficult.

When children are young, especially in this six-to-twelve year age group, they don't need their parents to "solve" their emotions for them. They need their parents to be a compassionate "container" for their emotions, holding them with love in their emotional process. To be a compassionate container simply means to attempt to mirror the emotions of the child; for example, seeing the child's tears and labeling the expression sadness while being open to the reality that the expression may also be hurt or perhaps fear. The child is surrounded by empathic attunement when the parent is grounded in spiritual connection and feels reasonably comfortable with her or his own emotions. Mirroring allows children to develop empathy and the capacity to be both authentic and respectful, which is vital for healthy relationships.

In our narcissistic culture, we have decided it is not manly or mature to cry or to be angry at an unjust system, whether it is economic, social, or political. If we really allowed ourselves to feel all that is going on in the world, if we were grief-stricken by the fact that twenty thousand people starve to death every day and many more have inadequate care of every kind, we could be labeled depressed. So we tend to block emotions out of our consciousness through one or more defense mechanisms. These defense mechanisms allow us to endure the many emotionally overwhelming circumstances of our childhoods and all that goes on in our culture and the world around us at every age. If we overuse our defense mechanisms, we become disconnected. It is vital to reconnect with and honor our emotions, because it is our unshed tears that create the greatest acts of acute and ongoing violence in the world. Alice Miller, the Swiss psychoanalyst, wrote about the pathological dynamics of Adolf Hitler's childhood and how their hidden emotional charge got acted out on the world. In her book *For Your Own Good,* she states, "The stockpiling of nuclear weapons is only a symbol of bottled-up feelings of hatred and of the accompanying inability to perceive and articulate genuine human needs."

Awareness of and compassion for our emotions can lead us in the direction of our needs. They tell us of our satisfactions and hungers. As long as we are feeling authentic emotional responses to the inner and outer events of our lives, we will be moving in the direction of health and integrity. All of the emotions can be useful, unless we are cultivating excess emotional charge for the purpose of manipulation—such as staying trapped in fear so that others will take care of you when you are actually capable of allaying your own fears. Learning to respond appropriately to the nuances of our emotions improves the quality of our lives and the lives of the people around us.

One of the reasons we may avoid or deny our emotions is fear of what our emotions might reveal about us. In the following journey we will practice seeing deeply into ourselves through our emotions. Seeing into oneself and not running from what you find is extremely important to develop a healthy energy body. With a healthy energy body you will be strong, wise, and flexible in both ordinary and nonordinary reality.

We all need to heal at the level of our emotions by staying lovingly present as they flow within us. In the last chapter, task eight involved simply being aware of the body and its sensations. We will now build on our beginning body consciousness and take a similar journey to the emotions.

◆ Task One: A Journey to the Emotions

Sit or lie down in a quiet place. Close your eyes and bring your awareness to your body. You may sense the density or solidness of your physical body. You may then become aware of your emotional energy, which is generally lighter and more fluid than the physical body. Allow the emotions to flow as energy. See if you sense colors or images that suggest why these particular emotions may be flowing in this particular way. You may also feel physical sensations, such as heat for anger or shame, tingling or pulsing for excitement, or heaviness for grief or sadness. How do emotions express themselves in your body? Does what you are sensing have any valuable message for you regarding the journey of your life at this particular juncture?

After you have a general sense of the flow of your emotional energy through and around the universe of your body, place your hands over your heart. Feel the energy in your heart as you continue this journey. You may be able to acknowledge your emotions—anger, fear, grief, sadness, hurt, joy, contentment, calm, love, peace—with compassion, especially the emotions we have been trained to think of as negative. In this journey hold your emotions with openhearted empathy, kindness, and courage. It is also beneficial to let your power animal be with you for support and protection and to know that Mother Earth is the loving container for all our emotions all the time. You may journey to your sacred place as you hold yourself lovingly in your heart.

CONNECTING TO CREATIVITY

Our emotions often lead us to our creativity. Being deeply moved or awed by visual beauty may prompt an artist to re-create or capture it, as Ansel Adams did in his photographs. I imagine that Sylvia Plath's exceptional poetry was in part motivated by grief and anger about her distant father and her feelings as a woman in the patriarchal world at large. I'd like to think that Martin Scorsese's violent films are an attempt to master fear of organized crime, senseless killing, and the reality we all face that the human mind can seriously twist under too much of the wrong kind of pressure.

If we believe that our emotions can lead us to creative action, we have no need to fear them. We can channel this energy for our own healing and for the healing of the planet. Very often it is our artists who invite us to look at life and to see situations and dynamics that we would otherwise avoid looking at more closely. John Steinbeck invited us to look more closely at the plight of the migrant workers in *The Grapes of Wrath*, and Marvin Gaye moved us through song to understand the implications of the Vietnam War and what we were and still are doing to the environment. We all can utilize emotional insight and creativity in our own ways.

When I decided I would study drama and dance in my first semester of college, I knew that I was on the right path. I realized that nurturing this part of myself had been and would continue to be my salvation. In the early grades of elementary school, before my stepfather's influence completely dampened my spirit, my friends and I were always creating plays and performing songs and dances. I could fully enter the world of the three bears, the flying gulls, or whatever we were enacting. In those early years, I had a strong sense of dynamic creativity that was juxtaposed against the severe abuse in my family. My high school studies were basically devoid of creative focus. This allowed me to hide from the terror of my family life in the left side of my brain, focusing on the logic of math and science. But on my own time I also wrote poetry, played guitar, and sang.

It is sad that we live in a culture that provides minimal support for creativity. We see it as optional. For example, the city school system I attended for elementary school has recently experienced a budget crisis and cut the art, music, and dance programs. Creativity is usually the first thing to go. But creativity is vital for our health and our integrity.

In the six- to twelve-year-old stage, we are still resolving the developmental crisis of industry versus inferiority. If we receive the support to do and to express, we begin to have a sense of ourselves as capable creative beings. If we do not get that support we can begin to feel inferior. Later, as adults, we may sense that we are not flourishing fully and that something is missing, and we may not feel worthy of support to express all that we are. To successfully resolve the spiritual aspect of this developmental crisis, we need to find a way to be supported as we dance in the full light of our being at every age.

Before doing this next exercise, have ready any materials that support you in the ways you usually create, or ways in which you'd like to create. For example, if you are a painter or have always wanted to be one, have paints and paper or canvas available. If you are a dancer or have always wanted to be one, you may want to play inspiring music or have it handy.

◈ Task Two: Journey to Creativity

As in the previous task, journey into your body, your sensations, and your emotions. Breathe deeply and fully to support this connection to your self. Really *feel,* allowing yourself to move into the heightened awareness of your own depth and aliveness. This heightened awareness allows you to experience nonordinary reality simultaneously with ordinary reality. Allow images to flow from any of your senses—sight, sound, smell, touch, or your general kinesthetic (motion) sense.

Ask yourself, "What am I experiencing in my legs? What am I experiencing in my arms? Physically, emotionally? What am I experiencing in my torso, especially in my pelvis and my heart? What am I experiencing in my shoulders, neck, and head?" Whatever you feel, let it flow as the energy it is.

Still in a journeying state, allow yourself to sit or stand. Begin to swirl the sacred, creative bowl of your pelvis, the home of the second chakra. If you are sitting cross-legged, put your hands on your knees and circle your pelvis, tailbone circling on the earth while the crown of your head circles on the sky. You will also feel yourself circling around the sitz bones. Be aware of and honor the process of swirling the creative energy in the sacred bowl of your pelvis. If you are standing, this movement will be the same as the hip circles in chapter 1, task seven.

Feel the sacred, creative energy spiraling up from the bowl of your pelvis through the spine, to your heart, down your arms, and up through your throat, brow, and crown. Allow this energy to empower any images that have come to you. Connect energetically through the materials you have chosen for yourself. See them and let yourself breathe as you appreciate their presence in your life at this moment. Sense how they will support you in and become part of your creative process. Feel yourself connected to Mother Earth. Feel how she supports the flow of your creativity. Imagine yourself as the light of creation as you move through the vehicles of body, of emotion, of mind and soul, and of the media you have chosen for yourself.

Now, physically connect with your materials and see what you feel compelled to create. What do you wish to paint, to dance, to write, to collage, to play or otherwise express? Allow yourself at least ten minutes to be completely absorbed in this activity, though it could go on for hours. Allow your creativity to express the truth and beauty of your emotional life. If you'd like, you can share your creation with a friend or loved one.

CONNECTING TO THE POWER OF WATER

As I mentioned earlier, the second chakra corresponds with the element of water. Our physical bodies are composed of at least two-thirds water, just like the surface of Mother Earth. We would die very quickly without fresh water to drink. It is not that surprising, then, that we have a deep and powerful emotional response to water.

I have experienced the following task many times, and its impact has deepened over the years. At some point during my middle childhood years, I started to deliberately spend time in the bathtub. The water soothed my pain and washed away some of the icky feeling I got from my family and upbringing. The water also held me in a way that felt safe and warm, with a kind of tenderness I couldn't find anywhere else. During these years, I started to have terrible stomach pains and sometimes diarrhea and discomfort in my bladder, and the bath would help to soothe my stomach and the anxiety that came from feeling that my body was out of control.

In my childhood, the bath was the only full embrace that was not poisoned by someone's sexually abusive agenda. This provided me with an opportunity to understand the healing energy of water in deeper and deeper ways. I understood the lifesaving quality of water, even as I was drowning in my need for affection. In the water I could be held by something lovely and warm. At this stage of my life, my father often brought me to swim in pools, lakes, and at Rye Beach. It was always difficult for him to get me out of the water, except to eat lunch. My skin would turn blue and prune up, especially on cold Memorial Day weekends, but I would still want to swim around in whatever sacred body of water I was in. I could be a young dolphin, playing in and around my spiritual mother.

◈ Task Three: Taking a Nurturing Bath

To do this nurturing, cleansing task of taking a bath, fill your tub with water at a comfortable temperature and add a cup of sea salt. If your bathroom has a window, open it. Light a candle. Submerge your body and feel the water all around you. Feel its subtle movement. Breathe. Feel the motion of the water responding to your breath. Feel the very gentle waves.

Feel the movement of the water within you. Feel it in your tissues, cells, spinal fluid, blood, lymph, and joint fluid. Feel the fluid within you and the water around you, moving with your breath. Feel the continuum.

Attune yourself to the quality of the water, its fluidity. Feel what that means. Ask the water, within you and all around you, if it has a message for you.

Imagine what it was like to be in the womb. Feel yourself float in the womb of this bath. Feel the water as a sacred mother goddess.

Imagine yourself reborn as you get out of the bath and wrap yourself in a soft blanket and lie down and relax. Breathe and receive the continuous gift of the water, born new into the embrace of your loving, nurturing heart.

When you are ready, you can journal about this journey.

◈

One of my sacred places will always be Long Island Sound and the special experience I had of her when I was a child on a boat, gliding on her depths. Though my family didn't take many photographs, I have seen snapshots of myself at age six at the helm of a sailboat, in shorts and a floppy pink hat. From an early age, I loved the parting of the sea as we harnessed the wind in the sails and the boat moved through.

By the time I was eleven or twelve, my mind was waking up to a new level of consciousness, as was my body. The premature loss of my innocence had pushed me very early to the edge of much-needed growth and support from Spirit. At this age, I was coming into a new understanding of myself and the possibilities of connection to Spirit through Mother Earth and the elements, especially the water.

⟞⟞ Task Four: Journey to the Water in Your Sacred Place

Lie down, relax, and allow yourself to journey to your sacred place as you did in chapter 1. Experience your sacred place with all your senses.

Find the water in your sacred place. Follow it. Follow the streams to the rivers, to the ponds, to the lakes, to the oceans. Swim in the waters of your sacred place. Feel the qualities of the water. Feel the fluidity, the contact, the nurturing.

Journey inside your body, feeling the streams, rivers, lakes, and oceans, the blood and lymph, the synovial, cerebrospinal, and tissue fluid. Feel the connection of your body to Mother Earth.

On this journey, invite a power animal or spirit guide connected to the element of water to present itself to you. If an animal or guide appears, ask it if it has a message or any guidance for you. This guidance might be connected to the energies of creativity, emotion, or sensuality. When you receive this message, thank your sacred place and spirit guides, return to ordinary reality, and record the experience in your journal.

As a child sailing on Long Island Sound, I instinctively understood something about the relationship of the angle of the boat and the sails to the direction the wind was blowing from. As if I was born with it, I had a sense of how to maximize the force of the flowing air with the greatest possible fullness of the sails, while moving on a course toward a specific point. At six and seven I understood that this was a healthy power. I was using instinct and logic together, utilizing a force in nature with respect, while moving toward a goal. I received great pleasure from this process. My mother and stepfather would drink quite a bit on the boat but because I knew I could steer and swim, I felt confident.

In the relative vastness of the water and sky, I felt I could allow myself to be vulnerable. The sea and heavens seemed changeable, emotional, and passionate, like me, so perhaps they provided some mirroring for my ever-searching soul. I already had so many burdens and unfortunate secrets to hold, which I could release to the sea. I never felt judged by the water, sea, or sky. As I moved into prepuberty, it seemed clear that my position on the boat was in the bow, standing directly with the elements, away from my family. Here I learned to undulate with the swell of the sea.

In the following task, we will explore moving the body in ways that will help us connect to the element of water.

✦ Task Five: Moving Your Body like the Water

The Wave

Standing with your feet hip-width apart, lift your arms as you stretch and open the front of your body (fig. 2.2, p. 64). Reach up high, then bend your knees and sweep down toward the earth, like a wave sweeping down and out toward the shore (fig. 2.3, p. 64). Breathing in, lift up like a swelling wave (fig. 2.4, p. 64); then breathe out, sweeping down, releasing to earth (fig. 2.5, p. 64). Repeat this several times, feeling your fluidity and power as the wave. You may wish to make wave-like sounds.

Fig. 2.2

Fig. 2.3

Fig. 2.4

Fig. 2.5

The Tide

Start with one leg comfortably in front of the other, with both feet on Mother Earth. Your legs are still hip-width apart. Rock forward so your weight is on your front leg. Leading with your heart, lean slightly forward. After you have rocked forward, rock back, leaning slightly in that direction as you put your weight on the back leg. Your toes and balls of your feet stay on the earth throughout this exercise. Your back heel will lift as you rock forward, and your front heel will lift as you rock back. Shift your weight a few times, forward and back. Feel the water in your body as you begin to move in this forward-and-back wavelike movement.

The Flow

Now we'll add a movement in the rib cage that will cause the spine to begin to undulate. Begin in the same stance you were in for the Tide, but switch feet, putting the opposite foot in front this time. Draw the breastbone forward and then up as you inhale. Then, gently draw the breastbone back as you begin to contract the upper belly. Roll through the spine, drawing the breastbone down, without collapsing or hollowing out the chest, as you tightly contract the lower belly and gently pull the navel toward the spine as you exhale. Remember to keep your knees unlocked, or slightly bent.

Repeat this movement—breastbone forward, up, back, and contract the belly—as you roll through the spine. Bring the pelvic bowl completely back under the rib cage before you bring the rib cage forward, up, and back again. As you do this movement, feel the sensuality of your body. Breathe in as you lift the breastbone forward, breathe out as you draw it back and contract the abdomen from the ribs to the pubic bone.

Feel the flow of the cerebrospinal fluid as well as the lymph and the blood as you undulate. Let these gentle movements support your connection to the sacred element of water.

Take some time here to allow these movements to bring you to your sacred sensuality. Sacred sensuality is connected to the integrity of the body, the fluids, the breath, and the relationship to Mother Earth. You may want to continue dancing in a sensual way. Or take a walk in nature, where you allow yourself to take in all the elements with your senses. You may want to make love with your partner, feeling the wave motion in your spine, at your core. Do what helps you connect with the pleasure and life-force energy that comes from being connected to your sensuality in this spiritual way.

To balance the second chakra and continue connecting to the element of water, it is important to find a water *huaca,* or sacred water object.

When I was a child, the holy water spoke to me from its sacred bowls in the Roman Catholic Church. "I emerge from the earth. I am always here for you to bless yourself with, to create a protective cross of spirit around your heart." From the time of my First Communion, I blessed myself with this water. You can use your sacred water object to bless water, changing it into holy, healing water for yourself, your loved ones, and healing partners.

My water huaca was given to me by my teacher, supervisor, and therapist at Hartford Family Institute, Naomi Bressette, a very powerful shaman. When I was thirty-one years old, after I'd suffered a trauma I will talk about in later chapters, she was able to see that I was still in a great deal of physical and emotional pain. During a therapy session, Naomi gave me a beautiful scallop shell from her medicine bag, its color a warm and sweet coral, a second-chakra color in the orange family. In my small healing center, which is called Birth of Venus, I have a copy of Botticelli's painting of Venus emerging from a scallop shell. This shell has been a womb for me, allowing me to give rebirth to the aspects of myself that were fragmented, bringing them back into the whole of my energy body.

⟨⟩ Task Six: Finding a Sacred Water Object

You can simply walk anywhere in nature to find your water huaca. To invoke the energy of the water more fully you can walk in the rain, or on the shore or beach, or after a swim. You are looking for a sacred object that holds the energy of the element of water. Most of my students find shells, sea glass, or stones smoothed by the caress of the sea, but something else may call you with its own reasons. Be open.

Ask the energy of the water to share itself with you through the presence of this huaca. When you find your huaca, thank it for appearing in your life. Thank the spirit of the water, the Water Goddess, for her presence in your life.

Hold your huaca to your heart and your navel center. Feel its energy. Let it nourish you. Ask your huaca if it has any messages for you about your creative, sensual, passionate, emotional journey. Listen with the heart in your pelvis. You may sense an opening there. The pelvic heart is the heart from which we create future generations. (In the introduction to their meditation, Opening the Heart of the Womb, Stephen and Ondrea Levine explain that men can also experience this pelvic heart or womb with profound healing impact.) We can consider the safety and quality of life for future generations from this pelvic heart. We need to engage this heart to protect the integrity of our natural environment.

NURTURING HEALTHY SEXUALITY

The second chakra is connected to our sexuality. Hopefully, six- to twelve-year-old children do not yet experience an adult sexuality. This stage brings them physically to the beginning of the possibility of an adult sexuality with the onset of puberty. But I believe that children of this age can have a sacred sensuality, enjoying and experiencing the world, the elements, and appropriate affection in a way that strengthens them and brings them knowledge and a pleasurable connection to their bodies and nature. If the parents' sexuality is spiritually connected and they have a rich intimacy with each other, then their children have a good model for creating sacred sensuality for themselves when they are ready in their next stages of life.

Children experience their sexuality in the context of this developmental crisis, industry vs. inferiority—they are busy developing a sense of competence about themselves as gender identified beings while they are becoming aware of what it means to be female or male in the culture of their homes and the culture at large.

When my mother gave birth to me, she was quite young and married to a deeply troubled man who spent a great deal of time unemployed and unhappy because of his mental illness. As a child, I did not receive a positive sense of what it meant to be female. My mother seemed unable to nurture or protect me but rather sacrificed me to her second husband. I learned to be ashamed of my body and myself. I learned from my mother to be powerless and ineffective with respect to advocating for myself in a healthy way. This is something we have both had to unlearn over the decades.

Through the millennia, women have been split into virgin/whore, wife/mistress, good girl/bad girl, and other dichotomies both within themselves and in the Western social mind set. This was demonstrated by the life of John F. Kennedy, who had his proper wife, Jackie, and his mistress, Marilyn, who committed suicide. In the triangulation with my parents, my mother was the wife of my stepfather, and I was the mistress, a role I did not volunteer for and received no pleasure from. This deeply split my energy.

In the best of circumstances, it is a tragedy to live in the flatness of a role, even if it is the role of an exalted virgin. It is painful and overwhelming to be condemned as the whore, as I was, the container for the shame of a man who did not have the courage to own his own energy, emotion, impulses, shadow, and wholeness. Many women in our culture carry this dichotomy inside them as energy-consuming conflict, rather than experiencing natural, spiritual wholeness as sexual beings.

Another important spirit guide played a role in resolving this conflict in my own psyche, and she became a pivotal being for my integration. When I was ten, my fifth-grade teacher, Ms. Patterson, played us music from the rock opera *Jesus Christ Superstar,* and I begged my mother to get it for me for Christmas. I played it and played it so I could hear the voice of Mary Magdalene come to life in song. I was captivated by this other Mary. At ten, it was important for me to hear her passion and sexuality, as I had been awakened prematurely to mine. I was moved by how she struggled with the dynamic force of love.

Somehow I understood that this was just one portrayal of Mary Magdalene, and not a very complete one. But when the writers dared to allow her to be a central character in the life of Jesus, this allowed me to begin dreaming about who she really was. She wasn't discussed at all in my Catholic religious instruction, but from gospel readings in Mass, I knew she was the "sinful" Mary who is redeemed by her connection to Jesus, who casts out her demons. This is also how the much-needed concept of redemption found its way into my psyche, especially with regard to my sexuality, which was violated at home and condemned by the Church.

But there is a whole other aspect to this Mary that made her the ideal choice for me as a spirit guide for soul retrieval. In my twenties, I became aware of her connection to the kundalini energy, the divine feminine earth energy discussed at length in chapter 1. This was affirmed for me as I read the gnostic gospels, and most recently, *The Gospel of Mary Magdalene.* Mary Magdalene speaks about the importance of acknowledging the origin of matter, its roots or the kundalini energy. And in this gospel, when Jesus teaches about becoming fully human, he suggests the importance of passionately embracing both the divine masculine and feminine. He honored Mary Magdalene in her fullness as a woman as he honored the divine feminine energy she embodied in all its expression.

At the writing of this book, my daughter is ten years old. I frequently speak to her about what a joy it was to have her grow in my belly and nurse from my breasts. I speak to her about how amazing it is that women's bodies can do these things. To the extent that she can, she understands that menstruation is when the special blood that supports the woman's body when she grows a baby leaves the body because there is no baby growing that month. I hope to continue to give her a positive sense of what it means to be a woman while I share my awe and joy at the magnificent creative processes that we are heir to as women. There are equivalents of this for boys and men, ways to tell them about how they are part of the magnificent process of creation. We can share stories with male children about how they were created by the love of both parents and how their fathers were present at their births. We should pass on to our children the creative, enjoyable, sensual, respectful aspects of sexuality so they can be confident about this aspect of themselves in a nonexploitive way.

The energy center of sexuality spins around the sacred bowl of the pelvis. The pelvic bowl and the procreation of our species are connected to the cycles of the moon. Women often menstruate in sync with the lunar cycle and the males in their lives respond to these powerful cycles.

The moon and Mother Earth act as mirrors for our sexuality, fertility, and creativity. Mother Earth is the ultimate fertile being in the sphere of human life. Her creativity, as it manifests in all the animals, plants, fruits, grains, vegetables, flowers, and seeds, provides for our existence and fertility. We are made in the image of Mother Earth, and the sacred body of the moon pulls on our inner tides, governing the flow of fluids and sexual energy in our human pelvises, our fertile, procreative center. Embracing the poetic and spiritual aspects of our connection to Mother Earth and Grandmother Moon allows us to sense more fully our fertility and sexuality. This next task will help you connect with the cycles of the moon as you feel her gravitational force pulling on you—the sacred, beautiful embodiment of Mother Earth.

❧ Task Seven: Connecting to the Cycles of the Moon

For a month, find the moon each night and use a calendar to follow its phases. In your journal, observe what you feel during different phases of the moon. What do you feel as the moon is waxing, full, waning, and new? How does the moon pull on the rivers, streams, and oceans that flow and move in the temple of your body?

How do you feel emotionally during different phases of the moon? Are there phases when you are more inclined to feel sad, angry, joyful, fearful, or at peace? If you are a woman of childbearing years, when do you ovulate? When do you menstruate? Are there times when you feel stronger or weaker? More introverted or extroverted? Is sexual desire more or less present at different lunar phases?

These observations and questions will bring you into a more conscious, intimate relationship with the moon. Grandmother Moon is a wonderful support for our ongoing passion, growth, and creativity. This second chakra becomes more balanced and empowered as we connect with her.

If you continue to observe and question your connection to the moon for at least three months, you will begin to notice patterns in how the energy of the moon affects your life. There is a cyclical pattern as the months progress throughout the year.

My daughter and I howl at the full moon. We have done this since she was two. I am the mommy wolf and she is the baby wolf. There is a sweet surrender in drawing this sound upward from the earth to the light and gravitational pull of the moon.

RETRIEVING PARTS OF YOUR SOUL

Most of the rest of this chapter will focus on the vital shamanic task of soul retrieval. I will include some of my own experience with the process and describe how I arrived at the protocol for soul retrieval that I believe works best. Soul retrieval is a very creative process, a powerful way to reclaim lost or wounded pieces or aspects of the soul and integrate them back into the whole. We emerge from a successful soul retrieval with a new sense of authenticity, value, and worth.

Pieces of the soul split off in times of trauma. When we are forced to choose between the full expression of our soul and our connection to our parents, this is trauma. When we have to suppress or repress the natural release of emotions around a wound, this is trauma. When other people act out their emotions on us, whether intentionally or unconsciously, this can create trauma, especially if a child is not permitted to make appropriate boundaries with an invasive parent or other source of authority. When we are overwhelmed and don't have adequate support to meet the life tasks we are given, this can be trauma. It is also trauma when we are abandoned. Soul retrieval heals trauma by reintegrating the fragmented parts of the soul with the whole.

Most people who take on the job of parenting in our culture have not successfully resolved this second chakra crisis of industry versus inferiority for themselves at a spiritual level. Perhaps they achieved according to the culture and their parents' wishes, or to make money, but were not supported when they sought to follow the path of their soul. So when they see their own children stepping into their light and creative expression, they get fearful or resentful and try to repress that expression or smash it in some way. Consciously or unconsciously, the parents' fears control the children, keeping them from exploring all their creative potential. The parent may even have the best of loving intentions but may be ignorant regarding how to be supportive in this way, because the parent had no example to follow. Trauma is often precipitated by the parents' inability to provide a safe container for their child's full emotional life and expansive spirit.

In an effort to survive with the most integrity possible, pieces or aspects of the child's soul get sacrificed for the sake of the whole, so that the whole can live in and through moments of crisis and trauma. A contract gets made in these times of trauma, in which the child agrees to put aside, leave behind, hide, or otherwise separate from the aspects of self that have not been supported or have been abused. This allows the child to survive with the bulk of her (or his) sanity and integrity intact, even if means behaving less authentically or believing she (or he) is deserving of neglect or abuse. The child, having no choice, metaphorically signs a contract stating that she (or he) will believe in this distorted, superficial, "in the cultural box," diminished version of herself (or himself) in exchange for support and approval, and to avoid abandonment, heartbreak, and in the severest cases, more serious ongoing abuses. This "adapted child" continues into later stages of childhood and adulthood with a sense, consciously or unconsciously, that something is missing: the "authentic" self.

All our parts must be brought to the heart, even those parts that, out of fear, believe in blind obedience to a rigid structure, rather than partnership in creation. It is time to bring it all to the heart so that we may dream from this place of wholeness, spaciousness, and beauty, and complete the great circle of human transformation.

The twenty-five years I spent in psychotherapy was in fact a long process of soul retrieval. Very often, it is best to approach soul retrieval gradually and as part of an ongoing relationship in which trust has been established. Depending on the intensity, duration, timing, and nature of the traumas involved in a surviving person's fragmentation, her or his ego may be quite fragile. In all healing work, but especially soul retrieval, it is important to be mindful of this.

By "fragile ego," I don't mean a lack of confidence or self-esteem, although these things may accompany a fragile ego. I am referring to the *ego* in the psychodynamic sense, as the part of the person that negotiates with the environment to meet needs and fulfill desires, maintaining the person's ability to function consistently and fully within the structure of the culture in which they live. You can recognize a fragile ego by hallucinations or extrasensory data that is disturbing or nonsupportive in nature, extreme mood swings, nonnegotiable emotional outbursts, excess rigidity, nonproductive bizarre thoughts, or a lack of ability to meet basic needs appropriate to functional adult life. If you have issues of this or a similar nature, it is vital to explore your past in the company of a qualified professional. If the ego is not strong in this sense, solitary exploration of the demons of the past is potentially dangerous. In the best possible scenario, a good psychotherapist is also a shaman.

When I started therapy, I had a fragile ego. I was eighteen years old, just two years out of high school, and it was very hard for me to maintain a functional external structure for my life for any length of time. I believe this was because my internal structure was at odds with itself and perpetually collapsing. Having emerged from the coldness, emptiness, fear, and pain I felt through most of my childhood, I was confused about how to best follow my path.

So much of my soul had left my body and integrity through repeated trauma. By the time I left my family to go to college, it felt as though there was very little of me left. I knew I had to get back home to myself, but I wasn't sure how. I now know I had a body memory of being whole, because I felt that way in the womb and during some parts of my very young childhood when I lived with my grandmother. But once I was born and the abuse happened, I lost that sense of myself. My body was a frightening place to be when I lived with my family of origin, and it took many years of work on every level of my being to make it feel safe again.

A great deal of the soul retrievals I had to do centered on this second chakra, this age. This was perhaps the time in my life when the most damage was done without reprieve. In the previous stage of my life I had my grandmothers' nurturing and appropriateness, and in the stage that followed, adolescence, I found ways to free and empower myself. But middle childhood and prepuberty was for me the worst kind of scary hell. It was the most fragmenting time in my life. It included the physical and sexual abuses, both my parents getting remarried, gaining and losing three stepbrothers and a stepmother, and moving our home twice. My stepfather was around most during these years.

I am grateful that, at the time, my sexual energy was able and willing to absorb my stepfather's totally overwhelming, abusive energy. This way my system could contain and discharge the terror as the nightmares he was acting out on me became my tragic fantasies. Only in this way did I manage to not become psychotic myself. It was painful having images akin to the abuses he perpetrated on me flood me and create sexual arousal in my system. This is so sad and tragic, because sexual energy is such an expansive and creative energy and can be about the most wholesome kind of love and connection. I am grateful that there were other wonderful and romantic fantasies and experiences that produced this feeling.

Unfortunately, this was occurring against the backdrop of my Catholic experience. At this stage of my life, I began the sacrament of confession, which taught me that I must search my soul for deep flaws, expressions of continuing sin springing from the original one. I learned to blame myself for many of the horrors that were being perpetrated on me. I learned that I was especially shameful because of the sexual abuse. I knew as early as age eight that all things sexual and sexualized were sinful in the eyes of the Church. I realize in hindsight that Catholicism, combined with the particularly hideous dynamic of hatred and punishment that my stepfather inherited from his family of origin, was beginning to fuse the energy of punishment with my sexual energy.

Thankfully, over time and with the help of healers, guides, and therapists, I have been able to cleanse this dynamic out of my energy system. Through soul retrievals, I've been able to join what my stepfather tore apart. With great support I have been able to choose wholeness and the protection of love. Love precludes hatred, and it is hatred, not anger or true righteousness, that creates punishment and our collective illness around the misuse of power.

▼

The next task will introduce you to a simplified form of soul retrieval. Gentle soul retrieval provides you with an opportunity to begin to connect with the traumas in your childhood and to bring loving energy to the aspects of yourself that experienced them.

◄◆► Task Eight: A Gentle Soul Retrieval

A gentle soul retrieval involves going to your sacred place and having a sense in your heart about what it was like for you in your childhood. Even if it is sad, it is always safe and healing to have compassion toward oneself.

Have your power animal and spirit guides take you back to the places where you remember being hurt, enraged, or frightened. Once there, without reliving anything, embrace your inner child and bring her or him back to your sacred place to be healed and nurtured. You may hold a pillow as you cradle your inner child.

With love, breathe your inner child into your heart and wholeness.

We will now work with the full protocol for soul retrieval. For the first several times, and for some people always, this protocol is best done with a trained shamanic healer. Once you know the process, you may be able to do it formally or informally with yourself, a friend, or a client. Always see a qualified professional should the need arise. You may even want to just read this process and not execute it until you have read the rest of the book.

There are many different ways to approach the full protocol for soul retrieval. I will discuss the map for the method I find works best (fig. 2.6) and provide an example from my childhood to illustrate one possible way you could use the map. This will involve weaving together many of the other healing connections we have made so far in this book.

Before beginning a soul retrieval you must decide what you wish to focus it on. Do you sense a wound, especially from your childhood, that is not yet healed? Is there a disturbing story regarding an event or trauma that you will retell repeatedly? Or is there something you've never spoken about to anyone that needs to emerge? Is there an event or dynamic that compromised your integrity that you need to heal to move on to a place of wholeness? Any of these questions could lead you to a fruitful soul retrieval.

When you have settled on a focus, this will determine where you will be journeying in spirit for the purpose of reclaiming a part of your soul from trauma—the location of the event that caused this aspect of your soul to split off.

Before you begin, you will also want to clarify who will act as your spirit guide or guides. It could be the power animal you retrieved in your work on the last chakra, or an ally of the power animal. You may even have a "team" of guides established for this purpose of soul retrieval, as I do. *If you haven't yet made a strong connection to your sacred place and guides in tasks nine and ten in chapter 1, do not do soul retrieval work until you have.*

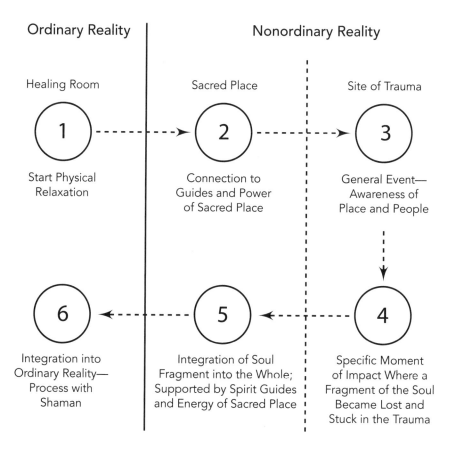

Fig. 2.6. Map of Soul Retrieval

❧ Task Nine: The Full Protocol for Soul Retrieval

As you approach **Step 1** on the map of soul retrieval you should be sitting or lying down on Mother Earth in any safe and comfortable room. You may want to play a shamanic drumming tape or have someone drum for you.

Begin to relax your body, your legs, arms, torso, shoulders, neck, and head, breathing in relaxation, breathing out tension. A deepening state of relaxation will help you to approach nonordinary reality.

In **Step 2** on the map, we move fully into nonordinary reality. Allow yourself to journey to your sacred place, experiencing it with all of your senses, letting it nourish you and fortify your strength. Before proceeding further, I suggest spending enough time here in your very familiar sacred place that you can easily come back to it any time you need to during this soul retrieval. If you find as you approach step 3 that you feel overwhelmed, come back to this step and gather strength until you feel ready to continue, or find an experienced shaman to help you.

In your sacred place, connect to your spirit guides. Invite the guide or guides that will support and protect you in these more vulnerable next steps to make their presence known. Talk to and/or make physical contact with these guides, asking them if there is anything you need to know before journeying back in time to the site of the trauma. They may share necessary wisdom or strategy for this soul retrieval, or they may simply reassure you, promising their protection.

In **Step 3**, ask your spirit guide or guides to lead or accompany you from your sacred place to the general site and approximate time of the trauma you are attempting to heal. With the help of your guides, survey the situation. Feel your guide or guides very present with you and ready to protect you if necessary, as you become aware of the details of your circumstances at this place and time. Feel the energy of your surroundings as you begin to enter the moments before the actual trauma occurred. Notice the details of what actually is happening, who is involved, what they are doing, and sense the energetic charge that will threaten your integrity. Invite your guides to make sure you are safe as you all create and adjust strategy as necessary. Keep in mind that you have come to nonordinary reality in this past time to retrieve an aspect of your soul and bring it back to the present, not to hang around. You may have emotional responses to what is occurring. Acknowledge them while continuing this task with purpose, knowing you will have the time and support to process them in step 5. You must be very focused in steps 3 and 4.

Step 4 brings you to the specific moment when a part of your soul was severed in this place. Your adult self, with the support and protection of your guides, will now confront the person or persons who are hurting you. If necessary, the guides will act on your behalf to confront the situation and the wrongdoer. The child who is being traumatized is usually not involved in this confrontation. Spirit will help you and your guides to know when to stop the trauma and use spiritual powers to free the soul fragment. More and more of my clients are stopping the traumas before they occur in nonordinary reality, addressing the energetic intentions of the aggressor or traumatic circumstance, providing protection for themselves in this layer of their stories. Before leaving the layer of nonordinary reality in this step, check with your guides and inner knowing to make sure you have said and done all that is needed to free the soul fragment from the traumatic circumstance, and that appropriate verbal and energetic boundaries have been made in response to any inappropriate action.

In **Step 5** on the map, you return with the soul fragment or traumatized inner child to your sacred place under the protection of your guides. Here they help you to draw healing energy and cleansing from your sacred place. The fragment of your soul that had been split off is reclaimed and integrated into wholeness. Your guides are most important here as they help you to hold this newly connected part of yourself with great love. It's important to thank the guides and sacred place before returning to ordinary reality. (If you should forget, thank them whenever you remember.)

In **Step 6** on the map, we connect back to ordinary reality. We land in our physical body and process the experiences and events with someone who is safe and conscious. While feeling your feet on Mother Earth, take a little time to sense your body as it holds your new energetic integrity. Here, we can integrate the retrieval's meaning into our consciousness, including new life-affirming beliefs and contracts with ourselves. Perhaps you will become aware of an image or symbol that embodies your new wholeness. It is good to journal about this shift in your sense of integrity or verbally share it with a loved one.

To give you a more tangible sense of how this process can unfold, I will now describe how I used it to heal the split between two aspects of my traumatized inner child: Peanut and Suzie. I'll begin by recounting how this split occurred.

On a typical Saturday I woke up and headed for the kitchen to get a bowl of Frosted Flakes. After I ate, I would go into the living room and hope for a morning of uninterrupted cartoons. Usually my brother, a year older, would wake up, too, and change the channel. Then we'd start to fight. My stepfather would come out with his belt. My brother would run to his room, and I would end up on the floor getting hit with the belt. I'm not sure which was worse: the pain of getting hit, or my fear of the very intense and strange animal sounds my stepfather would make when he was hitting me. I remember trying to get away from him, moving like a crab, my legs stinging and burning as I urinated on myself in my nightgown. When I think back, I can never remember what happened after that. I can only surmise that I disassociated, leaving my body, my consciousness splitting off so my nervous system would not short-circuit more completely or permanently. When I did finally return to my senses, I was often in my closet, the only room in the house that was really mine, where I felt safe.

My sleeping mother never heard my waves of outrage, pain, and fear. When I tried to tell her what had happened, her eyes would glaze over. "So don't fight with your brother," she would accuse. The unfairness and brutality of this seemed obvious to me but was never seen by anyone else. Something important in me shrank to the size of a peanut.

On some Saturday mornings, I would think that going to watch TV, given the circumstances, was a bad idea. So I'd stay in the room that I shared with my mother and stepfather. I could pray and read and color. Sometimes when I stayed in the room while my mother was sleeping, my stepfather would ask me to massage him. He liked to be caressed lightly or tickled on his back, and he made sounds I didn't understand. My skin started to feel like it no longer belonged to me. I remember him touching me this way on my arms and legs. This made me feel weird and terribly frightened. I was already scared of him because of the beatings, so I didn't feel I had any power to make him stop. I lost my voice in these moments, swallowed by fear, as I became a previously unknown self.

This part of me became Suzie, the name my stepfather called me. She could handle this challenge with a brazen quality that emerged from the feeling that I was already damaged and had nothing to lose. The other part of me, Peanut, stayed hidden in the closet. Sadly, I became two girls: one who participated in abuse because I needed any attention so as not to starve emotionally, and one who repented for my "sin" of having no other way to meet my needs.

Both aspects of myself suffered integrity-compromising abuses. I believe Peanut absorbed the brunt of the physical abuse and went deep inside, as well as in the closet, for protection from painful, confusing, and humiliating assault. I believe Suzie absorbed the brunt of the sexual abuse, disassociating and extending herself too far, getting affection and attention that was not offered in response to any other action, leaving her anxious and full of someone else's shame. Peanut turned to her conscience overzealously and began to beat up on herself. She embraced Catholic morals wholeheartedly and condemned herself. She hid in her shell from people, affirming her aspirations to be a good girl, and committed herself to harsh judgments, which created a safe but lonely and painful distance from other people. Suzie tried to embrace the attitudes of her mother and stepfather, the brazenness, and she hid her irresponsibility to self and spirit. I wanted to be whole but was hurt in response to it. Rather than totally sacrifice some part of myself, I split in two instead.

This is the soul retrieval I am examining here: myself at age eight. I know before going on this soul retrieval journey that I will have to retrieve two "selves," because the two halves will make a whole.

I have a team of guides to support me in soul retrieval. I embraced Mary Magdalene as my spirit guide for this work because of her connections to both the divine feminine and masculine energies, as both are needed for healing. And I embraced her as a redeemer because she had life experience, power, knowledge, and lived "out of the box" by choice, even though she was judged and condemned as a whore. I felt she could understand me and recognize my soul. As I've already discussed, Guiding Eagle and Eagle Woman are important spirit guides for me in general, and certainly in soul retrieval.

I was thirty-seven years old and separating from my husband when I explored my own second chakra and realized it was severely fragmented from the traumas of my childhood. At Rye Beach, a place where I spent much time during my separation and always feel a special closeness to my guides, I began this soul retrieval journey by sitting near the shimmering water, breathing gently into my body and Mother Earth, eyes half closed and unfocused. . . .

▼

When I feel relaxed and ready, I journey to my sacred place, a valley in the desert with a beautiful stream running through it. Here, I connect with both Marys (step 2). I know I need both of them to reclaim my split eight-year-old self. And Jesus is also there, a powerful man-king who can hold the fullness of the divine feminine energy, instead of needing to falsely split it into two parts. My eagle parents are also here, perched in the cliffs, watchful and loving.

My spirit guides make a circle around me energetically. They each share an important message with me about the process we are about to undertake. These messages are not primarily in words. They come through their eyes as they gaze at me. I feel their love penetrate my heart. Even otherwise fierce Eagle Woman feels deeply for me as her eyes tear in response to honoring all that I struggled with. I feel fully held by the collective of their presence, which says, "You deserve to be whole."

My spirit guides lead me from my sacred place to the apartment where I lived when I was eight (step 3). We gather there, getting a general feel of the place, its oppression and toxicity. I feel my guides here with me, protecting and guiding me. As we move to step 4 in the map, we go to the closet to find Peanut. Surprisingly, it is Mary Magdalene who sits with her. Peanut doesn't trust her at first, because she thinks she is sinful, but she is struck by the kindness of Mary M.'s heart, the warmth of her smile and hands, and the gentle softness of her body. There isn't much room in a closet, so they have to be close. Peanut has not had tender physical affection without an agenda since Grandma Margie moved to New Mexico a couple of years ago. It is at first confusing, and then a relief.

As Mary Magdalene and Peanut open the door and leave the closet, my stepfather and a priest try to stop them, yelling, "She needs to repent." But Mary Magdalene demands that they move out of the way, ordering them to "Look in a mirror!" There is a vibration to her voice, much like an earthquake. Peanut is surprised when the priest and her stepfather leave to find a mirror. Mary Magdalene brings Peanut back to the sacred place.

Next, Mother Mary brings me to the bedroom where Suzie is being "caressed" by her stepfather. She demands that he stop what he is doing. She directs a powerful light at him, and he stops immediately and backs off and then seems to be paralyzed. She demands that he "look at Suzie and see how she feels." At first my stepfather mumbles, "Uh . . . she likes this. . . ." Then Mary gets angrier and louder. "Look at her! How does she feel?"

"Uh . . . she's scared. . . . She's alone."

"You should be ashamed of yourself. Go process your own shame

so you don't deposit it in others. You need to discover and heal the source of your shame. In the meantime, you do not deserve to be around children," she scolds him. Then she gathers Suzie up and brings us back to the sacred place, followed by Jesus and the Eagles.

Suzie, Peanut, and I sit together with Mary Magdalene, Mother Mary, Jesus, and the Eagles as we begin step 5. The spirit guides and I surround the young girls. It is so peaceful in the sacred place. First, the girls take in grounding energy from the earth. Then, they are bathed in the warm, crystal-clear waterfall and flowing pool. All of the toxic energy from my family is washed off them. Both girls feel how they are made of the energy of water. They dry off in the warm sun, caressed by the gentle, sweet air.

Jesus is between the two Marys. His aura is nurtured deeply by their presence and it, in turn, holds them both with reverence. The young girls feel their connections to the two Marys. They feel held with love and acceptance. And as Jesus has the power to hold the two Marys, acknowledging them each as multifaceted whole women, both with sexuality and nurturing divinity, the two girls merge, once again becoming a whole girl with multiple facets and authenticity, held in safety and with honor. Mother Mary explains that she conceived Jesus through a spiritual, sexual union with his father, and Mary Magdalene explains that she is Jesus' partner and wife. They are both healers and wise women in their own right. It becomes clear that everyone in the circle is whole and complete. The integrated child sits on my lap near my belly and connects to my second chakra, integrating into the whole of my energy body. There is no need for any more sacrifice of myself. I express my deep gratitude to my guides who have supported me in coming to this knowledge.

In step 6, I feel myself sitting on Rye Beach again as I bring my consciousness back to my physical body looking out over the gentle waves. I am aware that through the soul retrieval experience with my guides I learned that I did in fact deserve to be whole. As I feel the sand beneath me, the warm sun above me, the salt air around me, and the sacred water moving toward me with the rising tide, I realize that the two adapted children within me became the authentic woman of the waves. It was she who made the waves or expressions of truth regarding my experience that were necessary, even though my mother couldn't handle them. I learned to ride the waves of despair and challenge on the boat—and in life—with the support of all the elements.

▼

Soul retrieval helped me to learn compassion for myself—for the choices I had made and for my powerlessness to do anything different in the face of what was done to me. Through soul retrieval you can learn to hold yourself in your own heart. Healing into integrity comes from this place.

After you have done a soul retrieval, it is good to anchor it into your energy body through the practice of ujjai breathing. The focus required for this breathing technique allows you to be fully present in every fiber of your being as you weave in the retrieved pieces of your soul.

Ujjai breath is a sounding breath, and the sound is like the waves of the ocean. This is a wonderful breath to do any time you want to relax and connect to the element of water. It gives us the power to hold and integrate our emotions so that healing can happen on a very deep level. We can surrender our wounds to the healing power of the ocean. This breath has supported me in becoming the woman of the waves. With this breath, I can shapeshift into the glorious ocean that covers three quarters of the earth's surface.

⊰⊱ Task Ten: Ujjai Breath

To perform ujjai breathing, take a deep breath in and exhale as though you are trying to fog up a mirror. This contracts the back of the throat. Now, breathe in and out through your nose with the back of the throat contracted. You will produce a sound like the rising and falling of the ocean waves. Breathe deeply into your belly with this ocean breath.

Don't think about anything in particular. Just breathe and see what happens. Feel the ocean flow through your body, connecting the puddles, tide pools, and streams into the greater fluid whole of yourself as you integrate your emotions and emotional healing into the wholeness of your being.

With this breath I have given birth to myself, Venus from the shell, woman of the waves, into the fullness of Spirit and the four elements. And with this breath I gave birth to my daughter, Kelly, from her amniotic life in the womb, into my arms.

EMBRACING WHOLENESS, REJECTING SACRIFICE

There is so much sacrifice in our Western mythology. The Jews embrace Isaac; the Moslems, Ishmael; and the Christians, Jesus. In the Old Testament, Abraham was willing to sacrifice the life of his son Isaac to prove his obedience to God, and God demanded the exile of Abraham's firstborn son Ishmael. In the New testament God sacrificed the life of his own son Jesus, who was willing to die so our sins would be forgiven. Somehow, sacrifice has become an acceptable way to operate in life—whether it is the sacrifice of one group of people to the alleged greater holiness, righteousness, or entitlement of another, suicide bombings, the slaughter of Mother Earth's creatures, or destruction of the rainforest to serve capitalist imperialism and excessive consuming.

I would propose that it is time for humankind to address this paradigm of sacrifice wholeheartedly. In my work as a massage therapist, yoga teacher, psychotherapist, and shaman, I have never found a situation in which sacrifice was a healing dynamic. (Though there are important times when, after serious reflection, one must take a strong stand and risk sacrificing for the greater good—such as Gandhi's fasting for India's freedom or Mandela's decades in jail.)

I do believe that sharing material things with people who do not have what they need to survive and enjoy a reasonable quality of life is important, but this is not sacrifice, because the person doing the sharing maintains her or his integrity. I also believe that if we do not help people who do not have what they need to survive with a decent quality of life, we are sacrificing them, not for spiritual gain, but for our own material gain. This is a crime that goes largely unaddressed in this country. However, releasing what we truly do need because of a spiritual theory that it serves some higher purpose is insanity. To heal humankind we need to embrace our wholeness, including emotional consciousness and expression, healthy creativity, and spiritual sexuality.

In her pamphlet *Sent by Earth,* a response to the events of September 11, 2001, Alice Walker writes about the Babemba tribe of South Africa and their response to a person who acts unjustly and irresponsibly. "He is placed in the center of the village, alone and unfettered. All work ceases, and every man, woman and child in the village gathers in a large circle around the accused individual. Then each person in the tribe speaks to the accused, one at a time, about all the good things the person in the center of the circle has done in his lifetime. Every incident, every experience that can be recalled with any detail and accuracy is recounted. All his positive attributes, good deeds, strengths and kindnesses are recited carefully and at length." We could learn a lot about transforming irresponsible behavior from this energetic dynamic. How much more powerful it is for the nervous system and the spirit to be reminded of one's capabilities and prior actualization of goodness than to be asked for a sacrifice. I believe it would be so much more powerful than punishment, which creates humiliation, shame, and a loss of self-esteem that then has to be healed before the person can be fully connected to Spirit again.

It is time to gather our soul fragments back to ourselves, the parts of us that got sacrificed, usually in our childhoods, because someone was immature, overwhelmed, or engulfed in a veil of ignorance and unconsciousness. It is time to know, through healing, what was sacrificed in ourselves and how not to sacrifice our own children.

By the end of this stage of my own childhood, I was wandering away from Christianity, but I often thought about the horrible way Jesus was punished for questioning laws that obscured the heart. And yet, as he died, he said, "God forgive them, they know not what they do." Even as he suffered the most awful unjustified punishment, he advocated ending all punishment. He died so that sins may be forgiven. He advocated that we change this paradigm of punishment and sacrifice. So who are we to perpetuate this old paradigm as we punish and sacrifice our children and fellow humans, rather than healing and bringing the hatred to the light of love? In punishment we obscure the spirit; in sacrifice we fragment the soul. In love we bring our weaknesses to our strengths and grow.

3
The Fires of Transformation
A Journey to Find Our Mission

The hot summer before my first semester of college was marked by the frightening reign of a local killer who called himself "Son of Sam," and a huge blackout in New York City. I was often seen wearing an orange polyester uniform working at the Howard Johnson's as a hostess. I was getting ready for college and reading books about the mysterious Bermuda Triangle. A compelling love interest developed that pulled me beyond all feeling I'd ever experienced before.

I'd invited him over but could only half believe it when he showed up at my door just after midnight, his blue eyes penetrating through the darkness. The universe expanded as I opened the door, smiling, offering wine, playing records that sang my soul: Jackson Brown, Neil Young, Carly Simon. With my parents away and my brother on the night shift, I knew we would have the whole night to ourselves.

I was sixteen and had never felt so intimately connected with another person. He revealed to me that he had attempted suicide just six months before our first wine-soaked kisses. I knew I had been almost that close to the edge many times but could never go over it. He had been on the other side and come back and was able to open up to me about how all the therapy he'd received helped him to transform his life.

The story of how he embraced transformation moved me in a way nothing had before. The steam of our tongues merged as I opened in a way I never had, as a new passionate being emerged from where I had previously been just moments ago. For the first time, I saw myself as a lover, surrendering to something far beyond anything I could have imagined. That night, we vibrated with a sexuality that had no bounds, expressing our young, expanding inner fires, lighting and inflaming each other, becoming the sun and all the exploding stars in the universe.

Mark's family was in the theater business and he'd grown up immersed in it. He took me to see my first Broadway play, The Basic Training of Pavlo Hummel, *starring Al Pacino. It changed my life. All of the fallout from the Vietnam War—the anguish, confusion, and rage— was captured on stage, raw and exposed for the nightmare it was. I watched, breathless and aching. I was opened to the knowledge that art could be a vehicle for blatant, powerful truth. I went on to register for acting classes myself.*

My dear friend Mark has been a lifelong catalyst and vehicle for my passion, love, truth, expression, and transformation. In spite of trying several times over the course of almost thirty years, it was not meant for us to be romantic partners, but he and I have a deep soul connection. He created crucial openings for me at this critical stage of development—to art, therapy, and a belief in the possibility of healing. In our own way, we have remained deeply committed to each other.

▼

Our inner teenager is embodied in the third chakra, the energy center connected to the element of fire. The third chakra is located in the upper belly, radiating yellow light as it spins above the navel, activating and balancing the adrenal glands (fig. 3.1). The solar plexus, the nerve bundle associated with the third chakra, processes energy from the fire of the sun. I have marveled at the instincts of the Siberian tigers at the Bronx

Zoo, simultaneously facing their upper bellies toward the sun's fire.

It is important to have a relationship with the element of fire. Fire is the element of transformation, passion, and commitment. Shamanically, the fire speaks to our hearts, burning away all that is false or unnecessary, revealing essential truths about our selves and our culture. This is its cleansing function. The fire also burns as our passions burn. To

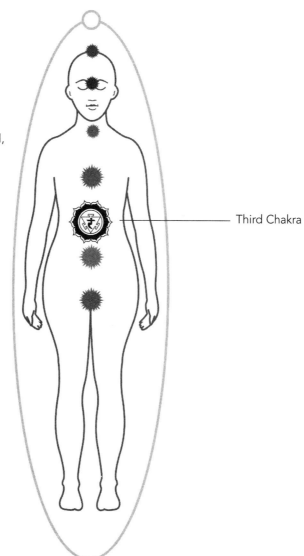

Color: Yellow

Element: Fire

Developmental Age: 12–18 years

Spiritual Strength: Will, Identity, Commitment

Developmental Crisis: Identity versus Confusion

Third Chakra

Fig. 3.1. Third Chakra

keep the spiritual fire of our passions aflame so we can grow personally and collectively, we must feed it. It is an ongoing process to feed the fire. Disciplining ourselves to do what we must to keep the fire burning becomes our commitment. The fire is strong energy to fuel the process of creation and the realization of true expansive power. Many of the tasks in this chapter are designed to heighten your awareness of this fire and strengthen your connection to it.

The challenge or developmental crisis of this time, which spans ages twelve to eighteen, is identity—having a core sense of who we really are with respect to our character, interests, values, and passions—versus role confusion. The major shamanic task of this time centers on finding a mission or a general theme or purpose for our life. At this stage, we start to know who we really are, what we care about, and the vehicles through which we may begin to express ourselves.

The hormonal dance of adolescence propels the emergence of passions—powerful emotions, appetites, and drives. Our passions generate the energy required to pursue what attracts us. By learning who we are and connecting to our will and focused, balanced power (as we will in the physical tasks in this chapter), we can move successfully to the mature act of commitment—binding ourselves to a worthy course of action.

Not knowing who we are and what we are here to do creates a great deal of anxiety and depression. Not living our mission can create great internal distress. I don't believe we can know all the details of our mission when we are teenagers, but we can be supported in finding out who we really are, what we deeply care about, and what we can do to express that in the world at large.

In the shamanic task of vision quest later in this chapter, we will call upon nature, the elements, and spirit guides to act as mirrors that reflect our depth and our core identities. They can point us toward the challenges we face in the world at large and our own unique abilities to logically and favorably affect them. The vision quest will help you find, expand, and/or deepen your sense of what you are here to do and how you may be able to do it.

Since adolescence is a time of surging hormones that fuel passion, spiritual guidance in this chakra is of great importance. When they are not being seen, mirrored, and supported regarding their core selves, teenagers can be hugely self-centered. But if someone takes the time to recognize, channel, and protect their passions, guiding them into productive and fulfilling commitments, adolescents can be magnificently creative and altruistic. We must channel teenage energy in ways that are nonexploitive and fulfilling, ways that add to, rather than detract from, life as a whole for everyone.

In some ways, we are very much stuck in this developmental stage as a culture. Here in the United States, we are figuring out whether our identity is focused on accumulating wealth at the expense of others, or being of service to make the world a better place for everyone. Part of where we get stuck in our culture is our collective addiction to materialism. We often emphasize the externals to our children, including clothes, cars, grades, and conventional behavior and appearances. Insufficient attention may be paid to who the young person truly is on the inside.

We are so addicted to materialism, and we sacrifice so much to it, including a safe, nontoxic environment, adequate social programs for people in need, and peaceful, respectful coexistence with each other and other nations around the world. Just like all serious addicts, we are even willing to sacrifice our lives. We have no reason to be surprised when our young people become addicted to tobacco, alcohol, drugs, sex, food, television, video games, the Internet, pornography, risk-taking, starvation (anorexia), and other behaviors. Their lives have been overshadowed by this enormous cultural addiction and all its global consequences.

In my early childhood my father was unemployed most of the time because of his illness and my mother worked at a low-paying job answering phones. When I was nine years old my stepfather made some money in the stock market, so for a few years we were able to enjoy a couple of the luxuries, such as the sailboat. But by the time I turned twelve he lost it all and then some and continued to be in tremendous debt through the rest of my childhood. So, my family was relatively poor. We didn't call it that, but we never had money for anything extra, even some of the things that other people in our affluent corner of suburbia considered necessities. There were moments when I was jealous of other people's clothes, cars, and exotic trips. When I drifted into wanting more things as a teenager, I was usually aware of not feeling good about myself as I was. I felt fat, awkward, unlovable. Through almost a decade, from ages twelve to twenty-two, I struggled with various addictions to food, alcohol, drugs, tobacco, sex, and television.

Until I was sixteen, I spent a great deal of time watching TV. I was addicted to the soaps I skipped school to watch, reruns of *Gilligan's Island*, anything that provided human contact that didn't hurt or insult me. While I watched TV, I mindlessly ate a lot of sugar. After a few years of therapy, I found better coping strategies. Somehow, when I had to choose between money and the expression of my soul, my soul always asserted itself. I could mobilize my energy around art and healing. I was finding my true depth and identity.

For me, one of the most appealing aspects of shamanism is that many indigenous people and their shamans do not wish to embrace the excesses of modern Western culture. It is considered living out of balance with Mother Earth to pursue such excesses. In our pursuit of appearances and materialism, we create a great deal of toxicity, much of which can be found in our sacred environment. To have the things we desire, we poison our environment, creating carcinogenic dynamics for our bodies.

Often, when our young people speak out to make us aware of things such as pollution, global warming, and other environmental issues, we call them idealists or impractical dreamers. Instead, we need to support young people in dreaming new choices and new ways of life that are productive and deeply fulfilling. We need to embrace them as teachers who can impart a fresh perspective on old problems. We need to dream a new system in which no one believes it necessary to exploit other humans and species, or pathologically reframes the exploitation as beneficial in some way for those being exploited.

As United States citizens collectively embodying the developmental stage of adolescence, we can allow ourselves to be mirrored by Mother Earth and embrace shamanic work that brings us to a living relationship with Spirit. To prepare for this mission, we need to be cleansed and encouraged to expand into the fullness of ourselves by the element of fire.

Healing this chakra requires that we fully acknowledge our past and present, personal and collective wounds and how we have misused our minds and power. Then we are free to throw our pain and unconsciousness into the fire, be fully cleansed, and go forward with our lives.

The shamanic tasks in this chapter conclude with a coming-of-age ceremony. By designing and facilitating this ceremony you are moving from exploring your identity to making a statement about who you have become. Since every aspect of the ceremony is infused with meaning it requires that you have questioned the status quo of the culture you were raised in and have kept what supports you and is worthy of keeping. With your passion and commitment, you will stand in the full power of your mission.

CONNECTING TO THE ELEMENT OF FIRE

My grandmother Margie loved a good fire. Her house in Yonkers had a fireplace, and I remember the flames and the warmth of her hearth. When I was three or four, Grandma made a fire and put something magical (and, I imagine, chemical) in it that made all the colors of the rainbow, like fireworks. I was entranced and thrilled. My grandfather also made fires outside his house, burning the leaves he raked from the yard. As they crackled and popped, their smoke made the neighborhood fragrant. During the summers I spent at my grandfather's house at Lake Champlain in Vermont, we also had fires at night when it got cool. He built fires outside after we went fishing in the morning, so we could cook the perch and sunfish we'd caught. Nothing was ever so delicious!

Margie's tiny house in New Mexico also had a fireplace. Perhaps it was the warmth from the fire that would bring the tarantulas. She was often visited by them, as well as by owls. When I stayed there with her when I was seventeen, we would sit in front of the fire after the sun went down. Even though we didn't have the same connection to each other that we'd had when I was younger (she was better with younger children), it was important for me at this stage in my life to remember that someone had once really seen me and loved me deeply and hadn't been afraid to express it. I tried to throw the broken dreams from the last decade of my childhood into her fire so I could move on, go back to college, and continue to be creative with my life. I believe it was with her fire as witness that I affirmed my dreams to act, write, and dance. I know my parents did not consider it a practical choice, but when I returned to New York, I was burning to go back to school to pursue my dreams.

This first task will support you in approaching the fire safely, while beginning to establish a relationship to it. The fire mirrors the passions that burn within us, revealing the truth about who we are. Very often, we have to allow the things that other people have imposed on us as important to burn away, making room for what is truly important to us.

◄❈► Task One: Journey to the Fire

Go to your sacred place. Experience it through your senses. The more you surrender to your senses and the details of this journey to your sacred place, the more powerful it will be.

Find the fire in your sacred place. Feel the power of the fire there. Draw it to you. You may find the fire where you least expect it. It may be an actual fire, a volcano, lava, geothermal water, or a fire animal, guide, god or goddess, or huaca. It may be the fire in your DNA or the mitochondria, deep in these cellular molecules and organelles.*

---

*One Amazonian shaman I studied with explained that DNA was photon light and our cosmic connection to the fire of the stars. We are all made from the atoms of exploded stars. Jeremy Narby also writes about this in his book *The Cosmic Serpent*, "DNA emits photons with such regularity that researchers compare the phenomenon to an ultra-weak laser."

Allow the fire to engulf you, feeling it happen. It may literally be a sunbath. Or you may jump into the volcano or be swallowed by a dragon, to emerge cleansed. It may be a cleansing ritual performed by your fire guide. Allow yourself to be cleansed, even if you must "die" to be reborn.

You may have a deep sense of old perceptions, beliefs, and energies burning off. You may see yourself and the world in a new way. The fire may tell you what you need to know about your truth and deepest self. You may go wherever Spirit, the unconscious, or your imagination leads you.

Come back to ordinary reality and record the journey in your journal.

Task Two: An Everyday Fire Ceremony

To connect with the fire, go outside. Feel the sun. (If you have concerns about your skin being at risk, go out at a time when it is not so bright.) Feel it penetrate you. Take it in. The sun burns brightly, even above the clouds. Feel the energy of fire outside you joining with the fire within you. We find the fire within us in the DNA and the mitochondria of the cells. Perhaps you can also feel fire in your belly, especially at the level of the solar plexus, where the third chakra resides.

Go inside. Light a fire in the fireplace or light a candle. This place by the fire may be your special meditation spot. Connect with the grandparent energy of the fire. Feel the support for the spark of creation that is you. Confide in the fire about your dreams for humanity and your mission within those dreams. Release your insecurities, knowing you've resolved the crises from the previous chakras. Feel your wholeness. Let the energy of the fire transform you as you clarify your mission and develop the capacity to tolerate your passion. Breathe and allow the fire to be a container for your passion and for your mission. Express your gratitude to the fire for its support.

Adolescence can be a powerful time when we try on all the boxes (political affiliations, religions, philosophical orientations, career possibilities, lifestyles, self-images) provided by our families and the culture in which we live, and decide if our spirits can thrive within them. Very often, people carry these boxes into adulthood because of fear, even when the boxes no longer serve them in any way. The box becomes home, but home is not a fulfilling place.

In this next task, we will become the fire through movement. The fire has its own dance that can act as a channel for the expression of passion, supporting our creative possibility. As you dance you will become the fire, blessing yourself with its energy. This will enable you to burn off the bonds and energies of unsupportive structure and limiting beliefs as you move your body. When my fellow shaman Leigh Reeves and I lead our fire ceremonies, we ask the participants to release what they no longer need into the fire. Leigh calls this "a garage sale for the mind." We all can get in touch with old, illogical, and invalid beliefs about ourselves and others that limit what we do in the world. When we are ready, we can throw these boxes into the fire and learn to be free.

❧ Task Three: Becoming the Fire through Movement

We will now explore moving like the fire. Fire sizzles and pops and leaps and flickers. The movement of the fire tends to be staccato, and its instrument is the drum. Ancient people have danced around the sacred fire to the beat of the drum. Start this task by playing some music that is exclusively or primarily the drum.

Head-to-Toe Vibration

Standing in a place where you can move freely, with your feet about hip-width apart, begin by allowing the whole body to vibrate, to shake, to shimmy. Vibrate and bring your arms up above your head as you inhale. Vibrate and bring your arms down as you exhale. You can intensify the vibration by allowing the knees to bend slightly. Feel all your organs vibrate, and allow yourself to enjoy this sensation. Vibrate the hips first, then vibrate the shoulders and chest. You can vibrate the shoulders by allowing one shoulder and then the other to press forward until it has a life of its own, right, left, right, left. Walk, and otherwise move about as you vibrate your hips, shoulders, and whole body. After about five minutes, pause, breathe, and feel your body and its fire.

Hip Bump

Bend your knees gently as you stand with your feet hip-width apart. Rest your belly back into the sacred bowl of the pelvis. Gently thrust your right hip out to the right, as if you were trying to close a door with your hip. Repeat with the left. To the rhythm of the drum, press the hips out, right, left, right, left. Be gentle, so that the movement is a massage for the body, but move with the staccato rhythm of the drumbeat, so it is also stimulating and strong. Feel your organs gently move and release as you feel your fire.

Allow yourself to perform these movements gently, to the best of your ability. Be creative as you allow yourself to compensate for any physical limitations you may have. The most important fruit this exercise should bear is a connection to the element of fire. It is inspiring when you can feel the movement of the energy of fire within you, the sizzle, the heat. Let the fire energy you've generated support you in releasing what you no longer wish to be limited by as you fully embrace what is essential and magnificent about you.

❧ Task Four: Breath of Fire

We will now learn an ancient yogic breathing technique called Breath of Fire. It is contraindicated for pregnant women and people with abdominal cancers or untreated high blood pressure.

Place your hands on your belly. As you breathe in, your lungs fill, your diaphragm presses down, and your belly organs press out. You will feel your belly organs press into your hands here.

As you exhale, the lungs empty, the diaphragm lifts, and the belly flattens. At the end of the exhale, gently press the navel toward the spine using the abdominal muscles to release the last bit of carbon dioxide from the lungs.

Then, breathe in gently through the nose, feeling the belly expand. Exhale through the nose as you press the navel toward the spine, gently using the abdominal muscles. Begin to do this rapidly and rhythmically, like a dog panting, only through the nose. Feel the belly bounce. This energizes the third chakra and the solar plexus. It replenishes the adrenal glands when they are exhausted from stress.

Do this for about thirty rounds (one inhale and one exhale, thirty times). You may repeat thirty rounds up to four times. Feel yourself cleansed and energized. You may follow this with a few ujjai breaths to invoke the element of water if you need to balance or cool the fire; or do a few "earth breaths," drawing energy up from Mother Earth as you breathe in, releasing what you don't need anymore down into the earth as you exhale.

The third chakra governs the adrenal glands and the sympathetic nervous system. This aspect of our nervous system is an important component of the human survival mechanism that allows us to fight or flee in response to threats and danger. This survival mechanism is a wonderful gift from creation. But to do more than survive, to thrive both as individuals and as a culture, we must know how to balance this third chakra center and connect it to other centers and parts of ourselves that can be more creative, compassionate, and wise. If we are completely led by fear in seeking solutions, we will be severely limited in our problem-solving abilities. We need to meditate, journey, and heal ourselves so our responses to life's challenges and tragedies can change and become expressions of the wholeness of who we are. We need to embrace shamanic practice so we can use all of our creativity, compassion, skills, and perspective when approaching crisis.

Triangle pose, our next task, helps to balance the adrenals. In addition to mobilizing us in response to a threat, the adrenals also release cortisone type chemicals that soothe inflammation or fire in the body. So, Triangle pose is an important pose for regulating our inner fire. It can help us balance and contact our logical mind to know whether something actually is a threat or not and to stand strong as needed in the face of great challenges, in contact with all of our inner and outer spiritual resources.

This task will help you to make real choices about what you want to do in any given situation, furthering your own purpose and the mission of the higher good. Triangle pose is a wonderful, physical way to bring the body and adrenal glands into balance so that solutions to problems will come from a wise place, free from fear-based judgment and manipulation. As it is often difficult to sit still when you are in a stress response, Triangle pose can be a wonderful way to move as you relax yourself.

◆ Task Five: Triangle Pose

Stand with your feet about two hip-widths apart and parallel, and reach your arms out at shoulder height into a star position (fig. 3.2, p. 102). Leaning over to the right, touch your right leg with your right hand and reach your left hand up to the sky (fig. 3.3, p. 102). Inhale. Exhale back to the star position. Now, lean over to the left, left hand touching the left leg, reaching the right hand up to the sky (fig. 3.4, p. 102). Inhale. Exhale back to the star position. Repeat this exercise several times, slowing down more and more and breathing as you relax and balance your adrenal glands.

Now it's time to find a fire huaca, or sacred fire object. Finding a sacred object that embodies the element of fire and spending time with it each day also helps us to balance our inner fire. Over time I have learned that I contact the fire most fully by actually being in the presence of flame, and I am drawn to use candles in my healing of others. I mostly use candles as my fire huacas and have them in all the chakra colors.

Fig. 3.2

Fig. 3.3

Fig. 3.4

Lighting them is a powerful connection to the energy of fire and a reminder to focus my passion on the spiritual. I light a yellow candle to get in touch with the energy of this chakra.

But my fire huacas also include pieces of brick and dried leaves. It is wonderful to have nature gift you with a fire huaca, something that has perhaps been touched by a fire or the intense light of the sun. My students often find dried leaves, sticks, or pieces of coal from a fire. But do not be limited by these examples. Let Mother Earth give you the unique gift of your fire huaca.

◈ Task Six: Finding a Sacred Fire Object

Allow yourself to physically journey to a sacred place in nature. It can be any place at all, but if you happen to be near volcanoes or geothermal water or a place that gets a great deal of sun, this place may draw you and be the perfect place to find your fire huaca. Ask this place for a sacred object that embodies the power of fire.

Your huaca will call to you. You may hear its voice or it simply may demand your attention. When you catch sight of it on this sacred walk, somewhere inside your upper belly you will have a visceral, energetic knowing that it is your fire huaca. When you connect with your huaca, hold it in your hands or place it on your belly and ask it if it carries a message for you from the sacred fire about your journey. Listen carefully to the message. Ask clarifying questions, especially about passion, commitment, respect, your mission, and what it might mean to come of age in accordance with having fully explored, embraced, and asserted your own value system. Bring it home with you and put it in your medicine bundle. Thank your huaca, the sacred place, the fire, and Pachamama for this precious gift.

CONNECTING WITH PASSION
AND COMMITMENT

Joan of Arc became one of the most legendary figures in history as a result of her uncompromising passion for the truth and her unshakable commitment to honor it. She literally became the fire, rather than allow the political powers of the time to force her to give up her spiritual connections and true power, which flowed from her relationship to Spirit. This shows her monumental commitment to Spirit and her undeniable passion for serving her truth, her God, and her nation. In the George Bernard Shaw play *Saint Joan,* her character says, "I hope men will be the better for remembering me; and they would not remember me so well if you had not burned me." Many women of power in the time of the Inquisition were shamans or witches. They, too, were burned for refusing to sacrifice their passion and commitment.

I first discovered the true essence of Joan of Arc in my first acting class in college when I was sixteen. A woman in my class performed a monologue from the Shaw play. This was to haunt me for many years, and I went on to study and perform it myself many times. After Joan learns she is condemned to perpetual imprisonment, she takes back her statement agreeing to her prosecutor's version of reality and reclaims her own experience of life and her personal relationship with Spirit. She exclaims, "Light your fires! Do you think I dread it as much as the life of a rat in a hole? My voices were right. Yes, they told me you were fools, and that I was not to listen to your fine words nor trust to your charity." This is the voice of a young person stepping fully into the passion and commitment of her mission. She boldly rebuked those who would have her deny her passion and go back on her commitment.

Joan of Arc served God by leading men into battle, and that was hugely "out of the box" for the women of her time. She bravely claimed her true identity in a culture that demanded that women deny their individuality to play a subservient role. So, not surprisingly, she was killed, but not before she showed her mission could be accomplished brilliantly, making her statement about the absurdity of living in a restrictive cultural box, cut off from Spirit and her true passion. There were certainly complicated "national" and religious politics involved, but the important dynamic for this discussion is her commitment to the will of Spirit and the unique way she honored it. This commitment filled her with the power and ability to manifest loyalty, victory, and an authentic life.

Whenever I practiced and performed this monologue, I could embody Joan's passion and commitment to Spirit. I felt more energy in my arms and legs. My sense of clarity was radiant and intense, and to perform it well, I had to commit to Spirit myself. I loved to let down the wall between the actor and the audience and speak directly to people about connecting to nature, Spirit, life energy, and not letting the powers that be decide what is best for us.

Joan was so committed that she was willing to sacrifice her life for what felt right to her. As regular, nonsaintly human beings, however, we do have to keep ourselves alive to fight a sick system. My survival instinct kept me alive during my childhood so I could get out of my house one day, connect to Spirit, and create a better life for myself and help other people who struggle with circumstances that are not supportive of their wholeness. By connecting to our passion and committing ourselves to our true mission, we are able to survive destructive environments and heal ourselves and others.

When we make a commitment, we bind ourselves to a course of action that is an expression of who we are and what we are here on earth to do. That bonding requires energy. If we do not continually generate the energy to perpetuate the bond, it will break. If you have struggled with commitments of different kinds, you may not have sufficient energy in this chakra. These next exercises can be of great help. I believe they supported me in the commitment required to follow through and complete the writing of this book.

To get in touch with the energy of commitment, it is extremely helpful to physically activate the upper belly and the third chakra. This will help move and spin the center connected to power, will, identity, and commitment, and generate the energy to manifest them.

❖ Task Seven: Energetically Connecting to Commitment

1. Lie down on your back. Bring your knees toward your chest or shoulders and massage your back on Mother Earth as you rock from side to side. Center your legs and bring your chin toward your knees. (If this feels uncomfortable for your neck at any point, release your head back down to Mother Earth.) Do thirty rounds of Breath of Fire. Then relax the back and head down, letting Mother Earth hold you while you breathe normally. You may repeat this step several times.

2. Stretch out long on your back, arms reaching above your head along the earth (fig. 3.5). Breathe in. Breathe out as you draw the right knee in toward your chin using your belly muscles, hip flexors, and arms as you raise your head. The left leg will stay stretched out long as you bring the right knee in toward the chin (fig. 3.6). Stretch out long again while you inhale, legs and arms along the earth. Repeat with the left side. Exhale, bringing the left knee in toward the chin as you hug it in with both hands (fig. 3.7). Inhale, once again stretching and lengthening the body. Repeat this exercise for at least a minute, alternating between right and left, going slowly at first and then more rapidly in rhythm with a gentle Breath of Fire. You use the muscles in the front of the neck to lift the head, so do this very consciously and lovingly so you do not injure yourself.

3. After completing this exercise, relax on your back, feeling the belly rise and fall as you breathe in and breathe out. Feel your upper belly, your commitment center, your will center. Feel the strength and power there.

In this reclining meditation, ask yourself, "What would I like my will and energy of commitment to be connected to?" What do you love? What do you dream? Envision luminous fibers from your upper belly connecting to images or symbols of those empowering, satisfying commitments. Feel the reciprocity of satisfying energetic connection and the strengthening of this third chakra.

❖

Fig. 3.5

Fig. 3.6

Fig. 3.7

Getting in touch with this chakra and the energy of commitment in this way was a great help in motivating me to write this book, but I realized that I couldn't be committed to everything. There were old patterns, beliefs, and relationships that I needed to let go of if I was to have all the energy required to finish this book. Often we become aware that we need to let go of connections that drain our energy, making us unable to fully follow our missions.

There have been many ties I have had to break to continue my mission. Some of them have been heartbreaking to release, and some have been a relief. Ending my marriage to the father of my daughter was heartbreaking, but truly necessary for me as I continued on my journey. The following exercise addresses this necessary letting go.

I used this exercise to separate from my parents' inability to actualize their passions. They didn't believe in translating dreams into reality and seemed to have financial fears that may have kept them locked in the boxes that other people created for them. My mother answered phones in a major corporation, something women were allowed to do in the sixties, when she was divorced with two small children and needed a job. My father pursued engineering as a career. In some ways, it was a passion for him. And yet his disease prevented him from having a steady job when he was in his twenties and thirties. My stepfather also tried to pursue some of his passions but was not successful in the ways he hoped he'd be. The years I was in high school, he made a meager living renting apartments, which, thank God, kept him busy fourteen hours a day. He always said his dream was to teach literature to underprivileged children, but to my knowledge he never actualized this.

My parents had thwarted their passions and manipulated others, rather than looking at their own wounds, which desperately needed healing. My passion to grow propelled me to see more of the world by living apart from them. I severed layers of ties to them over a journey of years.

This journey began when I was seventeen years old after spending a year away from my parents, at college and with other friends and relatives. Newly motivated to study my artistic passions, I was spending the summer at home so I could make money for the next year of college. I worked full time at a bakery in Grand Central Station, taking the 5:30 train each morning. Having committed myself to addressing my depression holistically, I ate healthy food, took vitamins, and ran five miles each day. Sometimes I'd nap in the afternoon.

One day I was trying to nap and my stepfather was playing music very loudly so he could hear it on the porch from the living room. I asked him nicely to turn it down and he proceeded to get very angry at me, beating me up, knocking me down the stairs between the living room and the kitchen, yelling at me to get out of the house. I was terrified and angry, too, and told him I would leave after I got some pants on. (Since I was trying to nap, I had no pants on.) I was so upset I left the house without my shoes and walked almost a mile to the Irvington police station.

I told the police what happened, and in that summer of 1978 they told me they didn't like to interfere with domestic affairs and called my mother, who asked me what I did to provoke the attack. I told my mother I would never enter her house again unless she agreed that I never had to talk to my stepfather again. He used to threaten to beat me up if I didn't say hello. I never wanted to say hello again. To her credit, my mother stood up to him and let him know I would not be saying hello anymore. I said nothing to him for a very long time. This was the first of the destructive ties I would continue to cut for many years.

If you know you have committed yourself in ways that do not serve you, stuck in the trance of old beliefs or relationship patterns that are not healthy, this is a great exercise to practice until you feel that those ties are broken. It is called the scissors, and it works at both the conscious and unconscious levels. It gives our energy bodies the power required to fuel our true missions, rather than needlessly draining it to support the culture's and other people's manipulations. Once you release the old ties, you can see where the newly freed energy wants to go. It is true freedom to know we have the power to cut ties that are not healthy for us.

⊰❊⊱ Task Eight: The Scissors

1. Lie on your back and bring both knees up toward your chest. Then reach both your legs and arms directly up toward the sky (fig. 3.8). Allow the elbows and knees to soften. This is called Dead Bug pose. Allow the thighs to rest back into the hip joints and the upper arms to rest back into the shoulder joints. Enjoy the peace you can have as this dead bug.

2. When you are ready, bring to mind any energy draining ties that you feel ready to break or cut. It may help to visualize who or what you are tied to and what the cord or connection looks like. If it feels comfortable, open the legs and arms toward the floor at the level of the hips and shoulders, just like two pairs of scissors opening (fig. 3.9).

3. Close the legs and arms to criss-cross, right over left (fig. 3.10). Open again. Then close and criss-cross left over right. Inhale as you open. Exhale as you close.

4. Repeat for one to five minutes until you can't do it anymore, or until you sense you have cut all the ties. You will feel a clarity of energy around your belly and perhaps a sense of emotional relief.

5. Relax, knees to chest, and stretch the back. Then release the legs and arms to the earth.

Feel the unproductive and destructive ties broken. If it feels appropriate, you can wish all the best to whatever you have released as it finds new forms and healthy connections in the universe. Take a moment to feel and savor your freedom.

The third chakra is the center for passion. Passion helps us to find out who we really are because it has the power to take us outside of our usual behavioral patterns or societal confines. So it is essential to our development that we learn to value our passions and express them authentically.

Fig. 3.8

Fig. 3.9

Fig. 3.10

In our Western culture, we are usually not supported in expressing our passions in a healthy way. Perceptions of our passions are often filtered through our cultural imbalances. For example, our natural sexual passion is often seen as immorality. Teenagers may be instructed to use abstinence as their exclusive method of birth control, whatever their ages and developmental levels. In spite of some long-awaited legal shifts, gay and bisexual people are still judged by many as having an "unnatural" tendency. So rather than learning how to integrate and channel our passion in the direction of love, maturity, creativity, respect, and spiritual connection, we have a culture addicted to sensational sexual advertising, pornography, rape, and other violence. (I'm differentiating pornography from other erotic literature, film, and art that expresses sexual passion in a manner that honors it.)

I was connected to my passions at a young age because I was depressed, and only my passions could mobilize me. Passion was the only way for me to liberate myself from the depression that set in as the losses of innocence piled up. Unfortunately, in early adolescence my passion was expressed in self-destructive behavior. My anger was really starting to bubble up, and it took me a while to find the creative path. I was probably most lost between the ages of twelve and fourteen. I started to smoke pot and tobacco, and drink. I had seen *Rebel Without a Cause,* and I became James Dean's character. It would have been too painful in those years to fully let myself know that my "cause" was my parent's mistreatment of me and my very damaged self-esteem.

I kept close contact with my friend Debbie, whom I managed to get into all kinds of trouble with. She was fifteen when I was twelve. We had many adventures, hitchhiking around the river towns, getting drunk and stoned and fooling around with boys, sometimes going to bars. I thought I was terribly sophisticated. I realized many years later that our bond was most likely mutual loss, as she had lost her mother at an early age, and I had never had supportive parents.

I know that in my immaturity I might have hurt some people. This was the one time in my life when I was trying to sate my own hungers without paying enough attention to other people's needs. There were a few boys whose feelings I know I trampled on. If we don't connect with the true power of expressing our passions and creativity in these adolescent years, we will express our power through manipulation and exploitation.

In the next task we will seek a spirit guide who can help lead us to balanced fulfillment and actualization of our passions. Without a spirit guide, passions can easily lead us into destructiveness, manipulation, and a misuse of power.

Mary Magdalene is one of my guides for passion. Through contact with her energy, I feel it is safe to let my passions dance through me, expressing themselves fully, without shame or apology. I experience her as a woman who was humbled by her experiences of life, a sincere student of Spirit who went on to be a great teacher in her own right. Love was at the center of her power, and she connected as an embodied human to Spirit. She did not let the sexism of the time inhibit her passion, mission, and commitment to her work. She loved life and truth. You will now journey to find just such a guide.

Task Nine: Finding a Spirit Guide to Support Your Passion

Go to your sacred place. Experience its evolving richness with all your senses. It may be wise to contact your protector spirit guide in your sacred place so you feel very safe and held in this journey. New adventures can bring up both excitement and fear.

Ask your spirit guide of passion to appear to you. This guide may appear to you in your sacred place, or you may need to journey beyond, perhaps to a place it has always been your passion to go or a place that you sense may be related to your mission. Your spirit guide for passion should have strong passions, probably similar to your own, and have the capacity to support you in pursuing them. You may identify with this guide, which will strengthen your own sense of identity. On this journey you may have an opportunity to do something inspiring together that expresses your mutual passion for some activity or cause.

When you find your spirit guide for passion, ask if it has a message for you about your passion and its expression on the journey of your life. Ask yourself what your next step is in supporting your passion. Feel the support of your guide in your energy body as you envision how that passion will be expressed. Ask this guide how she or he will continue to interact with you as you manifest this expression.

Thank your passion guide for being present in your life.

Begin a relationship with this spirit guide that will be supportive to you in honoring your passions. Perhaps you can visit this guide in non-ordinary reality on a regular basis and talk about what is close to your heart, or perhaps you can find a way to contact each other in ordinary reality. (For example, Dr. Martin Luther King is one of my spirit guides as we share a passion for nonviolent human evolution, so I read bits of his speeches regularly and that keeps us in touch.)

It is most empowering and crucial to our growth as individuals to join passion to commitment, and commitment to passion. It takes commitment to pursue our passions successfully; and without the fire of passion, our most sincere commitments can run out of steam.

When I was seventeen, I met Evgen Drmola, a theater director and complex man who was my model for bringing commitment to passion and passion to commitments. The first time I heard him speak, it seemed he was almost talking to himself in the basement of the fine arts building at the college I attended. His thick Czech accent enhanced his trancelike monologue. He seemed to gaze mostly at the ceiling and the floor. I wondered what this man could possibly teach me about "physical and vocal training for actors," the name of the course I was to take from him that semester. Suddenly, I was able to sense that rather than coming out to meet us, he was drawing us in. There was an amazingly rich world in his chrysalis, the deep inner place from which he created.

I was fortunate that he seemed to see something special in me and sought out my company. He was not seeking me out sexually as my stepfather had. He spoke of my beauty in a way that felt healing, comparing me to the subjects of great Renaissance art. I could identify with his depth, as I felt he identified with mine. We became good friends, an unlikely pair, as I was seventeen and he was in his early fifties. Sometimes souls just meet, and age has nothing to do with it. We were never romantic, though I found him an entertaining flirt. In the three years I knew him, he was married, and though he was separated toward the end, he was always loyal and in love with his wife. This was very healing for me as well, to see a man who was devoted and not acting out sexually.

He recognized the passion in me and cast me as Hermia, the fiery lover with a mind of her own in *A Midsummer Night's Dream*. He directed this play with such richness, helping us enter the dream world, connect to the power of nature and fairies, and recognize the magic we interact with in our unconscious. He honored this world through his interpretation of the play. The set was a large rootlike tree upon which the queen and king of the fairies lived, enveloped by a round platform representing a spiritual vagina, holding and allowing life to emerge from it. Looking back, I can see that this wonder-filled staging was an intricate Celtic shamanic world of nonordinary reality, aliveness, and adventure. Through Evgen, I learned that theater and art are expressions of nonordinary reality that bring us to our deeper and more expansive selves. He was committed to his passion for creating these worlds where people could see themselves and all that is heroic, conflicted, intriguing, human, and complex in all of us. He was always looking for the deepest and highest expression of every text.

When I was twenty, I returned to New York City to go to massage school. Evgen spoke about moving to New York himself. But shortly after I left, Evgen hanged himself, despairing over his wife's decision to leave him and the politics of the time, which prevented him from visiting his daughter in Czechoslovakia who was in need of him.

I was deeply saddened by his death, and I feel that this in part influenced my decision to pursue healing rather than theater. I felt that there was something individual, something deeper that I had to do for myself and others. I sensed there was something in me I had to continue to heal so I could prevent getting stuck inside myself the way he did, with no way out. The few formative years he was in my life taught me so much about fully living out one's passions, about being fearless in the face of new forms and risks, and about being committed enough to actualize visions. My passion for growth, which is a core value and an integral part of my identity, led to my commitment to healing work. He has certainly been present for the writing of this book. I can hear his deep voice with its thick accent, sighing, "Ah, Suzie. . . ."

This next exercise will help you, through both physical movement and spiritual journey, to join the energies of passion and commitment so you can achieve fruitful expressions of your whole self and your mission in the world.

Task Ten: Joining Passion and Commitment

To begin, do the exercises from tasks seven and eight, including breath of fire, to generate a lot of energy in this third chakra area. For this purpose, see if you can push yourself a bit without hurting yourself.

Ask your spirit guide for passion to be present as you exercise your commitment center. As you do the exercise, envision your passion guide in your sacred place. Feel yourself fully supported in your energy and will, your spirit guide sharing your nonexploitive, fulfilling passion.

When you've done the third-chakra kundalini exercise until you can't do it anymore, relax and ask your spirit guide in your sacred place, "What passion should I channel this energy of commitment into?" or "How shall I commit this energy of passion?" Listen for the answer. If the answer seems right to you, feel the energy channeling into that passion or commitment. See the body of your sacred commitment infused with the power of your passion.

You may also ask your guide how to safely express the passion and commitment in your day-to-day life in ordinary reality. Leave the altered state of nonordinary reality with at least one specific shamanic task to undertake. Thank your passion guide.

The task you emerge with could take many forms. For example, if your passion is to write a book your guide may suggest journaling each day. Or if your passion is shamanism your guide may suggest you make a pilgrimage to meet and learn from a gifted shaman. Your task commitment would then involve creating and attending to the details of this plan, initiated and sustained by your passion.

FINDING AND HONORING YOUR VISION

All the work we have done in these chapters so far culminates in the crucial shamanic task of the vision quest. At some point, it becomes vital to know who we are and what we are here to do, even though that is subject to change. It requires great courage and openness to really ask what we are here to do, to listen for the answer, and to follow through with action.

On a vision quest, you will isolate yourself from communication with other humans and technology and quiet your mind for an extended period of time. When your mind is still it finds its natural balance and your spirit guides, nature, and your own soul and spirit can communicate with you, giving you a clear vision of your identity and your mission. This helps you to understand deeply who you are, without distraction and manipulation, and to come to know the spirit guides that will step forward to support you in doing what you are on earth to do.

The vision quest can be done in many different ways. If it feels safe to you, it can be very effective to plan a full day, from sunrise to sunset, to do your vision quest. It is not good to cut it short, except for safety reasons. It is important to quest within a space that provides for physical safety. I have often fantasized about going off into the woods for days, on my own, to be with Mother Nature exclusively. I know this would not be safe for me, given the violent fantasies that people still actualize. Instead, I have spent a day in the local woods. This is a relatively safe-feeling place for me.

Bring what you need to feel safe. Given the nature of how crime occurs in our culture, women may have very different needs than men. I have found that having my cell phone with me, but turned off, is helpful. This is part of what is nice about the local woods. I also keep a Swiss army knife with me and maintain vigilance regarding what is moving around me. You may want to have a friend with you to function as a guard of sorts, but you need to have silence and solitude to listen to the communications of the spirits on your quest. Think about your needs and keep them in mind as you plan your quest.

You may want to fast, partially or completely, according to your biological needs. Because we often use food as a distraction, by fasting we can sometimes hear the deeper spiritual messages. Some people can use fasting itself as a distraction—so know thyself. Do what brings you closer to wholeness and the messages of Spirit. Again, consider safety, including blood sugar levels, hydration, and other concerns.

If you have difficulty inviting a vision to come to you during your vision quest, it may be important to go back to chapter 2 and do some additional soul retrieval work. Soul retrieval helps to create and fortify our core strength and integrity, which is required to successfully quest. You need to have a strong energetic core to bear the truth of who you are and what you must do in this life.

My eagle has always come to me in my vision quests, showing me how the pieces integrate to make the whole. He has helped me to recognize that my mission is about integrating the aspects of ourselves, helping people to heal the energy body so we can come into full integrity as the human race. Each of us has all the energies and colors inside us, and on my vision quests, the eagle has shown me visions of us in many circles weaving together a magnificent web of power. Any time I tried to drift a significant distance from a path involving the healing arts, a painful crisis arose so Spirit could let me know that I was to remain on the healing path with the love, support, protection, and guidance of the eagle.

✦ Task Eleven: Vision Quest

Once you know where you are going, how long you will be there, and whether you will fast or not, secure what you need for safety and bring along your medicine bundle with your huacas. Now it is time to surrender to the experience. Feel your connection to Mother Earth, your guides, your huacas, the elements within you, and the elements around you.

It is good to walk for a while, allowing nature to cleanse your aura of the clutter of your life. This can take quite some time, but after an hour or so of walking in a nature area, you will feel considerably different. This is usually when the vision quest begins. At this point you can either continue to walk or you can find a beautiful place to sit. Feel free to move your body in any way that's needed. Open yourself to communicate with Mother Earth and all her beings. Acknowledge that it is her you have come here to meet.

Ask the basic or the deeper questions about who you are and where you are going. Set your intention to receive the answers. Let Mother Earth and all her beings (including the four-legged, multilegged, and winged), the rocks, plants, trees, and the elements, deepen your questions and then answer them. Receive their communications. Perhaps they will attempt to make themselves understood through words, movement, image, dance, song, energy, telepathic or empathic communication, or symbol. Receive the gift of the experience. Feel deeply.

Beings may visit you in both ordinary and nonordinary reality. Both types of connection are very valuable. If your journey is successful, by the close of this communication you will have received a profound message about who you are and what you are on earth to do. If you end your quest knowing what your mission is, it is important to state it before you leave the sacred place where you did your vision quest.

At the end of your vision quest, express your gratitude. It is good to leave an offering of tobacco or corn meal for Mother Earth and all her beings. It is also good to offer your promise and commitment to use your visions to make a nonexploitive, fulfilling contribution to the circle of life.

You may need to do additional journeys or other introspective work, such as speaking with friends, teachers, or therapists, before you fully find your mission. But when you can articulate who you are and the contribution you are here on Earth to make, you may want to return to the place where you did your sacred vision quest, if you can, and tell Mother Earth and her sacred beings what you have come to know.

Hold to your vision. You may need to anchor it in a special place in your heart. Bring your hands to your heart and sense how you can embrace your mission with deep love, care, and commitment. Many forces in life attempt to distract us, consciously and unconsciously, from our understanding of who we are at our core and from our mission in this life. It is important to return to our knowledge of ourselves and our purpose over and over again. If we get distracted from this too often or for too long, we will feel a sense of loss or depression.

This brings us to the last task for this chakra, dreaming or redreaming a coming-of-age ceremony for yourself. We will journey in nonordinary reality creating a relevant and powerful ceremony in a sacred place that specifically supports who you are. In this ceremony, you will acknowledge your passion, accompanied by the guides that support it, and you will make your commitment to your mission with witnesses. This coming-of-age ceremony is a chance to acknowledge what is important to you as an adult in this life. It is a journey, so it can be as simple, elaborate, or exotic as you need it to be. In this ceremony you celebrate the ripening of the fruit of your true, core self.

Your actual coming-of-age ceremony in ordinary reality may or may not have been everything you wished for. You can decide if you'd like this coming-of-age journey in nonordinary reality to revise or add to the one you had, create a complement to it in the realm of Spirit, or completely redo it. If you didn't have a coming-of-age ceremony, you're starting from scratch and are probably very much in need of this task to heal your inner teenager.

 Task Twelve: The Coming-of-Age Ceremony

Go to your sacred place. Imagine all your loved ones there, as well as your spirit guides and power animals. Feel your presence in your sacred place, surrounded by your loved ones. Take in the support.

Envision your ceremony. Where are people standing? Are there sacred objects in your ceremony? How are they used? What are you wearing? Is there any significance in your garments? What development is this event acknowledging? Your first menstrual period, learning to drive, voting for the first time, or some other milestone? What does it mean to you?

Are any of your loved ones speaking at this ceremony? What are they saying? When you get to speak at this ceremony, what are you saying? Is there a time when you can state your mission? Do you have a new name as a mature adult? Is there any other activity you get to perform as part of this ceremony?

Allow yourself to vividly imagine this ceremony and journal about it while you are still in nonordinary reality.

Though I had explored various religious and spiritual traditions in my teens, I did not have any type of coming-of-age ceremony until I was a grown woman. The ceremony I describe here honored my sexuality as a woman and my powerful, equal, conscious standing in society. It was very important for me to be acknowledged as an adult woman in my full, vibrant, sensual, creative, intelligent power. This ceremony was so powerful for me that a part of myself remains in it always, being acknowledged, honored, and nourished so I can continue to do my healing work.

▼

I am standing in the center of a sacred grove of trees that has provided deep healing for my wounded, troubled soul in the past. It is the day before my nineteenth birthday, and I have come to realize that I am committed to a lifestyle and career that embodies both creative expression and healing consciousness. By creating a relationship with theater, dance, poetry, and therapy, I have come to know that this is my path.

In a private moment of preparation, I am lying on the damp grass, naked and warmed by the summer air. I connect to Mother Earth, feeling held, solid, yet released. I know there are so many layers of her depth always supporting me. Among this grove of trees, there is a sacred circle of women who live and practice spiritual arts, and one of them leads me to the sacred waterfall in the woods, just beyond the grove, where we will hold the ceremony.

The waterfall pours down on my shoulders, washing away the burdens and tensions of so many relentlessly difficult years. I swim around the bubbling pool at the base of the falls. My guide leads me to warm myself on a smooth rock in the sun.

As they light the sacred fire on the patch of earth at the center of the trees that had just held me, a few of the women dress me in silks, like scarves, in the colors of the rainbow, tying them around my chakras. The individual pieces become a beautiful dress, and I am covered in sheer, wispy softness from head to ankles.

I hear the drum. There is one man engaged in spiritual practice with the circle of twelve women. He drums, and I feel it vibrating in my bones. The resonance calls me to dance around this sacred fire. The women are waiting for me as I enter the circle, dancing. I know I am affirming my commitment to my path of consciousness and creativity.

The outer fire further ignites my inner fire. The drumming moves me to dance wildly. The sweat glistens on my skin. I begin to unwrap the veils from my chakras, starting with my crown, letting in the light from the heavens, invoking my highest wisdom and connection to Spirit. As I dance around the circle, I throw the veils one by one into the fire, unveiling the inherent spiritual talents that live in each center in all of us, the talents that will support me on my mission. The colors of the veils turn the fire into a magnificent, multicolored light show. I remember the magical fire in my grandmother's hearth in my childhood.

Once again I am naked, all the cells of my skin expertly caressed by the cool air, dancing my mission, my passion fully emerging as it connects to my desire to reach out to the troubled and beautiful world. As my bones quake, my skin is wonderfully alive, reaching out to return the touch of the air. My circle of guides applauds my dance and desires. I am given a priestess robe and pronounced one of them, to stand in the sacred circle and to work jointly with this group on the transformation and expansion of the human mission to include joy, passion, respect, and balance.

4
Sacred Inner Marriage
A Journey to Connection

The rich, deep sound of his heart, the unique echoes of living tissue, vibrated in my ears and through my whole being, almost as though my blood flowed with the warmth of his blood. I knew in that moment that I had been alone for too long, almost all my life. Nat, my third therapist, had a respectful sense of the woman I was trying to become. After we had worked together for about a year, he invited me to put my head on his expansive chest to hear the beat of his heart. He talked about the bonding sound of the heartbeat, how babies in the womb and infants resting their heads against their parents' chests bonded by hearing the heartbeat. He knew I had been denied the opportunity to bond with my parents and wanted to provide a corrective emotional experience for me. I can still feel him stroking my hair, whispering "Sweet baby."

I felt such a profound power as I rested in the arms of someone who had no agenda for me other than my own growth and healing. This may have been one of my first experiences of intimacy without fear. My heart was connected to another in simplicity and sweetness, as I was truly dependent on him to help me grow. I felt something open in me that had perhaps not been opened since the womb. I was a flower tended by a sincere gardener.

▼

This chapter focuses on the fourth chakra, the heart chakra, which spins out from the center of the breastbone (fig. 4.1), enveloping and energizing

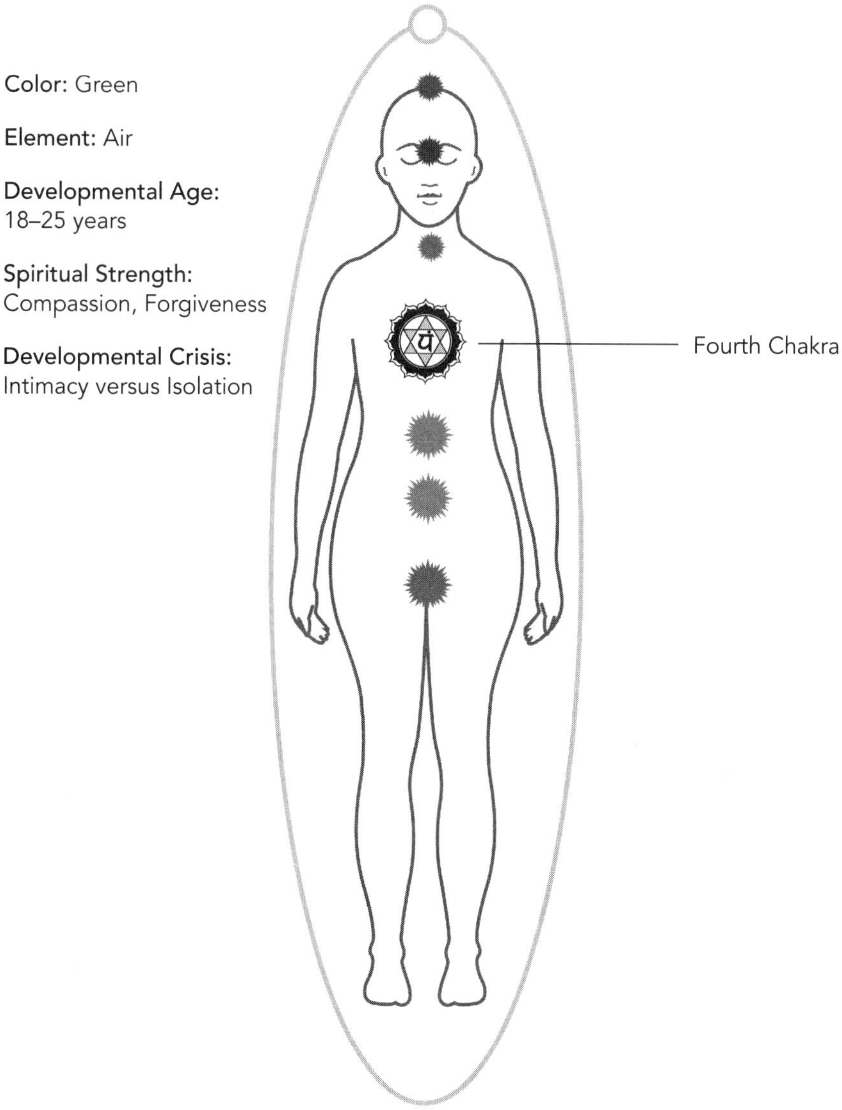

Color: Green

Element: Air

Developmental Age:
18–25 years

Spiritual Strength:
Compassion, Forgiveness

Developmental Crisis:
Intimacy versus Isolation

Fourth Chakra

Fig. 4.1. Fourth Chakra

the heart and lungs. It is the center of the soul, connected with the element of air. This chakra embodies the qualities of compassion, forgiveness, and loving kindness—the powerful energetic dances of the heart.

When this heart chakra is connected to our third chakra, the chakra of fire in the solar plexus, we can be powerful enough to make enormous shifts in consciousness. Dr. Martin Luther King Jr. invoked the power of love as he helped to lead a movement that made huge changes in some very insane and damaging cultural behaviors: "God grant that as men and women all over the world struggle against evil systems, they will struggle with love in their hearts, with understanding and good will." Much of the insanity unfortunately continues, so we must strengthen ourselves in this center, strengthening our love, compassion, and understanding.

This chakra embodies the developmental crisis of intimacy versus isolation that occurs between the ages of eighteen and twenty-five. Through shamanic work on this center we embrace and explore our own inner dualities, including the animus (male aspect of self) and anima (female aspect of self) so we can heal our intimate relationship within ourselves. This prepares us to proceed with the outward manifestation of intimacy: having a healthy relationship with a lover or partner in ordinary reality.

From this fourth chakra we learn to extend our hearts in harmony and fullness. In our hearts we have the power to recognize and hold duality, our own and other people's, with courage. I believe the truest definition of courage is fear supported by breath. Thankfully, this chakra expresses the element of air, providing us with all that we need to breathe fully so we can be truly brave and loving. To connect in an enduring, committed way, we must create a strong relationship with the element of air. As we increase our capacity to breathe consciously, we develop our courage to love.

CONNECTING WITH THE ELEMENT OF AIR

Breathing comes from this heart area; the lungs cradle the heart chakra. The breath is so powerful. It is a sacred energetic container. When we breathe with intention we ground ourselves—consciously connect our physical and energy bodies to the earth. From this grounding we build the support to embrace the electrifying charge of love and the fear that accompanies opening our hearts. When we breathe and pray, we are always connected to power in our hearts, the center of compassion. This can ensure that we will follow our loving intentions with responsible action.

❖ Task One: Cleansing with the Element of Air

Go to your sacred place. Experience it through all your senses: see, hear, smell, touch, and feel it. Take in nurturing nourishment from your sacred place. Connect with the elements from the previous chapters: earth, water, and fire. Then, contact the air. Ask air to fully reveal itself to you here in your sacred place.

Allow yourself to sense the air in everything. There is air in the soil, water, plants, animals, and all around you, caressing your skin. Your sacred place will send you a special sacred manifestation of air—a hurricane or tornado, a huge winged creature, or an air god or goddess, for cleansing. Interact with this manifestation of air so you can cleanse old, tired energy out of your heart chakra. Allow the air to clear away the unconscious clutter of ignorance that blocks compassion. You may feel the wind sweep around and through you, energetically cleaning out whatever forces keep you from contacting the deep love in your heart. An air guide may have a profound message for you about how to release your old wounds at the level of your heart, freeing your soul to evolve.

Give yourself fully to the cleansing that your sacred place and the element of air offer to you, even if it feels initially as though you may be consumed. Feel yourself in your journey dancing with the air. Let your spirit soar and expand. Feel inspired.

You may feel the storm or passionate encounter subside. Feel the peace in your sacred place. How do you feel having been cleansed by the air?

We will now do some movements to invoke and feel the energy of air in the body. The process of becoming expansive, loving beings is supported by connecting consciously to the air within us. We will end this task by performing an ancient yoga pose called Tree pose. We are literally bound for life to our reciprocal relationship with trees, especially at the level of air here at the fourth chakra. We breathe in oxygen and breathe out carbon dioxide. They breathe in carbon dioxide and breathe out the oxygen we need for life. In this way, we are profoundly and irrevocably linked to trees through our breath.

It can be hard for us as an industrialized, technological people to acknowledge or honor this profound interdependence. This balance allows life to continue on Earth. Honoring this balance is the most basic dynamic of respect, and yet the "civilized" part of the human species has been destroying it. By doing the exercises in this section, you can experience the connectedness, the beauty, the love, and the patience of trees in your own energy body. They are magnificently balanced in a way that we, in human form, can only aspire to understand. Perhaps the nature of their physical life has forced them to be more conscious in some way.

Trees stand still for long periods of time, developing an ever-deepening relationship with Mother Earth. Perhaps by moving with the air, as trees do in the wind, we can deepen this relationship ourselves.

⋘ Task Two: Moving with the Air

Take Wing

First, we will fly. Stand with your feet hip-width apart and your spine lengthened. Feel the earth underneath you, the air all around you, and the sky above you. Let your arms fly, sweeping up to the sky as you breathe in, sweeping down toward Mother Earth as you breathe out. Connect heaven to Earth. Feel yourself as a great bird, angel, god or goddess, or great winged creature. Feel how your spine moves with your wings as you breathe. The front of your spine opens as you breathe in and reach up. The back of your spine opens as your arms come down and you breathe out. Feel the deepening of the breath. Through the breath, we draw in *prana,* the healing light that is the life force from the heavens.

Swaying with the Breeze

Now we will shapeshift into trees swaying in the breeze, allowing our bodies to embody the form and essence of the trees. Still standing with your feet hip-width apart, reach your arms up toward the sky, allowing them to become tree branches. Feel your roots reaching deeply into the earth, through layers of soil and water and rock. Feel your branches reaching toward the sky and your leaves reaching toward the sun. Feel the air moving all around you, and allow yourself to begin to sway and move in response to the air on your bark. Feel yourself as the tree, and feel yourself breathe as the tree.

Tree Pose

Now we will do an ancient yoga pose called Tree pose. There are quite a few ways to do it, many of which can be found in yoga books and videos, but I will describe the most basic here. From your standing position, shift your weight over one leg. Sense how your balance shifts as your weight shifts. Focus your gaze on a point about six feet in front of you on the earth so you can balance more powerfully.

When you feel you are balanced firmly on your standing leg, bring the other foot to the inside of the standing leg. You can place the sole of the foot at the opposite ankle with the toes on the floor, or at the ankle with the toes off the floor, or at the height of the calf, knee, or thigh, depending on your flexibility and balance (fig. 4.2, p. 130). Bring your hands into Prayer pose by touching your palms together at the level of

Fig. 4.2

Fig. 4.3

Fig. 4.4

your heart. Feel the palms gently press against one another. When you feel balanced and ready, you can extend your hands/branches up toward the sky (fig. 4.3) and open your leaves to the sun (fig. 4.4). Draw the energy up from the earth through all the chakras. When you are ready to release, repeat on the other side.

Our next task will be finding an air huaca. My air huaca is a quail wing given to me by my friend Susan a few years after we both finished massage school. Susan was also studying shamanism at the time and she used one wing of a dead quail she'd found for smudging. (Smudging is cleansing the energy field of a space or around a person, using the smoke from burning sage, cedar, or sweetgrass, often by making sweeping motions with feathers.) Susan thought I should have the other wing. Even though we've barely been in touch through the years, I know she went on to become a chiropractor, and I'm sure continues to be a shaman in her own way. I have often wondered if she kept and still treasures her wing of this sacred quail.

◈ Task Three: Finding a Sacred Air Object

Take a walk in a beautiful nature area that invites your consciousness to contact the element of air. Breathe. Feel your wholeness and your connections, to your heart, to people, to your guides, to the elements, to all beings and spirits everywhere.

Ask Spirit for a sacred object that embodies the spirit of the air, one that will support you and any others you wish to help. Often, winged creatures leave feathers that we can find. My students often find feathers or branches with leaves to use as air huacas, but do not allow the mind to limit you. Let spirit and your heart lead you to the heart of your air huaca. Perhaps this huaca will help with issues of compassion, love, and intimacy, healing sacred connections.

Trust Spirit to lead you to your huaca. When you find it, give thanks.

Spend some time hearing its messages for you. When you are ready, place it in your medicine bundle.

I remember Ellen, who was my therapist for twenty years, asking me to tell her how I envisioned my heart. When I looked exclusively through my wounded eyes, my heart was glass, fractured into shards and fragments, sharp and inert. Ellen asked me to consider that my heart could be a strong muscle, perhaps bruised, but resilient. This image felt warm to me, and I could sense that perhaps I had a heart like Nat's inside me: living tissue that could pulse through decades as I encountered the wholeness of life, reminding me of my resilient spirit.

I was able to connect more strongly to my heart and deepen my compassion and love through my study of massage and yoga. I learned techniques to help alleviate headaches, stomachaches, and back and neck tension. I felt I could extend my love to people through my hands and actually help them feel better. By the time I went to the Swedish Institute, I was very aware that my arms were an extension of my heart. Energies flowed through me from earth and heaven to support my heart and my ability to care for people in this way.

In yoga, there is a *mudra,* or hand position, called Prayer pose, which you did in a previous task. The hands come together, palms touching, over the heart. This is an acknowledgment of the spiritual heart and the place of compassion inside where we always wish the best for every soul, our own and all others. One breathes deeply in Prayer pose and says "Namaste," which is a Sanskrit word meaning "The light within me honors the light within you."

Task Four: Journey to Your Heart

Place both hands over your heart. Feel the warmth of your hands on your heart. Let the warmth of your hands heal any old wounds there. Breathe into the heart. Feel the heart center rise and fall with the breath.

Breathe in the loving attention you are paying to yourself. Breathe out fear and any sense of abandonment. Feel the connection between the energy of love and the sacred vessel of your heart itself. Feel the heat and warmth in your heart and how it radiates out to your whole body through your circulatory system, and feel how the energy of love circulates through your energy body, touching every aspect of who you are. Feel blessed by the love that you are.

Extend your right hand out from your heart in the direction of anyone to whom you would like to extend your love. Send this person the energy of love from a distance, or touch her or him, right here, right now. Feel how the love moves from your heart through your arms and hands.

You can also feel connected to the spirit of the shamans here, including the people alive on Mother Earth today and the healing ancestors who are still with us in spirit, including Jesus, the Marys, Buddha, St. Francis, Mother Teresa, and so on. Let your heart be strengthened by the presence of their love.

MARRYING THE INNER MASCULINE AND FEMININE

As mentioned at the beginning of the chapter, this chakra of the heart embodies the ego state of the eighteen- to twenty-five-year-old and embraces the developmental crisis of intimacy versus isolation. It is during this stage that we seek to join the masculine and feminine, both within ourselves and within a bond, partnership, or marriage to another. If one were spiritually conscious at this age, one might get a sense of the strengths and limitations of one's inner male and female and heal what needs to be healed. If that were the case, perhaps the remaining years in this stage could be spent finding a wonderful mate in the world.

Since consciousness has not so far been a common cultural value, many people do not find the right life mate until much later in life and instead spend this developmental stage isolated from true, mature intimacy. This may be because most people do not have the knowledge or awareness to connect the masculine and feminine within themselves before they attempt to connect to another person. In these next few exercises, we will seek to heal this crisis.

The coming together of the divine masculine and feminine allows us to create new life and beauty in the form of a sacred relationship and possibly a child born of that relationship. This is the sacred spiraling dance of the DNA, the fruit of conception, which takes place in the seed in the plant world and the fertilized ovum in the animal world. Intimacy allows us to conceive of new energies and forms. I believe the quality of our intimacies greatly influences the quality of what we conceive and create.

Because of the abuses in my childhood and the culture, I have had to consciously heal the shadow side of the unevolved male and female that came to live inside me, the victimizer and the victim, the unequal and therefore sick power dynamic. Coming of age during the sexual revolution greatly delayed this process of healing, because with my baggage, I continued to allow myself to be exploited for a time, leaving me with more wounds to heal. Twisted sexual double standards and destructive dynamics remain in our culture today, and many people still need to do great inner healing before they are capable of creating true intimacy.

In the tasks that follow, we will first journey to connect with the divine inner feminine self, and then deepen this connection in the physical body in ordinary reality. There are often many aspects of the inner feminine that need to be addressed and healed in both men and women, because the feminine has been so devalued and dishonored in our modern culture. About ten years, ago I heard about an indigenous culture that had what I thought was a unique coming-of-age ritual for boys. When boys reached puberty, they constructed small clay "wombs" that they carried around with them every day. They were instructed to hold and make conscious contact with this womb several times a day throughout their lifetime. It was very moving to hear about this method of keeping in touch with the divine feminine in such a consistent, powerful, tangible way. Our own patriarchal culture discourages both men and women from connecting with divine inner feminine power. For us, a great deal of healing needs to be done in this area.

"Feminine power" is not an oxymoron, nor is it about manipulation and seduction. It is a power that comes from mastery of connection to the feminine elements of earth and water. This power is the fruit of a consistent, honest, respectful relationship with these elements, a deep understanding of the body and the cycles of life.

My women therapists and friends have greatly supported me in healing my inner feminine. It is through having a healthy, intimate connection to other women that I came to understand the beauty and power of what it is to be a woman. I am also in awe of my female spirit guides and aspire to understand the power they embrace. My therapist of twenty years, Ellen, has taught me a great deal about being a woman. Through all the years we worked together, I very much appreciated how grounded she seemed to be in ordinary reality, and yet she was open to all kinds of different healing theories and techniques. It moves me deeply to witness how she has nurtured me with impressive consistency. She has taught me more than I ever thought there was to know about the divine feminine quality of nurturing. Through her, I learned that it is the most powerful force in the universe.

In many ways our culture pressures us to conform to limited masculine and feminine roles, often to the detriment of the fullness of ourselves. Roles, though often necessary to provide a certain structure, can be superficial and keep us from the depth of ourselves. Shamans have traditionally embraced both the female and male, or yin and yang, aspects of themselves so they could benefit from the wholeness of their power. At the level of the energy body, we have both masculine and feminine energy. In our physical bodies both men and women have male and female hormones. Since most of us are in fact definitively female or male in body structure and hormonal balance we have nothing to fear by exploring the more recessive aspect of ourselves. After these journeys we will return to our definitive biological imperative, enriched by having the experience of the inner power we have explored and embraced.

❖ Task Five: Connecting with the Divine Inner Feminine

Allow yourself to journey to your sacred place, connecting in a strong way with the elements of earth and water as you did in chapters one and two. Then, feel how the earth and water flow together, such as when the ocean dances with the ocean floor and the shore. Feel how they flow together within your body, the fluids moving with the more densely formed bodies of the cells.

From a deep connection with the feminine elements, allow a vision of your feminine self to emerge from your sacred place. It may come from inside your energy body or may emerge from some other being, object, or direction. See this aspect of yourself being and moving in your sacred place. Begin to get a sense of what is meant by feminine power. Does this aspect of yourself have any outstanding physical, emotional, mental, or spiritual features? How do you imagine this self handling challenges in the world? Does this part of you need any healing or support? Has this aspect of yourself been impacted by past events or traumas that still need to be addressed?

Is there a spirit guide that emerges to support or heal this aspect of yourself? Allow this guide to heal and support your feminine self. This guide may listen to your story, provide a ceremony for your feminine self, or offer some type of nurturing hands-on healing work. This guide may share great wisdom about how to retrieve aspects of your soul and power from diseased events and cultural dynamics. You may even begin to do some of this work from your very first journey to the feminine.

As you are ready to gently emerge, come back to ordinary reality from your sacred place. Put on some music that your feminine self would like to dance to, music that expresses the feminine power that is you. See if you can be brave enough to physically express your feminine self. (This takes great courage for most men in our culture.) Feel how "her" energy fills and moves your body. Feel how she is solid, fluid, and strong.

Please journal about this experience and attempt to answer the questions that your divine feminine self has asked about how she is wounded and what she needs now to heal. They will lead you to a fuller understanding of yourself and what is required for your ongoing healing.

We will now take a similar journey to contact the inner male. Chances are, if you were raised in this culture, your inner male needs some healing. Men are taught to fear and feel humiliated by their emotions and their natural dependence on their mothers and Mother Earth. This creates so much conflict and stress. Men have been encouraged to scapegoat others while "acting out" rather than expressing emotions, as they often have not developed the character to contain and process them safely within themselves. Therefore, they are largely responsible for the crime of domestic violence that is rampant in our culture even in the most unexpected places. Men are also taught that they must always prove themselves, which unfortunately all too often results in a show of force and gain at the expense of others. This dynamic underlies our country's imperialistic approach to politics and economics.

Much of the healing of the inner male comes from cultivating a deep relationship with the elements of fire and air. Fire and air are as powerful as earth and water. But there is a natural aggression contained within the fire of testosterone that we need to learn to support in a healthy way in our culture. Perhaps some of these needs to express aggression get met naturally in indigenous cultures in which men do a lot of the hunting. This is a useful channel for aggression. Aggression, akin to passion in many respects, is a powerful expression of life force and is necessary at times for life to continue. As Fritz Perls, the father of Gestalt psychotherapy, discusses in his book *Ego, Hunger and Aggression,* even eating requires aggression, to bite and chew and swallow. So we need this powerful thrust for our very lives.

Unfortunately, aggression is such a strong force that when it goes out of balance, great damage can occur. When aggression moves from being channeled in relationship to Mother Earth to provide for the survival needs of food, clothing, shelter, and consensual sex, and instead fuels wars, killing, slavery, genocide, rape, and pollution that poisons our children's bodies, it is time to bring it back into balance. I believe that aggression needs the container of a spiritual relationship with Mother Earth for it to be a constructive force in the lives of all beings. Cultivating this will be a powerful healing for the divine inner masculine.

My connections to Evgen, Nat, and my first yoga teacher, Swami Shantanand, greatly helped to heal my inner male. They were very different from each other, and together they provided a very full picture of heartfelt masculinity. My relationship with Nat was especially important, because I could truly allow him to be a father figure. It was also healing for me that there were many similarities between Nat and my stepfather, including interest in literature and the arts, fluency in Yiddish, big bellies, and broad facial features, and yet they were so different in temperament and character.

Nat was gentle and kind. He was also a powerful, safe container for the expression of my rage and aggression, helping me to heal my inner masculine energy and self that had been so distorted by the violence in my family. As I knelt in front of large pillows, Nat would encourage me to pound them with my fists while yelling my anger and pain. I would pound and yell until I grew weary and my voice gave out, and then I would sob until I felt empty and clear of that wave of wounding. This was a powerful act of safe aggression that allowed me to honor my feelings and perspective regarding the events that occurred in my family, helping to learn to make boundaries without emotional violence, healing my inner masculine self.

Evgen was the embodiment of responsible, creative passion. He was willing to stand right in the center of the authority of his genius, which he did with respect for others and their unique contributions to the whole of whatever he was creating. His boldness taught me to not be afraid of truly embodying what I know and to speak freely, with courage, the words that carry the message of my vision.

Task Six: Connecting with the Divine Inner Masculine

Journey to your sacred place, this time connecting with the elements of fire and air as we did in chapter three and earlier in this chapter. Feel how these elements are present in your sacred place and in your energy body. Feel the power of the fire and the air.

Feel your inner male self emerge from your energy body or somewhere else in your sacred place. Really see and feel him. Does he have any outstanding physical, emotional, mental, or spiritual features? How do you imagine him handling the challenges that arise in the course of living? Does he need any healing from events and traumas of the past?

Allow your sacred place to offer you a spirit guide to help guide and heal your inner male. Again, if you were raised in this culture, your inner male needs to learn about healthy interdependence and self-acceptance. He needs to continue to learn about how to develop himself and meet his needs and the needs of his friends, family, and community without exploiting anyone. Your masculine guide may encourage you to feel and express the full spectrum of your emotions regarding your life as he holds you with love and acceptance so you do not repress or act these feelings out on others irresponsibly. He will help you to understand that there is great power in this act of courage. He will help you to manifest visions for action that include an openhearted perspective and a sense of fairness for all beings involved, including yourself.

When you return to ordinary reality, remember to play some music so your inner male can dance through your body. Journal about the experiences of your inner male, gently answering the questions asked in this task. Feel how aggression can be a powerful force as part of the creative process.

Inner marriage is a sacred joining of the inner male and female energies, allowing us to always live with a full balance of the elements of creation within us. The enactment of sacred inner marriage allows for an inner resolution of the developmental crisis of intimacy versus isolation. This resolution may then be mirrored in our external life.

I have been privileged to witness wonderful marriages between my spirit guides. My eagle parents live and work together, finishing each other's intentions. They have been together through some centuries, and their connection has a wonderful flow. Guiding Eagle finds Eagle Woman's strength, clarity, and fierce protectiveness beautiful, and Eagle Woman is deeply moved by Guiding Eagle's gentleness and tenderness. They both have depth and perspective that keeps their relationship wonderfully alive. Even though they are older now, they are still romantic and look very young when they gaze into each other's eyes. Together they give birth to healing.

Jesus and Mary Magdalene are also a magnificent couple that has been in my consciousness since the *Jesus Christ Superstar* days. They are a very sensual and loving couple, and I believe that having spiritual exposure to their relationship has fueled my sense of what I have sought for myself romantically. I have always wanted love to be spiritual, creative, and passionate. Together, Jesus and Mary Magdalene created a model for healthy heterosexual partnership—a dynamic love in which they encourage each other to grow and express the fullness of their spirits in spite of any fear of loss or change. Unfortunately, the world at large has yet to embrace it.

To experience my own inner marriage, I have been led through a sacred Incan journey to join my masculine and feminine energies. As I have repeated this journey over the years, it has deepened and expanded to become the following ceremony.

He wears a white silk sarong that clings to the ripples of his powerful thighs, accenting his creamy brown skin. She wears a black sarong tied as a dress, contrasting with and caressing her milky white skin. They join hands by the gentle, receptive pool and thrusting, clear waterfall of my sacred place, and they vow to put each other first, honoring all aspects of each other while supporting the passion and balance they create together. My guides surround them as they dance, swirling the yin and yang, black and white silk twisting and flowing. They weave their energetic connection to the depth of Mother Earth and the expanse of the universe as they dance. As they make love on the moss and soft pine needles of the warm forest, they whisper each other's names sweetly, acknowledging the grand wave that swells from their joining and crashes over them as they express their love, creating the seed of my dream.

You can do this next task to strengthen yourself, to find a partner, or to strengthen a relationship with a current partner. Whether we are male or female, gay, bisexual, or straight, we need to have a sacred connection between these inner aspects of ourselves.

⊰⊱ Task Seven: Sacred Inner Marriage

Journey to your sacred place. Allow both your inner feminine and inner masculine selves to emerge. Allow them to create a sacred marriage ceremony. Invite both of their spirit guides and anyone else who seems appropriate.

Envision the process of this ceremony. What do both parties need in the way of support to make this commitment to one another? Do they exchange vows? What do they say and promise to one another? Do they exchange sacred objects? How do the elements weave together in the sacred ceremony? How are your inner masculine and feminine selves supported by your sacred place, the elements, and the spirit guides as they form a healthy, beautiful commitment?

How does everybody celebrate? You may want to have one celebration or reception in nonordinary reality in your sacred place, and one in ordinary reality. When you return to ordinary reality, put on music and let your inner male and female dance together inside yourself. Feel them both within your body. Let them blend. Feel them dance around your spinal column, as the kundalini energy has both a male and a female spiral.

Feel the sacred masculine and feminine in each cell of your body, in the double helix spiral of the DNA. Feel how the sacred inner marriage lives in each one of your cells. If it feels right to you, you may envision or experience your inner male and female making love in the sacred reality of this deep inner dance. You may feel this in stillness or you may release your body into movements from this book or other spontaneous movement. Feel conception occur as you give birth to something new.

CREATING COMPASSION
WITHIN RELATIONSHIPS

The heart chakra is the center of compassion. In the heart, the expansiveness of compassion allows us to know and understand duality. By embracing the wholeness of ourselves within our hearts—the male and female, the light and the shadow, the strong and the weak—we learn to embrace others. We can hold differing opinions in the heart with grace; we can hold conflicts with compassion. Very often, this compassion can shift us to a core understanding of our conflicts with ourselves and others. Compassion can move us to hold a polarity to find its essence. For example, in my heart I know that greed and exploitation are truly attempts to become safe and maintain safety; there is simply a lack of balance of healthy aggression. With compassion, these drives can be channeled in a more creative way because there is a deeper understanding of the motivation.

I explored the idea for the next task in a workshop I took with Victor Sanchez, a powerful teacher of shamanic techniques who has studied intensively with the descendants of the Toltec people in central Mexico. From Victor, I learned that the ancient Toltec had a greeting. When two people would meet each other, they would say, "You are my other self." This goes a step beyond the Sanskrit "Namaste." In the Toltec greeting,

I hear our perpetual and often disowned humanity being acknowledged in another person. This is very important to do. If we do this, no one is "other," and therefore no one is available for judgment or exploitation. In the following task, the ancient greeting leads us to have empathy and compassion for others.

❖ Task Eight: "You Are My Other Self"

Take ten minutes out of your day to walk in a populated area. Silently, perhaps as you say "hi," also say, "You are my other self" to each person you meet.

Make a note about how that feels with each person, and perhaps why it may feel easier with some people than with others. See how you feel after ten minutes of greeting people inwardly in this manner. Does it get easier or harder as you go? How do you feel in your heart?

When you return, journal about your experience and any insights you may have gained from it.

We will now explore a task with a partner. This task of partner Tree pose is especially productive if you are working with a group, but you can also do it with any important person in your life. It feels wonderful to breathe and give birth to a new form while working together with another person. Allow yourself to sense the challenge of balancing with someone while being close and touching them. Release yourself to the joy of being successful and the humor of falling over and trying again.

❖ Task Nine: Partner Tree Pose

Create a balancing Tree pose together with another person. Stand side-by-side, back-to-back, or in another close position with your partner. Connect physically, shoulder to shoulder, hip to hip, holding hands, or back to back before you both lift one leg and come into balance to embody the tree pose described in task two. You may lean against one another's torsos, press the palms of your hands together, or if you are side by side you can press the sole of your lifted foot into the sole of your partner's lifted foot. Experience how leaning against one another challenges or perhaps enhances your ability to balance.

See how many ways you can do this. Find your own way to balance and create beauty and fun together. See how many shapes, how many different trees you can make together.

Observe how it feels to create this form with another person. How does it feel to create sacred beauty, balance, and perhaps comedy with another being?

Much of what we learn about intimacy we learn by observing our parents' relationship. We will now take a journey in which we invite our parents to heal any imbalances in their marriage or their relationship. This is an important facet of healing the balance and connection between the sacred inner feminine and masculine. We have all been deeply affected by what was healthy and what was unhealthy in our parents' marriage or relationship. This journey gives us the opportunity to work with it dynamically and in a sacred context.

It is important to honor your own experience here. If you didn't know both of your biological parents, you should choose the people in your life that you strongly sense have made the most parental impact on your energetic being. If your family situation is complicated, follow your intuition about what is required here, or come back to this when you've done the rest of the tasks in the book, when things may be clearer. In this case, several journeys may be required to address complexities.

Task Ten: Healing Your Parents' Marriage

Journey to your sacred place. Spend a little time there gathering what you need for yourself, especially strength, because we are all so easily affected by our parents' interactions with each other. Have your spirit guides and power animals with you for support, guidance, and protection. Take in all the healing energies you need for the integrity of your energy body.

Then, allow yourself to journey to a place that would have been familiar to both your parents. The place we are journeying to now may be a place that your parents actually enjoyed going to together, somewhere they always wanted to go, or just somewhere you think they both would like—as long as it is a beautiful, supportive, sacred environment for them. It could be a rooftop, someone's yard, a garden, a park, an exotic island, or another planet. Just search on your journey for a place where you know they both would have felt a bit more relaxed.

See them in this place, taking it in, enjoying the sights, sounds, textures, smells. You can even imagine them relaxing a little more than was characteristic for them. Perhaps both of them may also be a bit more conscious or present.

Ask this sacred place to provide a different power animal or spirit guide for each of your parents. Then pause and breathe. This sacred place may have wildlife that will offer itself for this purpose, or some spirit beings may appear who will help your parents feel safe, both within themselves and with each other. If one of your parents was abused by the other, it is especially important that the abused parent have sufficient protection and that the abusive parent have enlightened guidance.

Now, just allow them to interact in this sacred place, relaxed, with support, protection, and guidance. They will not be aware of your presence at all. Imagine them interacting in such a way that they make the relationship safe for each other on every level: physically, emotionally, mentally, soulfully, spiritually. This includes being loving to an extent that is appropriate to their actual connection. For example, if your parents have been divorced for thirty years, they would probably not want to hold hands in this journey, but they might want to agree to disagree about politics or whatever they argued about. If your parents' relationship was fraught with conflict, they will probably not fall madly in love in this sacred place. They don't have to resolve anything; they are just going to be together under these healing conditions with you as the witness. They will be together here in their sacred place, in a way in which they are safe and whole.

Perhaps your mother will stop criticizing and judging your father for things beyond his control. Perhaps your father will notice your mother's strength and beauty. Let the power animals and spirit guides support your parents in seeing each other and interacting from a more heart-centered place. Perhaps, as your parents interact, they will be honest and assertive about their feelings, rather than disrespectfully aggressive or passive-aggressive. If your parents were very heavy emotionally with each other, perhaps they will use humor and lighten things up. If they were sarcastic, perhaps they will acknowledge their real hurts and cry together.

Spend time observing your parents as they heal their relationship in this magical place. How do they feel together when they are both safe on every level?

When the healing feels complete, leave your parents interacting safely in the sacred place you found for them and come back to your sacred place.

Invite the experience to integrate within you, among the elements and your guides and allies. Ask yourself, "How does the shift in the energetic bond between my parents favorably affect my energy now? How do I feel having witnessed my parents come to a place of being able to interact or connect more healthfully and heart-fully?" Allow the energy to move within you as you process these feelings.

When you are ready, return from your sacred place to ordinary reality. How do you feel in your heart? Journal about your experience.

My parents' marriage sounded like a difficult experience for both of them. They got married because they were pregnant with my brother, and then had me a year after he was born. About a year after that they were separated, and after another year they were divorced. Because I was so young when all this happened, it never seemed to have very much to do with me. But I learned through therapy that I had some very deep-seated fears connected to this early instability, my personal experience with the fallout from my father's mental illness, and my mother being so overwhelmed and disappointed.

As long as my father was working, he continued child support payments until I was eighteen years old. But he had a hard time holding a job, and I realize now that this could be frightening for my mother, who I imagine got less child support at those times. She worked full time to pay the bills.

Because my parents seemed to have no fun of any kind when they were together, when I made this journey to support them in healing their connection, they seemed to want to have fun with each other, to have an ease with each other. I have very few pictures of my father, but my favorite was taken when he was about twenty-five, when he was on his honeymoon with my mother. He is in the back of a rowboat, singing, wildly gesturing with his arms as my mother takes his picture. On my journey, I saw them sitting by the pond where this picture was taken, just joking with each other about the other's human limitations: my father's boring rigidity and chronic tardiness, and my mother's flaky free-love irresponsibility. I do think it is possible over time to joke about such things, and about even more difficult things such as a bad temper, tendencies toward certain types of insanity, and coldness. In this journey I had them appreciate that they were both so young and in such a difficult circumstance. Everyone in the culture had difficulty acknowledging and coping with mental illness at the time.

They played tennis. They sat in chairs and laughed. They drank coffee. My father's sadness lightened. My mother's hardness softened. They were also at a loss with each other, and it was evident that they were not meant to be each other's life partners. They were kids who got into a situation in pre–Roe vs. Wade America. Unfortunately, so much pain came from this situation.

Something inside me relaxed after having taken this journey. Something in my heart, a compassion for my parents' collective humanity; and something deeper in my pelvis, in my creation center. I had more peace with myself as a sacred creation of my parents, Jane and Frank.

My mother and stepfather's relationship also required a healing journey. It would require a book of its own for me to try to explain how much damage my mother and stepfather's relationship did to me. I was triangulated into it in a way that was mostly to my extreme disadvantage. My stepfather made me into an extension of my mother; I became the part of her he could beat, yell at, abuse, and humiliate. At the same time, he put my mother up on a pedestal and seemed to worship her. My mother was willing to allow me to be the buffer or receptacle in this way. The clear advantage to her was better treatment, and I was sacrificed. This became more obvious as I got older. When I claimed my power to refuse to play this role, their relationship rapidly deteriorated and they separated.

The healing journey for my mother and my stepfather, which took place on a very beautiful sailboat on Long Island Sound on a very calm day, involved my mother and stepfather dealing directly with each other, without me to dump on or scapegoat. My stepfather had to confront my mother's intellectual apathy, and my mother had to confront my stepfather's meanness and sickness. They got to discuss, rationally, with no alcohol, how my stepfather once again disappointed her by failing financially, being manic depressive, being absent. My stepfather directly expressed his loneliness and lack of self-esteem, and how my mother was basically a trophy to compensate for what he felt he was lacking inside.

When they dealt directly with each other on this journey, I felt safe and protected, instead of feeling battered as I had when I was young. They also felt better about themselves, because they were being direct with each other. All of the manipulations had poisoned them. What they had done to my brother and me created some very powerful karma for them. Some of the karma cleared as they dealt courageously with each other. I felt more appreciative in my heart and powerful in my body.

▼

It is painful to write about myself at this stage of my development, espe-cially with respect to the topic of intimacy. This time was just before I acknowledged myself as a sexual-abuse survivor. In many ways, I was still acting out having been abused, largely by not valuing myself and still believing I had to be sexual to get any kind of love. I had a lot of work to do to get in touch with and begin to heal my inner masculine and feminine selves before I could find healthy partners with whom I could attempt the process of mature commitment.

I had begun to be sexually active in high school, in two different long-term (for that age) relationships. I felt cared for. I actually had some real intimacy with both these young men, and I still treasure it. Upon reflection, they were good experiences because I loved and felt loved, but I was really too immature for such intense relationships at that time. Unfortunately, this was followed by another incident of sexual abuse when I was sixteen, this time by my step-uncle, stealing the remaining crumbs of my self-esteem.

I remained in touch with my step-uncle for a few years after high school, as I felt he was my family, and, sadly, his behavior seemed nor-mal to me. When I was nineteen I moved to Boston for a year to go to the University of Massachusetts to study directing with Evgen. My step-uncle lived in Boston. At one point, I had to find temporary housing and, wearing his social worker hat, he found me a place to stay for a couple of weeks in an MIT fraternity house, which was very helpful. When he wanted a certain type of sexual payment for his actions, a light went on in my consciousness regarding how he had abused me. At this point, I felt empowered enough to tell him what I knew he had done and how very wrong it was. I also let him know that I never wanted to see him again. He had very little to say for himself.

Unfortunately, his actions had already taken their toll on my life. I spent a lot of the relationships in these years, eighteen to twenty-five, responding to the earlier abuse, trying to get love through sex, the only way I knew how. The love never really came, at least not in any way I could safely receive it. Since all the males in my family were dysfunctional or abusive and I had internalized this, I had to heal my inner masculine energy before I could achieve and maintain a healthy balance of power within myself. My inner feminine was just beginning to learn to step out of the role of victim and my inner masculine was internalizing the influences of Nat, Swami Shantanand, and Evgen, so vital seeds were being planted for healthier relationships to come.

A big change occurred when I turned twenty-five and began to deal with the sexual abuse directly, in an incest survivors group. I was able to move on to have relationships that were safer for me emotionally. I could honor myself enough to ask for safety. By having the courage to deal directly with and heal the wounds around my heart from the sexual abuse, I began to have the ability to be my own nurturing, protective parent and to choose partners capable of respectful, mutual love.

It took me until age twenty-nine to meet the man with whom I had my daughter. It would take a whole book to analyze my seven-year marriage. Since I had no healthy examples of intimacy, I learned a lot in this relationship. I learned about what I needed for safety and fulfillment, and what I could and could not give.

Ultimately, I left my marriage because of profound differences between my daughter's father and myself. In retrospect I feel I still did not fully know myself and my inner masculine and feminine selves at twenty-nine and perhaps chose a partner from a place of relative ignorance and lack of connection within myself. I needed to do more work on this chakra, and I feel this growth resulted in a necessary divorce. Though my ex-husband is in many ways a wonderful man and father, I didn't feel secure or gratified in my marriage, two important qualities of life I have provided for myself since becoming single again. Being divorced has felt unsafe at times, but I feel comfortable relying on myself.

I would have liked to remain friends with my ex-husband, but this has not been possible for him. We do our best to cooperate for the sake of our beautiful daughter. The great love we both have for Kelly and our mutual commitment to her care has enabled us both to learn to hold our conflicts with each other within our hearts with courage.

About two years ago, a man and I kissed each other. It was as if the currents of both our lives joined into a most powerful, sacred river of bliss. The core of the earth united with the outermost reaches of the universe. We have both experienced a great deal of personal growth work and we are committed to embracing life, centered in our hearts. We are both willing to acknowledge and confront whatever pulls us from this sacred center, including wounds from our previous relationships and conflicts and imbalances that remain as our souls continue to evolve.

There is an effortless place we create together that has never existed before. It is built on the foundation of the work we have both done to move in the direction of consciousness. It is the most beautiful mountaintop, with exquisite views. I feel this as the energy of a soul mate connection. He and I continue to navigate and negotiate the challenging everyday details of our lives.

Ongoing courage is required to keep the dualities within me communicating in my own heart and aligned with each other regardless of all that goes on around me. I do feel I have a soul family. My daughter is the love of my life, and we share a special closeness. I also have a handful of precious friends with whom I share love, my path of consciousness, and my daughter. I have learned to share so much more of who I am with those closest to me, to give and to receive, which can often feel more vulnerable than giving. I continue to breathe so I can be brave and learn more about love and compassion and handle the fears that emerge as my intimacies grow with the people I hold most deeply in my heart. I feel blessed to have this much love in my life. I have learned through the journeys and through my guides to balance the masculine and feminine energies within me, making me a whole person unto myself, ready to share myself fully with other whole, conscious people.

5

Portal to Your Dreams

A Journey to the Expression of Spirit

I sit in the womb of the goddesses, surrounded by the energies of my guides, and breathe. The plants smile in the window, the fountain trickles, the flames of the candles flicker, and the incense smoke smells sweet. The walls are the color of Bali sand. The room is across the street from an old town cemetery, and the lovely trees and sunsets bless my store windows. There are goddesses from many traditions in my front window, including Venus, Kali, Tara, Isis, Gaia, and Mary Magdalene. When people walk by, they are reminded of many rich traditions from cultures around the globe, of times when women's powers were not driven underground or murdered.

Just before my fortieth birthday, I manifested this healing womb outside my body. I had dreamed it for quite some time. For years, I had made house calls or worked in health clubs, hospitals, social service agencies, or holistic education centers so that my healing services would be available. I had often imagined having a womb or room of my own where I could invite people to be reborn. I am thrilled to facilitate yoga classes, craniosacral therapy, reflexology, psychotherapy, meditation, and healing shamanic journeys, all in the same place. Now, on any given day, people come to this sacred room for relaxation and blessings, and many of them comment on the energy or peace here.

▼

The developmental crisis seeking to resolve itself in this stage of life, from age twenty-five to forty, is generativity versus stagnation. If we are fortunate, at this time our knowledge of who we are and what we love manifests in the creation of meaningful work and family life. But if we are stuck in the swamp of previous unresolved developmental crises, we are unable to move forward with this process of actualization, and we stagnate.

The fifth chakra is the energy center of self-expression, specifically the expression of the truth of your spirit as you journey through this life. This actualization of self is both literally and figuratively the singing of the song of your soul, as the energy of this chakra spins out from the throat area (fig. 5.1, p. 154). A healthy fifth chakra will support a healthy larynx and thyroid.

From the shamanic perspective, this is the chakra that generates and contains the very powerful fifth element—ether. John Perkins taught me about ether, which he calls *arutam* (pronounced ah-ROO-tahm), a name that comes from the Shuar language and tradition. Ether is the pure energy of spirit that enables our dreams to manifest in ordinary reality. So this chapter includes tasks to bring you into connection with this element and invoke its power in pursuit of your dreams.

This is the place where matter meets Spirit. This is the chakra where we weave our dreams and distinguish them from fantasies and nightmares. Dreams are universally respectful, balanced, and vibrant manifestations of consciousness and energy. Your dream will be related to who you have found out you are, your identity and your mission, which you found in chapter 3. Dreams are about specific, concrete expression of our mission. For example, I discovered my mission was to help make the world a better place through creative pursuits and healing. In service to this mission I have manifested the dreams of my yoga and integrative healing studio, my shamanic healer training course, and my daughter. With the support of the energy from this chakra, we can create a wonderful life for ourselves and all the beings on this planet.

The spiritual, shamanic questions for this chakra are about how you proceed with realizing your dreams. Are you pursuing someone else's

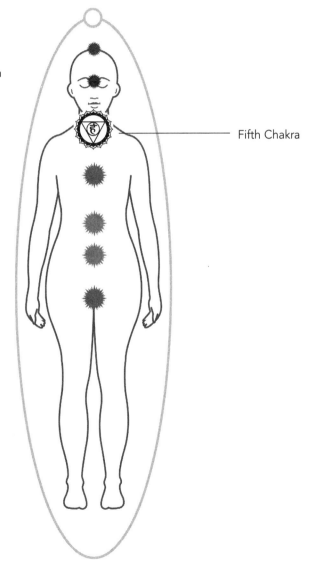

Color: Blue/Turquoise

Element: Ether, Arutam

Developmental Age:
25–40 years

Spiritual Strength:
Expression, Power to
Manifest

Developmental Crisis:
Generativity versus
Stagnation

Fifth Chakra

Fig. 5.1. Fifth Chakra

dreams, your parents' dreams, or the culture's, because you haven't successfully resolved earlier developmental crises? Do you choose to have a protracted adolescence and romanticize about what life should be, instead of taking productive action? Or do you dare to dream the sacred dreams you nurture and cultivate in your heart and use the energies of all five elements to actualize what you love? When you can start to answer this question with a yes, you will become a shaman and a shapeshifter.

The desire to express yourself effectively in the world, which is the energetic function of this chakra, may create a desire to go back and heal any unfinished business in the previous chakras. This is especially true if your energy is stuck actualizing someone else's dreams, mourning the tragedy of our perpetual human drama at the expense of your dreams, or still feeling too unloved in the young places inside yourself to have consistent empathy and compassion for yourself or others. Healing the energy body is not a linear process, as time is not necessarily a linear process, especially in the shamanic world. Growth is a web, always weaving between the past, the present, and the future. So in addition to tasks that focus on growth in this chakra, I have included tasks in this chapter that focus on healing persistent issues from the past. We always must be compassionate with ourselves in our process of growth.

Toward the beginning of this developmental crisis and period of life, I was severely interrupted by a trauma that ultimately led to the manifestation of my healing center. When I was twenty-nine, I was raped while traveling in Jamaica with my friend Patrice. I remember waking from the many nightmares I had afterward, in hot and cold sweats, drenched and quivering. I saw images of the ground falling beneath me and sharp, broken pieces of wood, metal, and glass swirling around me. I wondered if I could ever find a way to feel safe again. The deepest voices inside me asserted that I had to be able to transform my fears into a healing force, for myself and for the greater good. In a multifaceted process that would last a decade, I succeeded in doing just that. This chapter is about the journey we can take to transform a nightmare into a dream and to move past our fears to fully express our inner spirit and love.

The transformational journey that we undertake using the spiritual energy provided in this fifth chakra is a process of shapeshifting.

Shapeshifting can be described as change in the direction of heart-centered generativity. It is made possible by developing an affinity for magnificent life-enhancing ways of being. The tasks at the end of this chapter will use this powerful tool of shapeshifting to set us free to create the world we dream.

FINDING YOUR DREAM

We are all always dreaming, although often unconsciously. *Conscious* dreaming in the direction of life enhancement is a healing shamanic task. But before we can undertake that task, we must become compassionately conscious of our unconscious dreams.

This involves distinguishing between dreams and fantasies. Fantasies, in this shamanic framework, are by nature connected to our younger drives for gratification, usually immediate gratification. Sometimes it is helpful to look deeply into why you have a particular fantasy. Fantasies can reveal quite a bit about our deeper needs and how we need to grow and meet them in more fulfilling ways. For example, you may have a fantasy to build a mansion, with the finest marble and gold fixtures. In a shamanic context this may be considered out of balance as you would be taking more than you need from Pachamama. But there may be a dream to be found within the walls of your mansion of greatness—perhaps the need to make a huge impact on the community or world. The dream within this fantasy might be to create a school or yoga center for children.

Fantasies, especially those that are violent in nature, can also be old habits that arose in unhealthy energy patterns as an attempt to gain mastery over traumatic childhood circumstances. I spent a number of years working on releasing and transforming these types of fantasies because of the violence in my family. Violence is also imposed upon us by the larger culture, so we all have work to do to clear away the energy of these images.

In his book *The World Is As You Dream It,* John Perkins quotes one of his teachers, the powerful shaman Manco, with regard to making the distinction between dreams and fantasies. "Your people have great difficulty distinguishing between the two. You are overly rational, depend too much on the modern fantasy that science can answer all the questions and turn the world into a giant playground for rich gringos. You have convinced yourselves that you can control Pachamama, a fantasy that is wonderfully entertaining, but one that as a dream is terribly destructive." Manco's words reveal the important truth that if our "dreams" hurt other people, beings, or Pachamama, they are, in fact, fantasies or nightmares.

Dreams, in this shamanic framework, come from an older place inside and approach fulfillment with greater patience, perspective, respect, understanding, and courage, qualities that are usually not as readily or fully accessible in the younger developmental stages. We move from the realization of fantasies into the realization of dreams when we move into maturity.

You may choose to maintain some pet fantasies to rely on in moments of stress or indulgence (such as, on a particularly frustrating day, imagining winning the lottery or having wild sex with an attractive movie star), or you may want to transform a fantasy into a dream by recognizing the need that the fantasy is expressing and finding a creative (nondestructive), respectful (nonexploitive) way to meet this need. Some fantasies can never transform in this way, as they can only be hurtful if actualized in ordinary reality, but others require very little adjustment or rewriting to become safe. The more you learn about yourself through this process of shamanic practice, the more you come into the light of consciousness, and the more of yourself you will have available for support in actualizing your genuine dreams.

To distinguish between dream and fantasy, you can ask your dream if it is truly a dream and see if the answer resonates as truth in your heart. Start by observing your life in the present, and how your energy is dancing to create your current reality. Are you happy with it, and fulfilled on every level of your being? If not, you need to find a true dream that expresses your soul and spirit. It is important to avoid seduction by a fantasy or nightmare in this throat center chakra of actualization. We must take care that the dreams we bring to life in the realm of ordinary reality do not have destructive consequences.

In the mesa task that follows, you check your dream out with all the elements and related chakras. Before my studio, or the womb of the goddesses, came into being, I envisioned it and felt it. After feeling my daughter grow inside me, the womb felt like the perfect metaphor for a healing center. I knew the studio was my dream because I felt it in both my creative heart—my womb—and in my fourth chakra, or heart center of compassion and loving kindness. A great deal of energy then became available for me in my throat chakra, as I was aware of my need to express this dream in my adult life. When the holistic program at the hospital I was working at was closing, I decided to look for a space for my own center and had the energy to pursue that dream.

◆◆ Task One: Finding Your Dream

Journey to your sacred place. As always, experience it through your senses. Take in the safety, the nurturing, and the love. Feel yourself held in your sacred healing place.

Invite all the elements in your sacred healing place to cleanse you and dance with you. Take time to really sensually experience earth, water, fire, and air in your sacred place. Move with the powerful energies of these elements in your sacred place with great abandon and intensity. Perhaps you will stomp your feet on the earth, dive with the waterfall, leap with the fire, and swirl with the wind. Then pause, allowing the energies to whirl together. In the sacred integration of these elements you will feel the whole energy become greater than the sum of its parts. This new energy you generate, connected to all matter but beyond matter, is the fifth element—the ether. Feel it moving around you and through you. It has an expansive, powerful, indescribable quality of Spirit, different from all you have felt before. It opens an energetic portal you can enter so you can find your dream.

Connect to your spiritual protection and guidance by inviting your guides and power animals to be here with you in this sacred energy of all possibility. Feel connected to Spirit in your heart and with your whole being. Then, ask your dream to bring you to it. Invite it to call you. Perhaps you will hear the song or voice of your dream. It may be a deep hum, like the sacred sound of "om." Maybe you'll hear someone or something calling your name.

Notice if your dream calls you to journey into your body, to some place or element in your sacred place, or beyond your sacred place. Perhaps there is a person you have to see or a place in the world you need to go on your journey. Go wherever the voice of your dream calls you. A house, garden, town, city, mountain, country, the universe . . . anywhere and everywhere. It doesn't matter where you go in this journey, as long as your dream calls you there.

Feel your dream present itself to you. Feel yourself received by your dream. Your dream may present itself as an image, vision, being, symbol, song, or dance. Your dream may speak to you about its presence in your life, what it brings to you, and what it requires of you. When you feel you have learned all you need to learn about it at this point, return to your sacred place, where you may want to discuss it with your guides. When you are ready, thank your guides, the elements, and your sacred place, and return to ordinary reality.

When you come back from your journey, it is very important to journal about it. If the dream you encountered there resonates in your heart, start to develop your relationship to it right away. Ask your dream what the possibilities are for the process of manifesting it. What steps might you need to take in the world? Are there any old issues to be resolved first? The tasks that follow in this chapter will also support your relationship to your dream by teaching you how to generate energy for it, nurture it, and actualize it.

You may need to allow the meaning of your experience to unfold over time. Your dream may become your beloved; in the spirit of generativity, our dreams can sometimes feel like our children. Spirit will support you in your relationship to it.

GENERATING ENERGY FOR YOUR DREAM

It is important to address the previous four chakras, the whole lower part of the energy body, when starting to work with this chakra and the tasks of dreaming and shapeshifting. The lower chakras form our base and our core, and our best dreams come from having strength and integrity in this area. With these chakras healed you can start to feel that you not only have individual energy centers that are extremely powerful but that they connect to form a whole core of strength, and this core of strength radiates out to form your energy body. The desire to actualize fantasies rather than pursue an authentic and worthy dream usually comes from not yet fully meeting previous developmental challenges, and therefore not connecting these centers in a powerful, integrated way. After you have worked on the first four chakras the following exercises will help prepare you for the process of screening and integrating your genuine dreams.

As we have seen, ether or arutam is a powerful force. John Perkins taught me how to generate it, connect with it, and use it to manifest dreams. Everything one thinks, feels, and does has more power with arutam. This is another reason why it is good to heal your unfinished business in the first four chakras before you start to generate too much of it. Otherwise, the great power of the ether might be directed into unhealthy or destructive channels.

Part of the beauty in what John teaches lies in the reality that we generate arutam by being in deep communion with the elements of earth, water, fire, and air. This concept has a flawlessness to it, because the real power comes from the elements that connect us to the earth, our chakras, and our core. If we remain in our centers, then we can be sure our dreams will be respectful of the earth, ourselves, and our fellow spirits and beings everywhere. To be intimate with the elements from our core requires maturity—expressed as our commitment to do this work. This is the maturity required for ecstatic dreaming.

It is important to use the next task to know that your dream is in fact coming fully from your integrity and core. This is especially true if the steps toward realizing your dream will create some upheaval in your life. I needed to leave my marriage to continue to actualize my dream. I spent hours in therapy and performing this task to make sure this choice was coming from my core.

❧ Task Two: Constructing a Mesa

In this task you will assemble your sacred healing objects for the four elements in the shape of a tabletop (mesa is the Spanish word for table) or altar. To begin, define the space for your mesa on the earth by laying down a piece of cloth that has some meaning for you. Place your earth huaca on the part of the mesa that extends toward the south. Place your water huaca toward the west. Place your fire huaca toward the east, and your air huaca toward the north. (Various indigenous traditions place the elements in different directions. Honor your tradition if you embrace one, or, if your huacas need to be in different positions, listen to their wisdom.)

As you approach the mesa with great reverence, ask it for support in knowing if your dream is true. With your consciousness, enter or journey into the earth huaca and your first chakra. You will project and sense yourself inside your huaca as if it were a sacred dwelling or universe unto itself. You might be able to explore your huacas for a long time in this way, but you are here now just to ask your important questions. To journey to your chakras, breathe into them with your consciousness. Each chakra is an inner sacred place, the home of its corresponding ego state, with wisdom to share.

Ask your earth huaca and first chakra if your dream is true, and listen for the answer. Do this with each of the remaining huacas and the corresponding chakras. You will want to get a response in the affirmative from each chakra to know that your dream is, in fact, a genuine dream, rather than a spirit-less fantasy. You may also consult with your spirit guides for each of these chakras and elements. You can even consult with your ego states at each of the ages that correspond to the chakras, drawing on the wisdom they've acquired from resolving earlier development crises.

If you receive an affirmative response for each chakra, you are coming from the best integrity you can at the moment. If you receive a message from your guides, huacas, chakras, or any of your ego states that the dream you are presenting is not in fact a genuine dream, ask if it can be modified to reflect your full maturity and be a healthy manifestation of spirit. If it has that potential, consult with all your spiritual allies and find out how to transform it. In the unlikely event that it can't become a true dream, you can relegate it to the fantasy category and journey for a new dream. This process will have taught you about how to evaluate the truth of a dream, leaving you in a better position to recognize and respond to one that is genuine.

After consulting with each individual huaca and chakra, spend some time meditating on your mesa. Consciously enter the space in the center of the space created by the placement of the four huacas embodying the elements of earth, water, fire and air—this is the eye or heart of the mesa. Sense the powerful energy this sacred space holds. This is the etheric energy or arutam. This heart of the mesa is the portal to your dreams. As you meditate you can sense the vibration of the power to manifest and actualize here in this portal. This is the fifth chakra energy, ready to infuse your life with the ecstasy of having your dreams come true.

At this point in your process, you may want to find a sacred etheric huaca. Invite an etheric huaca to introduce itself to you. You may go anywhere in nature to find your etheric huaca, or this huaca could be a spiritual gift someone has already given to you, from nature or an indigenous tradition. If you look for your huaca in nature, you might connect with a seed; the potential for the whole plant or tree (the actualized dream) is present in the seed. Since the center of the mesa is the eye or heart of the mesa, so you may want to find a huaca that seems to embody an eye or a heart.

When you have found a sacred etheric huaca, you may place this huaca in the center of your mesa. Let it continue to gather energy from all the elements, kundalini from the earth, and prana from the heavens. In future mesa meditations, end by asking this huaca if your dream is true.

My fifth-chakra huacas were a gift from my daughter and a friend for my thirty-ninth birthday. They are amethyst quartz crystal hearts, a larger one that I use for the mesa at the studio, and a smaller one that I use for my mesa at home. I received this gift just before I manifested the studio. I feel that the hearts were a great support in bringing this dream into being. They have a wonderful feel to them, smooth, weighty, cool, yet very sweet. I believe they are a blessing since they support me in manifesting the sweetness of being through love.

▼

Task three is the culmination of many years of study in the ancient art of belly dance, during which I began to realize with the help of my guides that belly dance is the dance of the elements. There are sections of the dance that are performed to different types of traditional music, and I became aware that these different qualities of movement embodied the elements of creation. The floor movements are about connecting to the earth, the flowing movements about connecting to the water, the staccato movements about connecting to the fire, and the light, free movements are about connecting to the air. When one dances them over a period of twenty minutes to an hour, one generates energy that then becomes the etheric energy of arutam.

This uniquely feminine expression of power from an ancient Earth-honoring tradition was a vital discovery in my healing journey. The sexual assault I experienced in Jamaica wounded me deeply, both my sense of myself as an individual woman and how I experienced myself as part of "women" collectively. My sexuality needed to be honored and included in movement—not split off, repressed, controlled, and fragmented as can sometimes happen in certain styles of yoga or martial arts.

I had first been exposed to belly dance at twenty-two when I finished with massage school and went back to take acting classes. Serena, a very experienced and dynamic professional belly dancer, was my scene partner. Her studio was in the same building as my acting teacher's, and so I went to see her dance and to take a couple of classes. Though interested, it was hard for me to get my hips and pelvis to move in all the required patterns prior to resolving my sexual abuse issues. But this ancient dance remained in my consciousness. It seemed to keep presenting itself to me.

In my early thirties when I really needed it for healing my body, I found a wonderful teacher, Liana. Liana is very much a "show woman" with excellent technique. She also has a profound spiritual side, and she helped me to find my spiritual dance. The first dance I worked on was a veil dance. It was about the feminine spirit rising up with a colorful, flowing strength after much struggle. The movements of belly dance massage the pelvis and flow with the curves of the female body. When I danced, I could feel the energy move through me in a different way. The dance included an element of transcendence, and the knowledge that truth, beauty, and power do not have to be mutually exclusive qualities.

The following task utilizes the movements of belly dance to contact the elements of the mesa and to embody them physically and energetically. Belly dance has traditionally been a dance done by women, but I have taught this particular dance to hundreds of men in John Perkins's workshops. The power we generate with this dance can guide us out of stagnation to the fullness of expression.

❧ Task Three: Dancing the Elements

Recall the movements related to the elements in the previous four chapters. Hopefully you've gotten to practice them a bit. Put on some rhythmic music that makes you feel like moving. Let yourself generate the energy of the elements through the movements of your body. To move with the earth, stand with soft knees and feet hip-width apart, while you gently sway back and forth, making circles with your pelvis to draw the kundalini up from the earth. While you do these movements, experiment with feeling the energy of earth more deeply and generating that energy with the movement. As you dance on the earth, you may feel your own solidness, density, magnetism, and depth. Generate the power of the earth as you move with consciousness.

Continue with the flowing movements of the water (chapter 2, task five), the staccato movements of the fire (chapter 3, task three), and the breezy movements of the air (chapter 4, task two). As you dance to the music, move through all the elements, earth, water, fire, and air, with as much intimate contact and thoroughness as possible. Feel their individual qualities again, their life force. How you dance the elements is as unique as you are.

After you have enthusiastically danced and intensely connected to the elements for at least twenty minutes, you may pause and feel the arutam. As you did in the journey to your sacred place, sense the energies from the elements you've danced whirling together all around you. After a moment there is an energy that seems to transcend the others, to expand out from the dance of the other elements. This is arutam or the fifth element, the ether. It is an expansive feeling, as arutam is the element of all possibility. You pulse and vibrate and radiate with the energy of arutam, though you may actually be moved to stand in relative stillness, awe, and expectancy. You may sense a portal has opened to another realm of energy.

You may chant "a-ru-tam" several times, supporting yourself in allowing this sacred energy to move all around you and through you, filling you with the joy of possibility. Bring your dream into your consciousness and feel the energies dancing all around you.

The fifth chakra is the center where spiritual energy can cross the bridge to the physical world of matter. We will now perform the Bridge pose so we can bring more of this energy into the fifth chakra for use in dreaming and shapeshifting.

◆ Task Four: Bridge Pose

You begin Bridge pose by lying on your back, feeling Mother Earth under you, supporting you, cradling you. Always take the time to feel her nurturing and love. She is always there. Breathe in comfort, breathe out pressure, stress, and tension. Let it go to Pachamama.

Bend your knees so you can step the soles of your feet on the floor; your feet are hip-width apart and your heels are as close to your sitz bones as possible, without creating discomfort in your knees (fig. 5.2). Take a moment to come into greater contact with the earth by pressing the soles of the feet and the sacrum, the triangular bone connecting the creative bowl of the pelvis to the serpent of the spine, down into the earth. Press the whole spinal column down into the earth along with the triangles of both shoulder blades. The triangles of the sacrum and shoulder blades combine to form a larger triangle. Press gently down through this whole power center. Press the arms and hands down into the earth as they lie along the sides of your torso.

Now gently lift the pelvis, as if an invisible string is pulling the pubic bone up toward the sky, slowly lifting the spine off the earth one vertebrae at a time until your body forms a straight line between your shoulders and your knees. This will be at about a thirty-degree angle with the earth. Continue to roll up through your spine and come to a stop when your weight is resting on the space between the shoulder blades. Definitely avoid resting the weight on your neck. Continue to press into the arms (fig. 5.3).

In this posture, you will bring energy into the throat chakra. You can facilitate this further by gently circling your tailbone, creating a spiraling motion in the pelvic bowl and spine. This motion will create a nice massage for the tight, weary place between the shoulder blades and spiral the energy in the heart and throat chakras. You may want to chant "a-ru-tum," invoking this powerful element of transformation.

Feel the arutam, take a breath in, and slowly roll down, one vertebra at a time, feeling the wholeness of yourself received by the wholeness of Mother Earth and the power of her loving heart. Feel supported by the love of Mother Earth. Continue to feel the arutam and the sensation of consciously making the bridge between spirit and matter and matter and spirit, coming into knowledge of the process at every level of your being.

Fig. 5.2

Fig. 5.3

NURTURING YOUR DREAM

The seed of a plant or tree needs the earth, water, fire, and air as well as arutam to move it through the process of growth and successful manifestation. So does the metaphoric seed of our dream. As we have just journeyed to find our dreams and we are exploring how the elements empower them, we are still in the seed stage. This next task gives you a progressive image for this growth process that energetically embodies the dynamic of nurturing and realizing dreams.

⬦ Task Five: Seed to Tree

To do this task, go out in nature or put on a piece of music that is transforming for you. Start in Child pose (fig. 5.4) or curled up in a ball on your side. Now, be the seed. Physicalize it. Bring your dream into your consciousness. See it in all its dimensions and from all its different angles. Know that you, embodying this seed stage of actualizing your dream, hold the wholeness of your dream within you. Feel the universe of the tree inside the universe of the seed.

Feel yourself as the seed making contact with the element of earth. Feel your solidness. Relax on and in the bosom of Mother Earth. Release the energy of conflict from prior incarnations, of all that you were before you became this seed. Release to Mother Earth all your prior broken dreams and nightmares. Feel nurtured. Receive the rich magnetic energy that Mother Earth offers you, the hug of her gravitational pull. Feel your deep yearning as the seed to interact with all the elements and actualize.

Take in the element of water from within you and around you. Feel yourself start to germinate and sprout. Move onto your knees, reaching your hands toward the sky (fig. 5.5). Your center sprouts upward as you feel the solidness of your trunk, expressing your strength and commitment. Feel the instinctive intelligence of your roots as they shoot down into Mother Earth. Continue to feel warmed and held by her as the fluidity of your form continues to express itself as you unfold. See your dream beginning to develop as your creativity is supported.

Fig. 5.4

Fig. 5.5

Fig. 5.6

Feel your passion grow, your fire, as your branches reach up to make contact with the sun. Your leaves unfurl to open to the light, to make food and nourishment (fig 5.6, p. 169). Know that your dream is manifesting. Feel yourself breathe as the tree, sustaining life. Experience how the elements support the fully realized expression of your spirit as the tree. Know in every cell of your body what you are and what you have always been: Spirit. Express gratitude to the ever present etheric energy for supporting you in becoming the tree, shapeshifting into the embodiment of your dream. Envision, sense, and emotionally experience what it is like to have your dream come true in all possible fullness. Flower and make fruit as this tree.

HEALING THROUGH SHAPESHIFTING

You are now shapeshifting as you read this book, do these tasks, and move from being a seed to becoming a tree. I've learned most of what I know about shapeshifting from my work with John Perkins. Shapeshifting is possible because everything in the universe is of the same energy. We are all everything, and everything is us. We shapeshift or change all the time at the level of our feelings, our thoughts, our imaginings, our dreams.

Shapeshifting involves actually being that which you have previously wished to become. All shapeshifts happen through the presence and consciousness of the spiritual energy of ether, or arutam. Conscious shapeshifts happen because the shapeshifter is cultivating an alliance with that which she or he would like to become and inviting the presence of arutam so the old form or dream is released and the new form or dream is embraced.

John teaches that shapeshifting can happen at three levels. The first level is cellular, which describes the healing of physical illness or changing the physical form, perhaps into a different physical object or being. The second level is the intra/interpsychic or personal level, which refers to the healing of addictions, relationships, and behavioral patterns. The third level is institutional, which applies to shapeshifting at the level of organizations, including the societal institutions of business, education, government, politics, and communication.

John Perkins is a wonderful inspirational example of a man who reevaluated his dreams, and his journey unfolds along a path of ever-increasing integrity and courage. In the prologue to his book *Confessions of an Economic Hit Man,* John describes his gut-wrenching encounter with the aftermath of a dam that was part of a development project he had helped facilitate. Returning to Ecuador in 2003 to revisit the site of the dam, he recounts his visceral and mental response to the suffering this project caused for the indigenous people and farmers who lived along the river. Only "a few greedy men" truly benefited.

After a time, he was able to leave the company that facilitated this type of "development." He shapeshifted into a person who created a sustainable-energy company that set healing precedents for a troubled, selfish industry. The unveiling of his own shadow and the shadow of an entire economic and political institution through the writing of his book was a powerful shapeshift into integrity, and an expression of a bold new type of masculine power. Being willing to take responsibility and move directly through, rather than around, guilt and shame, to step into the light of Spirit while having wise dreams, is a shapeshift of considerable magnitude.

Prior to my formal training in the shamanic task of shapeshifting, I was able to experience a shapeshift around the rape I discussed earlier in the chapter. Rape is primarily, but not exclusively, a crime against women. Women have a long history of being blamed for the crimes against them. And we have blamed each other because, paradoxically, it makes us feel safer to believe we have a formula for avoiding rape. If we don't wear the short skirt, we won't get raped. If we don't provoke the angry man, we won't get beaten. I guess I, too, had previously been comforted by a "blame the victim" mentality. I listened compassionately to other people's rape stories but mentally made a note that I would never do whatever it was they did that got them into that predicament. I even had a therapist who was a specialist in the field of sexual assault tell me she was never raped because she could say "no" very strongly. The problem is, these formulas don't work—and we are making each other more unsafe by perpetuating them.

Since I was somewhat self-aware, having devoted myself to more than ten years of psychotherapy that included healing from sexual abuse, I knew the rape was not my fault. And having been through it, I understood that, short of having a crystal ball, I could not have stopped it from happening. Because I was able to clearly see that the rape was not my fault, which reflected a hard-won evolution in my consciousness, the victim-blaming dynamic in the culture became so clear to me. I had worked so hard for the whole previous decade to heal, be responsible, get sober, finish college, continue learning, and to build my healing practice, only to be victimized—which could happen to anyone. The worst part of the trauma was the blame that would come in subtle forms every time I told my story. Somehow, the personal became political for me in this moment in a much deeper way than it ever had before. I recognized the most insidious disease of our culture: blaming the victim.

So for the next five years, along with a few committed fellow survivors and colleagues, I created a theater company that addressed issues of sexual violence and the victim-blaming attitudes that perpetuate it. We performed our program for colleges, law schools, social service organizations, and spiritual centers. The workshop included emotionally explicit dramatic depictions of rape and the consequent disassociation of the soul from the body. There were improvisational and scripted examinations of sexist cultural dynamics, and responses from both male and female peers and "authorities." We encouraged the audience to dialogue with the characters. We always ended with a "take back the night" ritual, passing a candle, allowing every audience member to share according to her or his needs, sharing the light of healing and consciousness. This was a healing shapeshift, a redreaming of the nightmare for me and my two codirectors, who were also survivors.

Our project resonated out into the world. We were able to change how people were taught about rape prevention, at least here in Westchester County, New York. Programs began to shift away from teaching girls and women to say "no" more loudly, because people finally realized that the victim's actions were not the cause. Some powerful educators, especially of young people, developed curriculums to address the culture's need to embrace its responsibility for perpetuating this dynamic through victim blaming. These programs supported young men in deeply understanding issues of consent and the impact of their actions on others. This was a powerful fifth-chakra lesson about not letting your fantasy be someone else's nightmare.

Generativity and the actualization of dreams develop over the course of time. Elba, the Quechua shaman from Peru who taught me about the mesa, also taught me how to shapeshift to embrace the past, present, and future simultaneously—because in the shamanic realm they are all happening concurrently, at different levels, in different realities. To shapeshift well we must open our souls, minds, emotions, and bodies to this truth, even if we do not totally understand it intellectually. Our spirits already know this truth.

Elba spoke about the three-leaf configuration of the sacred coca plant, and how it was mirrored in ancient Incan architecture. She told me about the three animals that embody the qualities of the three states of being—past, present, and future—in her spiritual and cultural tradition. With Elba I studied the movements of the serpent, puma, and condor. I recalled what I'd learned about Egyptian mysticism from my study of the ancient art of belly dance, in which one also embodies the sacred beings of the serpent, the cat, and the mythical bird. Elba's teaching inspired me to write the following poem:

Three Simultaneous States of Being
Serpent sheds her past again and reveals a deeper self.
The spirit dances with the soul and life experience.
Serpent is the core, the spine, her heart moving with the waves

of energy from Mother Earth.
She is the past in the light of truth
the strength of magnetic resilience.

Jaguar is the present. Water and fire
the blaze, the sizzle, the steam.
In her acute awareness she hunts.
She assimilates.
She is.

Eagle is the air.
She sees.
She vibrates with her own majesty.
She carries our dreams to manifestation
on the breadth
of her wings.

The past is represented by the serpent. A serpent sheds her skin, leaving behind expressions of her past self and revealing her more authentic, ever evolving self. Serpents slither and glide in contact with Mother Earth, connecting deeply with her energy. The present is represented by the cat, who is connected to the elements of sinuous water and smoldering fire. As predators, cats have keen awareness that keeps them alive and present in each current moment. And the future is represented by the soaring bird connected to the element of air. From their vantage point above the clouds and with their piercing eyesight, birds can see far into the possibilities of the future, and they can carry our dreams to manifestation.

Every being exists on these three levels, and if we can become conscious of this, we expand our power and our positive impact. As we dance these three amazing animals, feel them, and know them, we can draw on the wisdom we've accumulated through our ancestors. We can have the support to be fully present here and now, and we can soar effortlessly on the winds of the future. We can dream and shapeshift our world.

◈ Task Six: Dancing the Three Simultaneous States of Being

Put on music. You may want to choose one piece of music that evokes each animal for you, or you can just play ongoing drumming music. Start to dance the animals, the three simultaneous states of being, one at a time.

Explore how the serpent and the ancestors are within you in the DNA of your cells. Invite yourself to coil. Feel your body as one long muscle. Propel your belly forward on the belly of Mother Earth. Feel how this consummate shapeshifter sheds her skin and perpetually renews herself.

Next, feel the grace, power, and awareness of the cat. Let yourself prowl, stalk, and hunt. Purr and bask in the sun.

Finally, open your wings and fly like the eagle. Expand yourself beyond the confines of your mind. Fly through the universe of your heart and the collective heart.

Experience how you have become a shapeshifter, embodying these powerful animals of spirit that provide the dimensions and layers of energy we need to realize our magnificence. How did it feel to embody the serpent, the cat, the majestic bird? How can their energy, wisdom, and presence help support you in actualizing your dream?

You may find that your fantasies and nightmares persist in spite of trying to contact your dream. If so, then an extraction may be required to remove what interferes with manifesting your dreams. The basic dynamic of an extraction involves removing or releasing something negative from your energy field.

Most often these negative charges are deep, old beliefs about not deserving the rewards and pleasure that would come from actualizing your dream. It is also possible a negative charge from another person or group of people may have attached itself to your energy field. This negative energy is usually generated when someone is irresponsible or vengeful in nature and has made you a target at a time when you were vulnerable. If soul retrieval does not dispel old negative beliefs and you are unable to dislodge negative energy directed at you by others through power retrieval (task six in chapter 6), extraction offers a different energetic approach to releasing these energies.

There are many ways to perform extractions. They include, but are not limited to, techniques that utilize eggs, crystals, movement patterns, sucking, and purging. It may be possible to find teachers for all these techniques. It is most effective to do this technique as a partner exercise, but you may also perform this extraction on yourself. This technique works well as a preparation for the shapeshifting healing session.

My favorite tool for extraction is a chicken egg. Eggs are so warm and sweet and have energy much like that of Pachamama herself. No old belief or negative charge can resist moving into the inviting womb of the chicken egg. I believe that people who extend negativity and create havoc and pain do so because they were not sufficiently loved in this or perhaps a previous life. The egg-womb will seduce this extension of their energy and begin basic, loving nurturing again. Although its shell is thin in a material sense, the egg is a very powerful container and transformer.

Because of the deprivation and abuse in my childhood, I had many old beliefs and negative charges that needed to be extracted, removed, and released. When I was thirty-one I developed cervical dysplasia, or irregular cells that are sometimes considered precancerous. This forced me to release my old demons as I received guidance. To fully heal this condition, I needed to both remove the toxic energy deposits and take in healing energies.

❖ Task Seven: Extraction with an Egg

I will present this as a partner healing. (Ideally, your partner is also working with the tasks in this book independently, or you are guiding the person through this process.) If you are not working with a partner, adapt this exercise for yourself.

To prepare the room for this extraction, generate your mesa. You may use your original five huacas unless you wish to reserve them just for your own healing. In that case, you may find other huacas for the elements that you are comfortable using to facilitate healing for others. Prepare a place for your partner to lie down, sit, or stand, as this healing can be done in any position. Use your partner's feedback and intuition for this.

Before you begin your first extraction, spend some time with one egg. Ask its permission to be used to help in this process of healing. (If it says no, ask another egg or see if it has any ideas about what you should be doing instead. Always ask for permission with each new egg.) Feel the energy, personality, and spirit of the chicken egg. Feel it in your hands. Let it talk to you. See if it has a message for you. Rub or roll it over your body. Shake or otherwise move it in your energy field. See if its energy changes as you do these things.

Is there anything you would like to release to the egg before you begin this healing extraction? Let the egg absorb it. How do you feel? If the egg absorbed a negative charge from your energy field you will feel freer and lighter and the egg may feel denser. You are beginning to develop very subtle energy discernment abilities here and this may take time. As the egg will have absorbed some of what you needed to release, even if it is simply general tension, you will need to dispose of it. Do not ingest it, but release it to the power of one of the four elements, earth, water, fire, or air. Bury or compost it, or put it in a body of water or fire.

When you are ready to begin this partner extraction healing, take a fresh egg or two. Don Jose, a powerful shaman from Ecuador, uses two eggs for cleansing; one for the body, one for the soul.

Invite your guides and your partner's guides to be present and helpful in the healing you are about to do. Ask your partner to clarify her or his dream by stating it to you. As the expression of the dream is resonating in the person's energy field, sense if there is any energetic dynamic that seems to be preventing your partner from dreaming or actualizing effectively. While you hold the egg or eggs, scan your partner's field by moving around your partner's whole body with your hands. The intelligence of the egg as well as your intuition will help you find and feel potential blockages created by old beliefs and negative charges. For the purpose of this exercise you don't have to differentiate or know what they are, though information that might be helpful may come through spirit to you or your partner as you proceed with the cleansing or extraction.

Trust that you will either feel or be guided to areas in need of extraction. Cupping the egg or wrapping your hands loosely around it, you may gently roll the egg on your partner's body, or carefully shake it all around her or him make scrubbing and brushing movements, or simply hold it in certain places coaxing the negativity to enter the egg. When you are done, the person's field will feel clearer, lighter, less dense. Perhaps if you had any sense of the presence of the negativity, you will feel it gone. Also, the egg will feel warmer and denser as your partner's energy field is cleansed.

While you process or talk about the extraction with your partner, both of you expressing sensations, emotions, and perhaps insights, you may leave the egg with the mesa so it is protected. Then your partner can take the egg that is holding her or his released charge, express gratitude to it and dispose of it within a day to the earth, water, or fire, whatever feels right and is available.

You are now ready to conduct a shapeshifting healing session. In this task you will generate the elements to support your partner in actualizing her or his dream. The elements cleanse and empower and open your partner to a greater alliance with Spirit in all its expression so she or he can generate a cellular, personal, or institutional shapeshift. If you don't have a partner to do this work with, adapt these instructions for working on yourself.

In John Perkins's book *Shapeshifting*, another of his teachers, the shaman Kitiar, describes what happens in a shapeshifting healing session:

[H]e announced that he would conduct healings on any people who felt the need. "This will involve a shapeshift," he said. "What I call a 'spirit shift' because only the spirits see it. To the rest of you I will be just an old man sitting here on my stool. But the spirits will see me transform myself into a great fire-breathing volcano. The mountain will blow its top off. A raging river will burst forth and rush down the volcanic slopes into the person being healed. This river will form whirlpools and they will suck the bad spirits out of the illness."

To prepare for your shapeshifting healing session you must establish safety on all levels—you and your partner should feel connected to supports, guidance, and protection. Feel surrounded by your spiritual supports, including your power animals and spirit guides. If necessary, you can refer to previous exercises and chapters to help establish this.

❈ Task Eight: The Shapeshifting Healing Session

Prepare your mesa in the healing room. Have your partner state her or his dream, trying to envision or experience it in her or his body and being as if it already is actualized. Bring in the four elements of earth, water, fire, and air through movement. Use your huacas as you move, dancing with them and/or other objects that evoke the elements such as incense, swords, candles, water, essential oils, flowers, herbs, branches, stones, rattles, drums, or other musical instruments. If there are songs or sounds you use to invoke the elements, use your voice as well. It is important to do this for at least twenty minutes. Take a moment to feel the dance of the elements around and through your partner.

To help heal and transform your partner, shapeshift into a jagged cliff, tar pit, deep canyon, tidal wave, waterfall, monsoon, erupting volcano, boiling geyser, exploding star, tornado, hurricane, or trade wind. Love this partner with all possibilities of yourself, your passion, the totality of your union with Pachamama.

Let your ecstasy push your partner over the edge, get swept away, incinerated, stripping away the veils while throwing this person clear to heaven so she or he may land, naked core self, here on earth smack in the center of the embodiment of her or his dream.

Feel how the fifth element, arutam, is activated as you feel the power to effect change at the etheric level. Invite your partner to feel the energy of manifestation following the dream she or he has expressed. Hold the space energetically for this to happen by continuing to focus on the energies of the elements and dance them if necessary.

Direct the energy of all five elements into your partner's dream. Let the energy flow into the dream, shapeshifting this person's life, cells, energy body, and energetic connections. Both you and your partner will feel more powerful and expanded after this healing session. Express your gratitude to all the elements and Pachamama.

It can be very helpful to redream our actual nightmares, the unconscious collages of images that move through our energy fields while we sleep, sometimes surfacing into our consciousness upon awakening. Our fears frequently reveal themselves through our nighttime dreams. We will often have nightmares when we encounter events that shake our security or violate our integrity. The human organism will attempt to gain mastery over our fears through nightmares.

The following task enables us to achieve this sense of control in a balanced way, bringing our consciousness to our unconscious. This task will allow you to connect to guidance and protection in a deeper way. We can be much more creative and generative with our healthy dreams when we feel we are supported and protected. We tend to be aggressive in a destructive way when we don't feel supported and protected. We get greedy, taking more than we need from Mother Earth and making unnecessary wars in a futile attempt to make ourselves feel safe. It is time to redream all our nightmares.

I needed to redream the nightmares that grew out of the rape experience. My beloved eagles flew around me to protect me from the shards of glass and sharp metal, weaving a cocoon of soft, yet impenetrable protective energy. As the ground was pulled out from underneath me, my eagles held me and flew with me over the land, showing how I, too, could fly. They accompanied me to my sacred place so I could heal and bathe in the energy of the elements. I began to feel my wounds shapeshifting into insight and wisdom, as my anger transformed into action.

⟪⟫ Task Nine: Redreaming Nightmares

Whenever you remember a fragment of a nightmarish dream, write it down or record it in some way. As soon as you can, set aside some time to review the events of your dream in a quiet and nurturing space. This time, as you recall the events of the dream, allow yourself to bring protection, guidance, support, and love to your fears. For example, if you dream of falling off a cliff, you may find a large bird who is willing to scoop you up long before you hit the ground, and perhaps even to take you on a wonderful adventure.

If you dream of being attacked by a band of thieves, a large bear may come to protect you. Allow yourself to resolve your nightmare using powerful supports to make you safe.

Express your appreciation to any and all of the protective guiding spirits you encounter that support you in redreaming your nightmares.

We can redream our collective nightmare: the problematic "American Dream." We can shapeshift. I know this because this fifth-chakra period in my life, though fraught with challenges and past baggage, taught me how to move on into the future with a powerful wholeness that has included manifesting new friendships, healing techniques, my healing center, and my daughter. I believe we all can generate our dreams for healing and beauty by practicing the tasks in this book, staying connected to Mother Earth, to our hearts, and to Spirit in its infinite capacity to express greatness.

6
Opening the Heart of the Mind
A Journey to Clarity

A couple of years ago, I got word through an acquaintance that the co-owner of a yoga studio in an adjoining town was leaving that partnership to open a large yoga studio across the street from Birth of Venus. I remember doing quite a bit of ranting and raving to friends. My flush of rage and fear was hard to contain.

My new potential competitor left a phone message, presumably to discuss her opening across the street. But when I called back a couple of times, she didn't return my calls. I left a message, simply stating that I supported my daughter with the money I made from my small business and that I thought she should reconsider locating her business across the street from mine. Then everything quieted down for a time, including me, and it almost seemed she might have changed her mind.

A few months later, on my birthday, I saw her sign in the window across the street. She was opening soon. This certainly was not the present I wanted. I got mad again, but less so, because it wasn't a surprise. When I calmed myself down and meditated about it, I could see from a place of clarity that what was most important was to recognize and accept the challenge this woman's choice presented to me. My faith in my dream and in my ability to provide material security for myself and my daughter was being tested, and this test had something important to teach me if I could expand beyond my fear and pay attention.

This clarity of vision came from the opening of my third eye, the center of the sixth chakra. The opening of the third eye allows us to see through the fog of emotion and fear, so we can separate ourselves out from the drama as we continue to fulfill our missions and actualize our dreams.

I had to allow myself to experience this situation energetically, centering myself in my third eye, contacting the light of wisdom and compassion. As I sat meditating on this situation, I realized that having a similar business so close by fueled a desire in me to transmit my message more clearly. I could use the energy of this challenge to support me in moving to a place of greater integrity. I called in the goddesses and my guides to protect, guide, and support me. I constructed my mesa. I connected to and danced the elements. I invoked the shapeshifting element, the ether or arutam. Many aspects of my practice started to grow in positive new ways.

In the seven years since I opened my small studio, I have watched yoga become more and more about props and products, people naming techniques after themselves, yoga schools trying to prove that yoga is a good "business," and so on. It seemed that much of the original spiritual intention of this practice was being lost. By opening her studio directly across from me, my competitor challenged me to commit more fully to my vision of yoga and healing.

I changed how I practiced and taught, and how I ran my business. I began to offer a Mother Earth–centered shamanic healer training program. I also created a yoga teacher training program and began to focus on the yamas and niyamas, the ethical principles of yoga, which I feel have been very much overlooked in recent years. In an effort to perpetuate the vital service-oriented aspects of yoga, I opened all of my yoga and meditation classes to allow anyone to come and leave a donation according to her or his ability to pay. Twenty percent of the donations are given to community organizations. As I called in the elements and my guides, the competition I was facing forced my altruism. Using the clarity and wisdom of my sixth chakra, I allowed that threatening energy to interact with and strengthen mine, not to paralyze it.

▼

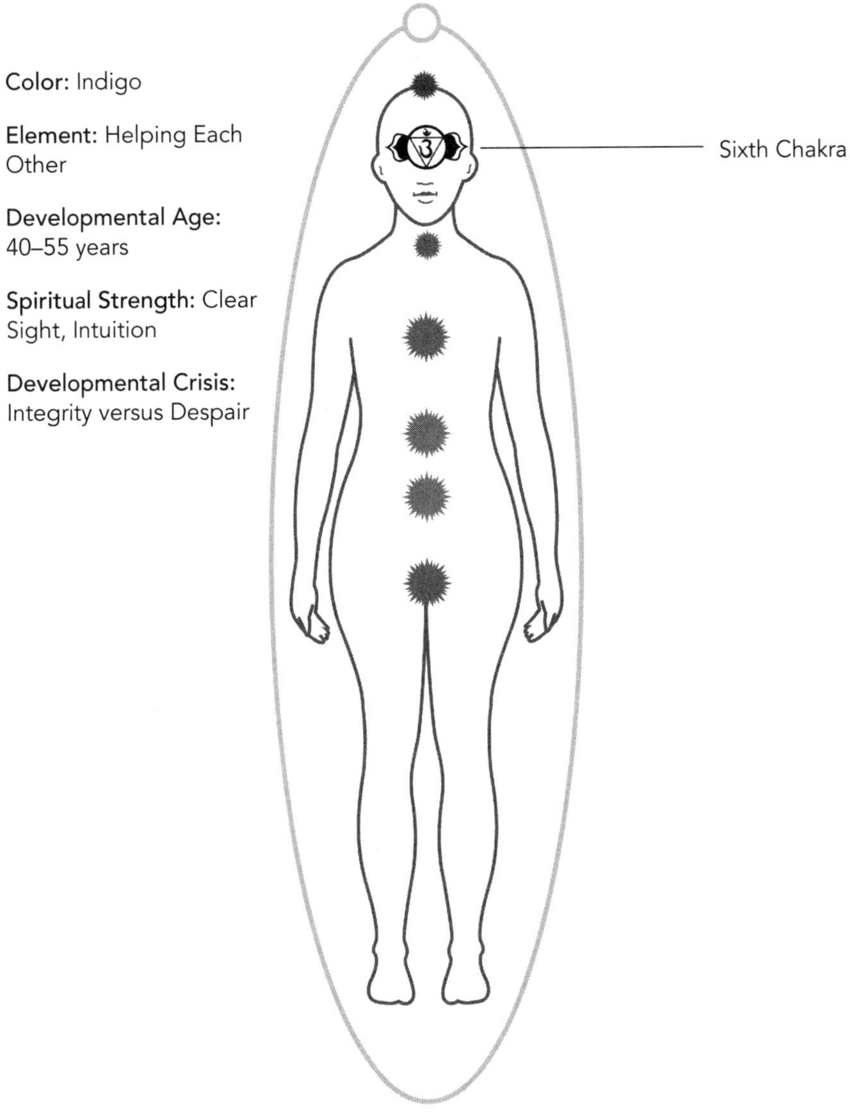

Color: Indigo

Element: Helping Each Other

Developmental Age: 40–55 years

Spiritual Strength: Clear Sight, Intuition

Developmental Crisis: Integrity versus Despair

Sixth Chakra

Fig. 6.1. Sixth Chakra

The sixth chakra is commonly referred to as the third eye. This is because its energy spins out from the center of the forehead or brow center and is associated with clear psychic sight and intuition. When we view our own and other peoples' circumstances from the third eye, we see with the light of compassion, nonjudgment, and knowledge.

The ego state contained in this center of the energy body is approximately ages forty to fifty-five, and the developmental crisis that opens itself for successful resolution is integrity versus despair. I believe this crisis is the "midlife crisis" that shows up with frequency in our culture.

In many ways, this can be considered the most crucial crisis. This is the moment when we get to ask ourselves if we have truly lived according to our own integrity, and if our lives have truly been the best possible expression of our souls. With or without shamanic consciousness, people may start to feel a sense of despair during this time of life if they have taken steps outside their integrity. It is very common at this stage for people to leave marriages, start new relationships, change careers, or make geographical moves to quell the inner angst that stems from choices that have been less than a spiritual, whole expression of the self.

The sixth chakra, like all the chakras, expresses an element or essential energy with specific qualities. The collective expression of these elements or essential dynamic energies are vital to empower an evolving humanity that is respectful of all beings and spirits everywhere. About four years ago, I learned about this sixth element from my then-seven-year-old daughter, who must have a wise woman on the precipice of middle age living inside her. I had come home for a day between teaching at two workshops a couple of hours north of my home, to play and swim with my daughter, Kelly. She asked me what I'd been doing over the weekend, so I explained the five elements, shapeshifting, and the dances I'd been sharing. She got surprisingly excited and exclaimed, "Mommy, I know what the sixth element is."

"Hmm," I said. I hadn't realized there was a sixth element, but hey, I was open to hearing about it. I started to get excited, too.

"The sixth element is helping each other," she said. In that moment,

I knew she was right. "Yes it is, Miss Kelly. Thank you." The element or essential dynamic energy of helping each other is the key to ultimately living in integrity rather than despair.

In middle- to upper-class culture here in the United States, at this stage of life some people begin to question if material success is enough. Just as decades of alcohol abuse may destroy the physical liver, decades of material abuse may leave a very depressed or hungry soul in its wake. As the reality of middle age begins to whisper through the wall of youth culture propagated by the media, we are forced to reluctantly acknowledge our own vulnerability and mortality. With the veil of immortality cast off, we may now become more aware of the difficulties of others who are far less fortunate.

Therefore, this stage of life becomes the ideal time to expand our awareness of all beings and spirits everywhere, not just the tiny bubble of any one particular country, race, ethnicity, or religious group. As we age and become aware of our mortality, the mortality that we have in common with all other humans, our budding spiritual consciousness can prompt us to ask ourselves if the material success we enjoy is in any way connected to people being exploited or to environmental damage. Here in this sixth chakra, where the element is helping each other, we must respect the dreams and vitality of others, as well as our own. At this level of self, integrity must include this connection with others, or we will remain fragmented and immature in spite of being accomplished at the art of material success. These important connections require the wisdom and skill of age. It is crucial for the continuation of human life here on Earth that we successfully resolve this developmental crisis.

If one has done the challenging job of resolving the previous developmental crises successfully, the good news is that there is much energy, wisdom, knowledge, and love available in this center to create new dreams of exquisite beauty. We will now do a series of powerful shamanic tasks to strengthen this center.

ENERGIZING THE THIRD EYE

I would like to begin this chapter by teaching a sacred prayer practice in which we are reminded that everyone and everything has a heart, and that it is our obligation to leave the world a better place than we found it. The inspiration for this body prayer came from a profoundly spiritual Mayan shaman named Mercedes. Upon meeting her, I was deeply touched by how her power seemed to lie in attending respectfully to the details of her relationships with the elements. She illustrated her devotion to the trees by perpetually reusing paper towels, honoring their source with gratitude. Her commitment to life is to allow her heart and her actions to touch all she comes in contact with, leaving everything in better condition than before the encounter. This promise to enhance life through love and reverence is the most deeply spiritual practice I am aware of.

In chapter 5, task two discussed building a mesa. This shamanic practice can create a portal into nonordinary reality and be a strong reminder of all the spiritual support and energy that is available to us at every moment of our lives. The prayer we are about to learn is a way to create the mesa in our minds and hearts. This "body prayer" consciously invokes the presence of the elements in much the same way the huacas do on the mesa. The body creates the mesa as it reaches in different directions, connecting with and radiating the elemental energies. I have found this prayer to be the most simple and powerful way to remember my place in the universe, in the heart of all there is.

◆ Task One: The Mayan Prayer

The words to this prayer are simple:

> *O heart of the earth*
> *Heart of the heavens*
> *Heart of all beings and spirits*
> *Heart of the wind and water*
> *Our hearts.*

As you say "O heart of the earth," gesture down to Mother Earth. As you say "Heart of the heavens," gesture up to the heavens. As you say "Heart of all beings and spirits," bring your hands into Prayer pose. Open your arms and sweep out to each side as you say "Heart of the wind and water." Bring the hands back into Prayer pose with "Our hearts." As you move your body while saying the prayer, feel how the physical body connects to the mesa and becomes the mesa.

It is good to repeat this prayer three times, feeling the connection to Spirit.

This third eye center is associated with the higher mind and the opportunity to live centered in one's higher self. In yoga studies the lower mind is sometimes referred to as the ego-mind. This is the mind and ego in service solely to the individual. Through our earlier developmental stages this is an appropriate place from which to function, as we must learn how to get our basic needs met by negotiating with the world and within ourselves.

Sometimes people get stuck here although they are chronologically at later developmental stages, resulting in much despair, anxiety, depression, suffering, and imbalance for the individual and surrounding beings. As we embrace the teachings of this sixth chakra and the dynamic element of helping each other, we manifest the higher mind through which the ego continues to develop in a healthy way. Now, in addition to meeting the needs of the individual, it can expand to also be of service to the light of spirit as it manifests in other beings.

It is important to stay grounded in the physical body as you go through this process to ensure that you do not lose sight of the realities of life, and you can maintain awareness of your own needs as you remain committed to gentle spiritual growth. At this point, I would suggest going through some of the physical exercises from the previous chapters, such as Cobra, the wave, Triangle, Tree, and Bridge, and doing at least one exercise for each chakra. This way, you make conscious contact with all the previous elements and energy centers while remaining grounded in the physical body.

Once we are grounded, we will move on to an ancient yoga exercise that allows you to contact and bring energy to your third eye center. It is called yoga mudra, and it is an excellent posture for opening and balancing this chakra. It assists the mind in appropriately bowing to the heart. This humbles and releases the ego-mind while strengthening the energetic link between the mind and heart. From this connection we center spontaneously into our higher mind and integrity.

⊰⊱ Task Two: Yoga Mudra

This posture may be done kneeling or standing, and I will present both variations.

Begin by kneeling, sitting back on your heels. Interlace your hands behind your back. Come into chest expansion position by pressing your knuckles down and your little fingers back as much as possible without lifting your shoulders (fig. 6.2, p. 190).

Bring your hairline (where your forehead meets your scalp) to the earth or floor (fig. 6.3, p. 190). Depending on your flexibility, you may remain seated on your heels, or you may have to lift your pelvis to get into this position. Make sure you keep your weight on your legs so you don't strain your neck. If you feel any neck tension, release this posture immediately or bring your hands down to the earth on either side of your head to support your body. There should be no weight at all on your head. If your neck feels comfortable, you may roll from side to side on your hairline. This position will bring a great deal of energy to the sixth chakra.

To do yoga mudra from a standing position, stand with your feet hip-width apart. Interlace your hands behind your back and come into chest expansion by pressing your knuckles down toward the earth and your pinkies back, without lifting your shoulders (fig. 6.4, p. 191).

Bend at the ankles, knees, and hip folds, reaching the sitz bones back and the head forward and down. Hang the crown of the head down

Fig. 6.2

Fig. 6.3

Fig. 6.4   Fig. 6.5

toward the earth as you press your knuckles, with the arms extended, up toward the sky (fig. 6.5).

In either position, affirm for yourself that your mind is balanced and your intuition is strong. To come out of the position, press your knuckles and hands back and down, and let your arms lift you.

Follow immediately with task three.

❖ Task Three: Alternate Nostril Breath

In this task we will let the logical mind (left brain), creative mind (right brain), and instinctive mind (cerebellum, brainstem) come together. This technique will balance the brain, supporting the creation and enhancement of intuition and connection to the higher mind.

Fig. 6.6

Allow yourself to sit comfortably. Join your thumbs to your index fingers on each hand, resting your hands on your thighs or knees, and gently follow your breath with your awareness. This hand position is called jnana mudra (fig. 6.6).

As you hold this jnana mudra, you can "brain balance." Sense or envision both sides of your brain. Imagine breathing into your right brain; then allow the energy from your right brain to flow into your left brain as you exhale. Breathe into your left brain; then allow the energy from your left brain to flow into your right brain as you exhale. Repeat for one minute. Then, sense your third eye in the center of the brow. Feel your balanced inner sight and thought.

It is also powerful to use alternate nostril breathing to balance the mind. Rest the index finger and middle finger of your dominant hand over the third eye center. You will use the thumb to block off one nostril and the ring finger and pinky to block off the other nostril.

Take a breath in through both nostrils. Block off the right nostril and exhale through the left. Inhale through the left, continuing to block the right nostril. Block off both nostrils as you hold the breath and let the mind balance. A balanced mind will feel free, still, clear, and quiet. Then, block off the left nostril and exhale through the right. Inhale through the right nostril, still blocking off the left. Block off both nostrils and let the mind balance. Block off the right nostril and exhale left. Continue with several more full rounds of alternate nostril breath, allowing the parts of the brain—the cerebrum, cerebellum, and the brainstem—to quilt together.

After finishing the alternate nostril breath, it is powerful to chant the sacred sound of "om," using the balanced mind and intuition to experience and know your deep connection to all there is.

My first experience as an expanded being, physically and energetically aware of the radiant light of my spirit, happened in Swami Shantanand's yoga class when I was twenty-three years old. While connecting to the sweetness in his heart, I opened to the practice of yoga and meditation. I embraced the postures and invited them to cleanse my body. The focus of my mind invited me to look for myself in a new place—the realm of Spirit. The meditation we practiced emphasized that the most essential aspect of who we all are is compassion and nonjudgmental clarity. I learned that if I am compassion and nonjudgmental clarity, I am Spirit.

Swami shared a lot of profound wisdom with his students, including some one-line gems such as "Even Jesus Christ had to go to the bathroom," and "Everyone has to go to the bathroom, but don't spend your life in there. Come out into the living room." The following ancient jnana yoga technique taught me to find myself, beyond the metaphoric bathroom of my lower mind.

This is a powerful jnana yoga meditation. Jnana yoga is the yogic path of knowledge. The knowledge referred to here is the knowledge of our true nature, that we are all spiritual beings having a human experience. Since the time I sat in Swami's classes, I feel myself grounded and connected to the earth, but expanded beyond all the ways in which I have limited myself. There is a joy and clarity that comes from knowing that we are this light of consciousness, this beautiful shining star.

⫷⫸ Task Four: The Shining Star Meditation

It is best to do this meditation after the previous movements, tasks one and two, and the breathing technique in task three.

Sit comfortably in jnana mudra and imagine a shining star between your eyebrows. Feel your body relaxed, your emotions still or just gently moving, and your mind at peace. If you have any remaining worries or concerns, see them all through the light of this shining star. Allow this light of your consciousness, compassion, and nonjudgment to bless you and whatever other beings are connected to your worries and concerns. Spend as much time as you need for this.

Now, allow yourself to become this shining star. Feel your expansiveness, your brilliance, your magnificence. Know that you are this light of consciousness, shining through the vehicles of mind, emotion, and body. Feel the freedom of this knowledge of self.

CULTIVATING ENERGETIC INTEGRITY

It is vital to cultivate clarity and consciousness at this stage of life. This enables us to stay centered in our higher mind, always evolving into greater integrity. Swami Shantanand used to say that every human is both perfect and not perfect. The perfect parts will always be perfect no matter what we do, and the imperfect will always be imperfect no matter what we do. If we acknowledge our negativity by seeing it clearly with our consciousness, we can protect ourselves from our own negativity and the negativity of others. This is the foundation of the nonjudgmental, compassionate mind. To have compassion for people—expanding to embrace them, whatever their struggles and circumstances—aids us in finding our own wholeness and integrity rather than the emptiness of despair. It is vital to support, but not enable, other people—respecting their integrity while not supporting their violent, destructive, or exploitive defenses.

This crisis of integrity versus despair is the life crisis in which I currently dwell, as I am forty-five years old at the writing of this book. The last several years have all been about taking determined steps into my integrity, despite fears of the unknown and apparent loss of security. As I approached this stage, I gave birth to my daughter, left my marriage, opened a yoga and healing center, worked with John Perkins, strengthened my friendships, started to develop a shamanic healer training course, and began the writing of this book. I have been asked by Spirit over and over to keep integrating, to keep addressing my despair about the state of the world by becoming more whole myself and sharing this wholeness with others.

I have also been asked at an interpersonal level to become more aware of other people and their hidden agendas, and who and what pulls on my energy for selfish purposes. In the home I shared with my mother and stepfather, there was ongoing manipulation. As a couple, they shared a skewed view of reality that was, most of the time, cold and heartless. I understand now that this inner darkness was from losses they had suffered and had never addressed or mourned in any helpful way.

This left me with a blindness to the manipulations and agendas of others. My parents told me that the abuse was for my own good. So even though much of what my parents did made no sense and outraged me, I became blind to their manipulations. I was left unable to see that other people, rather that being fair and just, might actually have less than sincere motives in their interactions with me and might go to any lengths to get what they really want. My blindness was strengthened by my need to believe that I could find fairness and justice somewhere. I guess I preferred to believe that it could be found everywhere except in my home. This romanticism allowed me to continue living, as I believed I could eventually leave my home and find love somewhere. But it did not end up serving me, as I trusted many unworthy people. It is only in the last few years that I have begun to find healing for this blind spot through these next two tasks.

I have taught these powerful tasks to my students. One student worked with these techniques to address issues regarding a couple of colleagues at her job. Two women she was previously friendly with were ignoring her, implying she had somehow been offensive. My student, who is an adult child of an alcoholic and has an overdeveloped sense of responsibility, was searching her memory for the offending comment or action, with no success. At the time this was troubling her, we were working on the following tasks in class, and she used them to explore her issue.

As this student focused on sensing her energetic connections (task 5), she saw these women sucking out her energy. This image made sense, as my student is highly creative and the two women she was referring to had been relying on her for a great deal of creative and emotional support, often taking up quite a bit of her energy and time. She had begun to feel drained as she realized that they were not willing to be helpful in kind when she was in need. So she had gently backed off with respect to offering herself in this way. During the task of sensing energetic connections, it became vividly clear that when she started to make better boundaries and attend to her own needs first the women had begun ignoring her, trying to capitalize on her insecurities and make her feel guilty. In the power retrieval (task six), she was able to reject the implication that she was not a nice person, retrieve the energy her coworkers had sucked from her, and affirm her right to make boundaries.

This next task is about seeing clearly, opening the third eye, and using this intuitive center. At this stage of honing our integrity, it is good to know where your energy is going and who and what manipulates it. In this task, you will free yourself from the web of illusions of others, so you can see your own fibers and their attachments more clearly. With that knowledge you have the power to redirect your energy back into your dream. This will ultimately help you feel more energized and healthier at every level of being. Learning to see in this way is the pathway to freedom and integrity.

It is important to balance the clear, wise kind of seeing with the compassionate kind of seeing that you do with the light of the heart, so that you stay centered in the nonjudgmental mind. This will keep you from unhealthy cynicism. It will also support you in distinguishing people's promises from what they are really able to actualize. If we permit ourselves to be fooled we are allowing manipulation, which usually results in despair.

In this task, you don't have to change anything yet. Just see. Do not lie to yourself about what you see. Be brutally honest about what is there. It can be extremely difficult to really know the truth of one's own circumstances, behavior, and energy patterns.

❧ Task Five: Sensing Your Energetic Connections

Allow yourself to journey to your sacred place for the purpose of clearly seeing your energy and all that it is connected to. In your sacred place, you can have all the spiritual support and protection you need to make this truly possible. Experience your sacred place through your senses. Connect with the elements. Ask your spirit guides and protectors to be present with you so you can feel their support.

Assume a relaxed position in your sacred place, nestled in the arms of the elements and your guides. Allow yourself to see or sense the main fibers that extend out from your energy body to other people, activities, and projects. You may envision or feel the energetic connections from each chakra, one through five, as you experience where your energy flows and what other energies flow to you. The fibers may look like rope or streams of light. They may feel like vines entwining or trapping you, heavy chains or a type of sticky substance. Invite your guides to help you experience these energetic connections so you can recognize them and begin to sense what might be required to disconnect if necessary.

Ask yourself about the nature of each connection. Does it feed you? Does it drain you? Is it pleasurable or painful? Is it a loving connection? Is it an abusive or exploitive connection? Is it desirable or necessary, or not? Does this connection enhance your life or your dream?

Be aware. Really see. Step fully into your courage. Are any of these connections manipulative in nature? Are they straightforward, or tricky? Is this how you want to relate to others? Is this how you want others relating to you? Ask Spirit and your guides, "Are my energy fibers connected to other beings and energies that support my integrity?" This is especially important in intimate relationships. Both people need to be willing to do the work Spirit requires of them and not drain each other.

When your feel you have completed this task for the moment, thank your spirit guides and your sacred place for supporting you in moving into courage to see clearly. When you are ready, come back from your sacred place into ordinary reality. Feel the difference this expanded awareness and clarity makes in your perception and your life.

After you have learned to see clearly and have done all the previous tasks in this book, you are ready to perform the shamanic task of power retrieval. It can be done either by yourself or with a partner. It is wise to have an accomplished shaman support you in power retrieval at first, someone who knows the process from direct experience.

As with the soul retrieval, you may need to do this task many times until you experience the full integrity of your energy field. It is wise to journey to the end point of each thread of draining energy that you found in the previous task and resolve the issue so you can be free.

To prepare to retrieve power, reflect on the previous task in which you became aware of what your energetic fibers are connected to. Sometimes, simply being aware that your energy is being drained can be enough to break or alter the connection. If this does not happen spontaneously, either you are still in conflict about the situation and perhaps not yet sufficiently invested in your own integrity, or someone may be energetically holding on to your power, stealing it, so to speak. If the latter is the case, you must energetically make a boundary and retrieve your power.

I will begin by sharing an example of power that was essential for me to retrieve. I spoke in the previous chapter about being raped. There was an important piece of my power I had to take back from the perpetrator of this attack. Though I had the wonderful opportunity to shift a lot of energy in ordinary reality through my work with the theater company, I still had this important piece of work to do in nonordinary reality. I felt as though the rapist was holding something important of mine energetically, something he was obviously not entitled to. It was something that should only be given voluntarily, but he had stolen it. He had captured both my sense of choice and an inner garden I had been cultivating with great care for some time.

For this journey to retrieve my power to choose, I led myself with support from my guides. Since the stealing of my power in the rape was so terrifying for me, I really needed to spend time feeling the safety and protection of my sacred place. My eagle parents accompanied me on this journey, along with the ancient circle of Celtic shamans, twelve women and one man, whom I introduced in chapter 3.

With the help of my guides, I was able to realize that the criminal act of rape does in fact rob the victim of her or his power to choose. In nonordinary reality, the rapist kept my power to choose in the room where the rape happened, in the form of a key. I became aware that this man held many keys from other women on a very large ring, letting me know that I was not his only victim. These keys were all made of a high-intensity light energy, and they hung on his bedpost, illuminating the room. The ring itself was rusting and ancient. I was aware also of cut flowers with similar energies of light and life all around his room. There was a huge crystal vase of fragrant lilies that I knew were from my inner garden.

My guides and I planned a strategy to go back to the scene of the rape. I could see from my safe vantage point (my sacred place) that the rapist was often sleeping. This was partly because of marijuana use and drinking. I also observed that he was very sharp and hypervigilant when he was awake. So I knew it would be much easier to retrieve my key and my lilies while he was sleeping, if that were possible. We observed his sleep cycle for several days in nonordinary reality and decided on a time when he would most likely be in the deepest sleep. This was no guarantee, but I felt comfortable with it as the best possible strategy. My inner desire to do what was necessary to get my power back was strong.

With my eagle parents and my circle of shamans, I went directly back to the room where I was raped, and I picked up the key ring. While I tried to get my key off, the whole ring broke. I received a message from the circle of shamans that I needed to return the other keys to the women they were stolen from. They told me I could do this by throwing the other keys up through their circle, and the keys themselves would know how to journey back to the women they came from. I held on to my key as I threw the others skyward. The light the keys created was blinding for a moment; then it was dark, except for the light from my key and the flowers in the room.

I saw the rapist start to shiver, and, as he had no blanket, I knew my time in this room was very limited. I grabbed my lilies in the crystal vase and began to ascend on the wings of my eagle parents. Just then, the rapist's vigilant eyes shot open and he tried to grab me, shouting, "No!" His fury was frightening. His ability to say the word "no," the "no" he didn't allow me, deeply disgusted me beyond anything I had ever felt before. There seemed to be some green slime that his nonconsensual sexual act deposited in me. This slime regurgitated out of my energy body onto him, like a net. It stopped him from being able to move at all. So I was free to return to my sacred place and its safety with my spirit guides.

Before leaving, I said a prayer for his healing, including the healing of his posttraumatic stress disorder. I know that men from all cultures and backgrounds commit rape, and there is never any excuse for it. But upon reflection, I have thought that perhaps issues of consent could get confused when a man has a long cultural history of his people being denied the right to give and refuse consent. This could certainly be the case for people of African descent in postcolonial, postslavery Jamaica, where I got raped. Before leaving, I also said a prayer for all our cultures for the healing of this ongoing insidious disease in which the will of one unfairly prevails over the will of another. Life continually provides us with challenging opportunities to center ourselves in our sixth chakra and connect to compassion and nonjudgmental understanding.

My power had once belonged to, and needed to be returned to, my chakras. I felt the flowers and the garden returning in my second chakra and pelvic bowl, and the key came back to my upper belly, or power center. I took time to feel the loving contact of my guides and the beauty of my sacred place. I connected with my inner male, who is loving and understands about respect and issues of consent.

As I received power, I realized the rape itself was a manipulation. The act was perpetrated upon me so I would feel less positively about myself. Once I understood this deeply, in my body, emotions, and mind, I was free. I became stronger, able to refuse to be diminished in the face of the manipulation or violation. I could see with greater clarity the patterns of energy people perpetrate to avoid growing into integrity on their own journey. There are now many traps I avoid, as I am freer to use my energy for my own creative, constructive, respectful purposes.

As you become aware that something or someone is draining or manipulating you, and this does not spontaneously shift when you recognize it, you can proceed with a power retrieval regarding this person or situation.

❖ Task Six: Power Retrieval

Figure 6.7 (p. 202) illustrates the six steps we will follow in this process of power retrieval. We will begin with **Step 1** on the chart. In a place where you feel protected, make yourself comfortable. Lying down or sitting are the most usual positions, but there are times when other positions, such as standing, may be best. Be in whatever position feels relaxed, but safe, to you. Here in ordinary reality, you will clarify the task you are about to undertake. Where are you going? What aspect of your power do you intend to retrieve? From whom?

Help yourself to relax as we move to **Step 2** on the power retrieval chart, approaching nonordinary reality. It is always best to support yourself in journeying by going to your sacred place so you can gather energy, power, and a sense of deep connection and wholeness. You will need all your strength for this power retrieval. It is also crucial to ask for a spirit guide or power animal that can support you in the retrieval

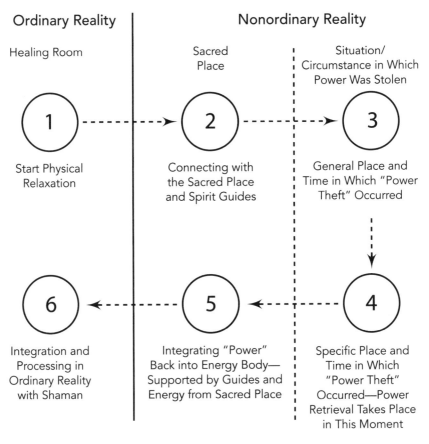

Ordinary Reality | Nonordinary Reality

Healing Room

Sacred
Place

Situation/
Circumstance in Which
Power Was Stolen

1

Start Physical
Relaxation

2

Connecting with
the Sacred Place
and Spirit Guides

3

General Place and
Time in Which "Power
Theft" Occurred

6

Integration and
Processing in
Ordinary Reality
with Shaman

5

Integrating "Power"
Back into Energy Body—
Supported by Guides and
Energy from Sacred Place

4

Specific Place and
Time in Which
"Power Theft"
Occurred—Power
Retrieval Takes Place
in This Moment

Fig. 6.7. Map of Power Retrieval

of your power and the restoration of the integrity of your energy body. You may have guides that are always present or new ones that appear for each particular journey.

From the vantage point of your sacred place, take the time required to understand the dynamics of the situation in which you lost your power. You can view the encounter from the perspective of watching it from your sacred place with all of your support and protection. You need to look at how the offending person or circumstance has stolen your power, and how she or he keeps it. Is the person hiding or guarding it in some way?

Ask your spirit guides to help you take back your power. Interact with your guides to plan a strategy to take your power back. You may ask your shaman to share ideas with you, supporting the plan you formulate.

Does your strategy involve a plan of covert or overt action? Is there a symbol or image for the power you are taking back? What does it look like? Will your power animals or spirit guides also function as bodyguards? Who will protect you, and in what ways? Do you need to confront the power thief as part of the retrieval, or is it enough to simply regain the object, image, or power? Talk these things over with your guides and trust your inner knowing.

Once you know your objective and have clarified your strategy, it is time to proceed with steps three and four on the power retrieval chart. **Step 3** is the process of returning to the general time and area where the trauma or power "theft" occurred, and **Step 4** is entering the specific moment in time and space where you can retrieve your power. You may move slowly or quickly from one to the other. Take the time required to find and retrieve your power, but do not linger longer than necessary.*

After you have retrieved what you sought in your journey according to your plan, check to see if there is anything the person or circumstance

---

*Note that, although the maps for soul retrieval and power retrieval are similar, the process differs here. In this power retrieval you yourself must retrieve your power in steps 3 and 4, as opposed to soul retrieval where a guide may take back the required soul fragment for you.

may have dumped on you that you no longer wish to carry. It may be a burden of some kind or a disowned shame that was slimed on you. What does this thing that was dumped on you look like? What are you returning? You may need to "forgive" that person by returning what she or he has made you responsible for, and by giving her or him your best wishes for handling the toxic energy or matter in a more responsible way next time, for the highest good of all concerned.

When you are done taking back your power and returning what you no longer wish to carry, return to your sacred place. This is **Step 5** on the power retrieval chart. Take the time here to feel the relief of giving back an unwanted burden, and to allow what you have retrieved for yourself to integrate. Is there a place in your energy body that the retrieved power strengthens? Your shaman can support you by seeing and understanding what chakras the power thief has manipulated, what fibers were attached to this manipulation, and how they were attached. The shaman can place her or his hands on this chakra, energizing it during the healing, addressing any wounds. What special support do you need for the release and the integration? Make sure your shaman provides these things for you, or provide them yourself. Have your guides help you see all the details of your inner strengths.

In **Step 6** on the power retrieval chart, you can return to ordinary reality after expressing your gratitude to your guides. Spend some time in ordinary reality sensing your increased power. Journal about your power retrieval experiences.

Once you have retrieved your power, it is time to put it to work clarifying any concerns you may have regarding your integrity and continuing to resolve this critical crisis. Ask yourself, "What does my soul and spirit require of me?" In the fullness of your power, it is possible to express the magnificence of your spirit in the service of "helping each other."

❖

EXPANDING YOUR CONNECTEDNESS

This last task is a journey or meditation to support you in evaluating and manifesting your dream in synchronicity and harmony with the energies of Spirit in the universe. We achieve integrity when our dreams and visions are congruent with compassion and clarity.

I was called to begin my shift into integrity about eight years ago, when Spirit asked me to put my shamanic work front and center. I began to see all the techniques I knew and the other professions I had engaged in as extensions of shamanism. I was being asked to integrate and expand my professional life, to fully actualize my dream. At this time, Spirit sent me a very special group of guides that have supported me in stepping fully into my integrity. I mentioned them in task six, power retrieval. They are my Celtic circle of twelve women and one man. What separates these guides from my other guides is that for the most part, I do not know the individual personalities of the beings in this sacred circle. Their power lies in who they are as a collective.

In this circle of Celtic shamans there is one being for each month of the lunar calendar (which has thirteen months). For women, these months may coordinate with the menstrual cycle, or the creation/birth cycle. This is a very sacred circle of cycles, and of life itself. This sacred shape holds the spiral of time, the cycles of the months and years moving forward into the future as we manifest our lives. This spiraling energy of time draws magnetic energy up from Mother Earth and light energy down from the heavens. Radiant spiritual energy emanates from all the beings in a sacred circle, creating a space where we can materialize our dreams and integrity over cycles of time.

Eight years ago I brought my challenged, almost broken postdivorce self to this sacred Celtic circle of beings. They offered themselves for my healing at this time and in exchange asked that I become as fully myself as possible in every way. In my journey I laid down in the center of the circle on the long, soft grass in the moonlight. They surrounded and filled me with sacred light energy and supported me in doing the necessary power retrievals so I could heal from the divorce. I envisioned my path as the shaman, all of my professions coming together as they have in this book. My inner selves linked arms and we walked around the path together. I was embraced by the sacred circle's energy, as it held me in my wholeness and invited me to see from many different perspectives (at least thirteen) what the benefits and possible problems would be as I manifested my path as the shaman. I was open to know who I might help as I embodied my dream, and who, if anyone, I might hurt.

The circle encouraged me to pursue this "helping" path, but in balance. I was encouraged to teach from my experience and to be humble and admit when I was ignorant. In this sacred circle I made the difficult decision to not have another child as it was my soul and spirit's truth that I couldn't give adequate attention to another child and my shamanic work. This circle also made it clear to me that I had to make appropriate arrangements to provide healing services for people who are financially challenged.

It is important to have the energetic support and perspective of a sacred circle of guides to help you manifest your dreams while maintaining your integrity. Most of the significant changes we make in our lives happen over time. There is a spiritual power in trusting the mystery of growth, opening, and unfolding. We need the guides to support us so we don't try to control everything and we can allow for new behavior to emerge that expresses our growth. You can't force a flower to open; it opens in its way and time. In this task, you will ask for a group of guides to support you in manifesting your dreams with integrity over the natural cycles of time, the moons, and seasons.

⬥ Task Eight: Connecting with a Sacred Circle

Ask Spirit for a circle of guides to support you in materializing your dreams with integrity, supported by the cycles of nature. You may wish to go out in nature to do this. You may actually find a grove of trees or group of large rocks that naturally form a circle. Ordinary and nonordinary reality may blend; an ordinary meadow may fill with nonordinary animals that will be your guides.

You may go to your sacred place and find this sacred circle of guides, or Spirit may lead you to a new sacred place, just for this purpose. Whether you are outside or inside, let yourself stand, sit, or lie down in the center of this sacred circle and feel its energy blessing you. Circles have a special healing energy. Receive this into yourself as the light illuminates any remaining confusion about your sacred path, providing you with an opportunity to see with clarity.

The purpose of this task is to allow the guides to support you in ever-evolving integrity. Is there a particular question you have for them regarding some incongruity of self and action that you are struggling with at this time? Do you want to step further into your integrity but don't know how? Ask them to help. Ask if they have any messages for you about what you may need to examine or rework as you move into greater integrity. Ask how you can best support others on your path in powerful ways, minimizing despair for everyone.

Feel yourself embraced in the perspective, support, and compassion of this sacred circle as you continue your growth. See your dream and integrity grow and bloom like a sacred flower.

This sixth chakra journey provides the opportunity for us as individuals and as a culture to step into the fullness of our integrity. Integrity is what will enable us to change the dynamics that are destructive to our environment and to the collective whole of beings. As we embrace compassion, clarity, knowledge of spirit, and balance, we leave the despair of incongruous personal and societal action behind and manifest the sacred garden of blossoming peace through integrity.

7

Channeling Universal Love

A Journey to Mastery

Today, when I think of my stepfather and his brother and all their pathology and cruelty, my consciousness traces back to their parents' issues and the histories that could have created such hurtful dynamics. I sense that the man who was my stepfather's and uncle's father was physically and mentally abused as a child, and so he abused his sons, especially my uncle, who claimed to be hit in the head with his mother's high-heeled shoes. My stepfather, who was the oldest, was made to work in the family business at a very young age because his father would go off to Florida to gamble on dog races. His mother turned him into a surrogate emotional husband, and there was a lot of pressure to perform as an adult, even before the age of ten.

I have compassion for the stories of these men, especially now that I have allowed myself the full range of my emotional life, including my anger and pain, and have retrieved my soul and power. It is time now for me to open fully to the love in the universe and attend to ancestral healing. I can do this from an integrated place, because all my lower chakras have been honored, enabling me to make strong boundaries and heal old wounds.

I dream for my step-grandmother a world where she could have left her marriage without shame and had her own voice and career. I go back one more generation to her parents, who had to leave Russia due to religious and cultural persecution. For them, I dream a world without anti-Semitism and other forms of racism. And I dream for my step-grandfather a childhood that was safe, so he could grow up with love and shift out of the perpetual adolescence and violence that left everyone else bearing the consequences of his actions. And lastly, I wish for myself that instead of learning about fear and ugliness from these men, I could have learned about the love and the beauty that is inside us all, waiting to be nurtured.

▼

The seventh chakra is the chakra of wisdom. This energetic vortex spins out from the crown of the head (fig. 7.1, p. 210), holding the energy body open to the divine masculine energy from the stars and the heavens. We are made from the atoms of exploded stars. We can contact the expansive energy and love of heaven and the universe and feel how it dwells inside us—an experience of boundless inner freedom.

We acquire our seventh chakra wisdom through deep connection to Spirit and by cultivating a comfort level with boundless inner freedom. Such expansive feelings require the nervous and energy systems to adjust; otherwise we may feel too open and vulnerable and may even shut down. Yoga, meditation, and service tasks such as those that follow in this chapter help us to hold and channel this expansive energy with greater comfort.

The seventh chakra embodies the developmental crisis of mastery versus distraction. In this place of complete freedom we can really grasp that love is not only possible without manipulation, it is the only way to truly love. In this center we can be open to all possibilities, profound healing, miracles, and joyful expressions of this love. This is the higher love Paul talks about in his letters in the New Testament and that Rumi expresses in his sacred poetry.

If one is still working at this age, fifty-five to seventy, there is a level of life mastery based on much conscious learning and experience. This mastery cannot be replicated by a younger person, no matter how enthusiastic or even brilliant. It is so important to honor and, especially, enjoy this aspect of our middle years. There is a great pleasure that can

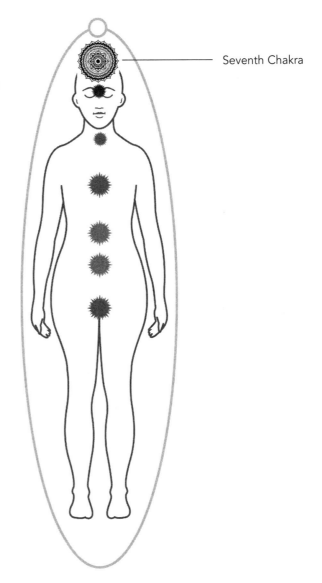

Color: Violet

Element: Loving Each Other

Developmental Age: 55–70 years

Spiritual Strength: Spiritual Connection

Developmental Crisis: Mastery versus Distraction

Seventh Chakra

Fig. 7.1. Seventh Chakra

come from basking in wisdom—which is done with great humility if one is truly wise.

Through the tasks in the previous chapters, we have worked to free ourselves from all the veils that obscure our true wisdom and our capacity for boundless love. All the tasks have created the opportunity to step up toward wisdom and the mastery of universal love, like a ladder we have climbed to the top. An important aspect of mastery is to know how to recognize and clear away that which obscures our connection to wisdom over and over again as necessary. Because we are human, we will get caught up in distractions. Busy-ness, information overload, and other dysfunctional personal and cultural patterns of behavior can distract us from our path of mastery. If we stay distracted, we don't grow very much and may lose touch with spirit, become apathetic, and feel like we are just going through the motions of a life without substantial meaning. But as masters, we reconnect to spirit very quickly.

I am, of course, writing above my head here; as I write this I am forty-five years old. But I have learned that we contain all of these ages, elements, and developmental stages within us, regardless of our chronological age. Through the process of deliberately cultivating consciousness on a spiritual path such as shamanism, development sometimes can be accelerated. It is possible to achieve mastery at earlier or later ages. If you have successfully completed the tasks in the previous chapters, move on to these tasks even if you are not "old enough." Be open to all possibilities without judgment. Our developmental stages are always evolving. Our chakras are always spiraling and radiating.

CONNECTING TO UNIVERSAL LOVE

My daughter, though very young, does in fact have a wise woman inside her who surfaces on occasion. At the same time my daughter told me about the sixth element, helping each other, she also told me about the seventh element, loving each other. By embracing the developmental challenge in this chakra, mastery of universal love, we get to love as

Christ and all the great masters and shamans loved. Having comfortably asserted our basic human needs and getting them met on all levels, this is our opportunity to become clear enough to be free to live life and to love without any agenda.

To connect to the universal love within us and in the heavens, you will first connect with the body, the elements, and Mother Earth for grounding by doing the Downward Facing Dog pose. In this pose, you will bring energy to the crown of the head, to the seventh chakra, to empower your sense of mastery and wisdom in this center as you perform the tasks that follow.

Before performing the Downward Facing Dog, it is best to go through all the chakras once again, doing at least one physical exercise from each chapter (for example, mountain, cobra, wave, triangle, tree, bridge, or yoga mudra) to warm up the physical body and the energy body.

⊷ Task One: Downward Facing Dog Flow

After you have completed the warmup, come into table position on your hands and knees. Make sure your feet are hip-width apart (fig. 7.2). Curl your toes under. When you are ready, press down into your hands and press your pelvis (your sitz bones) up toward the sky and a little bit back, so you are in an upside-down V (fig. 7.3).

To open the body and align into the V even more, feel your breastbone pressing toward your toes as the triangles of both shoulder blades press in the opposite direction. You can also feel the very crown of your head pressing toward your thumbs as your sitz bones reach in the opposite direction. You may chant the sound of "om" as you hold this posture.

After one to five minutes when you are ready to release this posture, come back into table position, then press back into Child pose—moving your sitz bones back toward your heels, resting your forehead on your hands or the earth—and release. Feel yourself loved by the energy from the heavens, sensing the light from the sun and the stars shining down on you illuminating every cell of your body, every fiber of your being.

Fig. 7.2

Fig. 7.3

Feel the energy in the crown chakra. Feel the energy available to you for the mastery of love.

From Child pose, curl your toes under and lift your knees as you press your pelvis back and down toward the earth, lifting your head and coming into a gentle, parallel squat. Then lift your sitz bones up toward the sky, coming into a forward bend. Slowly, roll your torso up, one vertebra at a time, until you are standing upright. Reach your arms up toward the sky, gathering the light from the heavens to you. Perhaps you can feel your crown chakra drawing the energy down from the heavens into your energy body. Breathe while connecting your own energy body to the energy of love from the universe, the atoms of the stars from which our bodies are made, and the light from the sun that warms us and keeps us alive. Express your gratitude to the loving energy and warmth from the universe as it supports your very life.

HEALING THE ANCESTORS

We are now ready to extend our connection with the higher or spiritual love in the universe beyond ourselves, to perform the important shamanic task of ancestral healing. In this task we will continue to develop our connection with universal love as we become masters of expressing it. We will look deeply into the experiences of our ancestors with compassion and understanding, and lovingly dream healing circumstances to hold their challenges so they may face or rise to meet them differently.

After connecting to the elements and strengthening yourself through the previous tasks in this book, you may be able to look back at your family, perhaps for several generations, and see the origins of imbalance and the consequent misuse of power. Very often, looking clearly at your parents' imbalances can allow you to see how they are related to the imbalances of their own parents and grandparents. You may be able to support the healing of souls for several generations back.

This happens in a layer of nonordinary reality that transcends time and space. Not only does it heal our ancestral energy, perhaps our ancestors themselves, but it also favorably affects us. The DNA in our bodies is the matter and energy most affected by our ancestors, and I believe it can be shapeshifted in some way through ancestral healing.

When you do ancestral healing, it is good to follow the lines of energy back as far as you need to—at least as far back as your great-grandparents. As shown in the map for ancestral healing (fig. 7.4), you will trace back one line or branch of the family tree at a time. A person with two biological parents will eventually need to do at least eight ancestral healings. If you have a family situation that departs from the two-parent biological family model, work with the people who performed the majority of parental responsibilities for you. There may be great gaps in information about some of the people in these lineages. These gaps may be filled in as you journey, or they may remain a mystery. Either is fine. Ancestral healing should not be a pressured task.

I would like to share my own experience with the ancestral healing journey as it may give you ideas about how to proceed with your own.

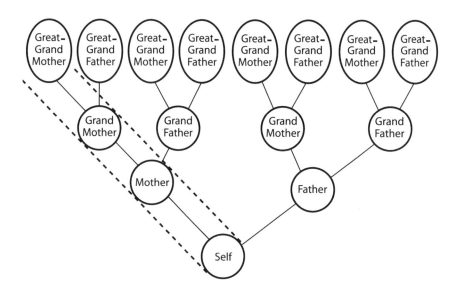

Fig. 7.4. Map for Ancestral Healing

Although I've done this healing with all my ancestors, I will focus in this example on my female, maternal lineage. This line is illustrated by the dotted line on the ancestral healing chart. I followed this line of ancestry back three generations, beginning with my great-grandmother and moving to my grandmother and mother. It is also possible to do this in the reverse order: parent, grandparent, great-grandparent. One or the other will feel right to you.

As with other journeys, it is important to bring along guides to advise and protect you when you do ancestral healing. For working with my mother's ancestry, Guiding Eagle and Eagle Woman were very helpful guides because the wounds in that line were about the imbalance of masculine and feminine energies, and my spirit guides are very balanced in this respect, both within themselves and in their relationship to each other.

I was strongly drawn to this process of ancestral healing six years ago when my mother was battling breast cancer, a disease that affects the DNA of the cells. Even before the well-publicized interruption of clinical trials for estrogen replacement therapy (ERT), my mother had already attributed the presence of the small and estrogen-receptive tumor to her decades of hormone use. ERT had been touted by my mother's gynecologist as the fountain of youth, and my mother took it without question for a long time. I saw this as further evidence of her personal pattern of passivity—a pattern that was clear to see in her relationships to her family, and a pervading cultural pattern for some women of her generation.

It has always perplexed me that my mother stayed married to my stepfather, even though he was consistently cruel and abusive to me physically, emotionally, and sexually. After having worked on retrieving my soul and power and forgiving my mother, I was still left with a sense of disconnection from her. This invoked sadness in me, as I know my mother is "my other self." Our same-sex parent is a profound developmental mirror.

I know that part of the reason my mother stayed with my stepfather was financial. Perhaps under these circumstances, it became easier to deny or distort what was going on. The unacceptable behavior became acceptable or justifiable. I knew this passivity had to come from somewhere. I knew there had to be traumas and patterns from past generations that needed to be looked at and healed. The first logical place to look was the women on my mother's side of the family.

Unfortunately, there is less information available than I'd like, because the people I would like to question directly have died. I have some vague second- and thirdhand information dating back to my great-grandmother, Alice. I have also had dreams and other nonordinary reality experiences about her that I feel fill in some of the information gaps. I do remember being held in her sweet arms and walking with her along the block around my grandma's house.

Alice graduated from Bucknell University in Pennsylvania in the 1890s, not a common experience for women at that time. I believe Alice had an adventurous spirit. She began to work for the railroad when she completed college, a career she gave up when she married and had children. At that time, "respectable" women could not do both. She raised three daughters, Helen, Inez, and my grandmother, Margie. All I have been told about my great-grandfather is that he was a "man's man" and never spent much time with his wife or his daughters. After the death of her husband, Alice stayed with each of her three daughters for a third of the year and used her minimal pension as spending money. She died at eighty-seven years old, when I was two.

As part of this ancestral healing, I journeyed to my great-grandmother, who told me it was sad for her to come of age when women did not have the right to vote and had to choose between career and family, a choice men have never had to make. I could feel her dilemma, her anxiety and frustration. I envisioned for my great-grandmother a world where women didn't have to choose, a world where she could have had her career and family. It felt good and healing to offer my great-grandmother these wishes and dreams. I felt her smiling.

My maternal grandmother Margie always seemed like Mother Earth to me. She cared for her yard, her house, her husband, her children, and her grandchildren with a gentle force that seemed to be unconditional acceptance. She also spent years fighting with my grandfather, who was very withholding of attention, affection, and money, especially with women. By her late fifties, Margie was terribly angry with her husband and chose to divorce him. She moved to the New Mexico desert, where she lived among the rattlesnakes, tarantulas, jackrabbits, quail, and owls. I believe the solitude in the desert was peaceful for her after years of abusive verbal arguments with my grandfather. But in some ways, it was also sad that she had to live in relative poverty in the middle of the desert, with no car, just to have this peace.

In my journey to my grandmother, I saw her as a teenager in a world where she would have been supported as a female in finding out who she was and what her mission was. My grandmother was drawn to children, to loving and supporting their self-esteem. I envisioned her being guided to get a college education in early childhood education or play therapy. Although I believe she still would have lived modestly if she had had a decent income, I know she would have had a greater sense of being in control of her own destiny. Margie also loved nature. I envisioned her as an educator in this area. I see her smiling, just to have someone recognize her strengths.

During the summer before she entered eighth grade, my mother developed chorea, or St. Vitus's dance, a neurological condition that created temporary paralysis on one side of her body. She had always been something of a tomboy and was probably being forced to "feminize" herself. Her symptoms, shaking and losing control over her movements, perhaps expressed her rage at her parents and at the culture that did not allow her to dream her own dreams as a woman.

From the time I was seven or eight, any time my mother and her college friends got together, they went on and on about their escapades, painting a picture of an idyllic, outrageously fun, two-year-long party. I only recently learned that my mother lost her virginity when she was raped on a date during her first semester in college.

To heal my mother's adolescent self, I imagine her feeling she could feel free to know and express her true self and receive acceptance and love from her parents and her peers. I also hold healing images about my mother's college experiences. I imagine self-actualizing experiences growing out of her college life. She designed and constructed sets for her college plays, so I dream her having a career in set design and construction. These healthier self-assertions support her throughout her life cycle in making integrity-affirming choices on every level of being for herself and her children. This journey to heal her life feels like it connects me to her in a deeper, healthier way.

The protocol for this journey is less structured than others in this book, which is one reason why it is vital to have practiced the other journeys before undertaking this one. When you are ready to do ancestral healing, it is important to be thorough, to feel the feelings, to allow your spirit guides to support you in facing all you need to face. They can help you to weave the healing scenarios and energies, and protect you against being confused, manipulated, or retraumatized in any way. Offering compassion and empathy is very healing, especially when your soul is whole and you have retrieved your power. You can understand your ancestors and their choices through the perspective of the powerful universal love we are connecting to and expressing in this chakra, while having the wisdom to honor your own genuine response to their actions and how they may have adversely affected you.

❖ Task Two: Ancestral Healing

You can start this journey to heal your ancestors in your sacred place. Experience the elements there with your senses. Connect to your spirit guides and huacas. Feel very nourished in the present moment. Feel how you have cultivated a spiritual family through your own conscious efforts. If for any reason you do not feel this, it is best not to proceed at this time. Go back and do the earlier tasks, perhaps with a professional, and then return to this journey when you feel supported.

As you feel this nourishment and all of your supports, ask Spirit for a guide to lead you on this ancestral healing journey. Follow the spirit guide that emerges to support you with this journey. If it is not a guide you have already developed a relationship with, spend some time with this guide to develop trust and rapport. When you feel comfortable and ready, ask this guide to lead you where you need to go for the healing of your ancestors. This guide will lead you back to heal the traumas that formed the dysfunctional patterns in the energy of your ancestors.

You will be drawn by your consciousness to choose the ancestral line that you wish to and are ready to follow. Envision your parent, grandparent, and great-grandparent, remembering what you know about their lives and the decades in which they lived, sensing their energy.

When you have fully envisioned an ancestor and understood the limitations, traumas, choices, and behaviors that crippled this person's energy body, send your ancestor a healing dream. This dream can be a shapeshift for your ancestor's family, culture, or behavior. Allow your ancestor to fully experience a healthy, supportive dream, and know that the dream will echo through his or her descendants and back to you.

It is important to recognize and retain all the strengths of your ancestors. As you reflect on your journey for ancestral healing, recognize the strengths and wisdom of your ancestors. Ask yourself, what did they have to offer you that served you well in your life? Along with challenging behaviors, were there also threads of wisdom? What spiritual gifts have been passed down to you through the generations? How did your ancestors show their love?

I know that from my great-grandmother I received intellectual and literary curiosity. From my grandmother I received a sense of earthiness, playfulness, and a capacity for nurturing. From my mother I received a sense of adventure, as well as openness toward people from all backgrounds and respect for their dignity. I am grateful to have these gifts and to pass them on to my daughter.

In the next task, we will honor and physicalize these gifts.

❧ Task Three: Connecting with the Strengths of Your Ancestors

Sit with the knowledge you have gained of the gifts of strength, love, and wisdom from your ancestors. Let yourself feel the gifts emotionally and receive them energetically. Feel fed by the love from your ancestors as the energy of their gifts spirals into your DNA and spinal column. Feel their strengths empowering you at your core.

Recall the poem about the three states of being: past, present and future. The serpent is the past, holding the energy of the ancestors. After connecting to their strength and wisdom, put on spiritual music and dance the serpent to feel your ancestors in your spinal column and DNA. This is the power of your past. Sway your spine and undulate while embodying deep knowledge of your strength.

CHANNELING

The beings and energies that dwell in the realm of Spirit have much wisdom to share. Channeling is the process we engage in to bring forth this knowledge and love from the realm of spirit to ordinary reality, for ourselves or for someone else. When you channel, you bring forth universal love through the instruments of your body, energy, voice, words, and images. Channeling is an exceptionally powerful tool for facilitating spiritual connection and growth for ourselves and others. It provides the opportunity for healing love and specific wisdom to come through so you and a partner can heal into greater integrity and fullness of being.

I am fortunate to have studied many healing modalities and to have a large body of spiritual and therapeutic knowledge. However, the way I combine these techniques and apply them is greatly influenced by channeling my guides and spiritual energies. Much of this book and the content of the classes I teach is channeled information. I creatively collaborate with my guides. Many of the shamans I have spoken with over the years have told me that the most powerful shamanic knowledge can come through clear channeling and direct information from Spirit.

At this point in your journey you already channel your guides. You hear the messages, the communications from your spirit guides. I'm sure there have been times when it has been appropriate and beneficial to pass on these communications, perhaps when you have performed a shapeshifting healing or if you have supported a partner through the soul or power retrieval process. What the guides share is often so perceptive that it becomes natural to pass these gems of wisdom on to our friends and family if they are struggling with issues. Sometimes the guides just extend loving energy so our loved ones can receive more love than perhaps we have in our own individual well at any given point in time.

This next task will support you in enhancing your channeling abilities as you organize them into a thorough protocol that embraces the integrity of the energy body and all your spiritual strengths. This task is ideally suited to this developmental stage because we have used the previous tasks to embrace love and clear away our old baggage from the past so it will not cloud what we will bring through from spirit. Now we may be ready to be a clear channel for Spirit.

Just as we distinguish fantasies from dreams, it is wise to distinguish helpful, accurate channeling from potentially confusing or harmful messages. Usually, confusing and harmful messages occur when personal baggage and self-centered agendas from the person doing the channeling are clouding the process. Spend time with your guides processing the value of the information that comes through so that it is useful and supportive for all concerned. Before you share any information with the person you are channeling for, ask Spirit if what you are about to share comes from Spirit and Love, to ensure that sharing it will serve the highest good of all concerned.

Sometimes my guides share all of their perceptions of a situation, but it is clear the person I am working on would be flooded with too much information if they heard every detail or they may not be emotionally ready in that moment. You can ask Spirit what and how much of these perceptions and messages to share with your partner in this task. This process will prevent sharing too much too soon with someone you are working on.

The skills you have developed from the tasks in chapter six to perceive clearly how energetic fibers connect to you will also help you to know if any counterproductive energies are pulling on you and interfering with your channeling. If these troubling connections are not released just by witnessing them, do more power retrieval work before proceeding with this channeling task.

You may find, as I have, that certain guides live in or are strongly connected to particular chakras and their spiritual strengths. If so, you may journey to a particular chakra by breathing and bringing your consciousness to it, making contact with that specific guide if you feel it would be an important source of love, wisdom, or energy for healing yourself or your partner.

✦ Task Four: Channeling Light, Love, and Wisdom

You may prepare for this task by generating the mesa to connect with the sacred energies (see chapter 5, task two). You may also go to your sacred place to meet with your spirit guides to energize, cleanse, support and protect yourself to best perform this task. Ask that all channeling done in this protocol will come from Spirit, for the highest good of all concerned.

When you return to ordinary reality, set up a mat or massage table for the partner you will be channeling for. Refer back to Hands-on Healing with Kundalini Energy (task eleven in chapter 1) and to the chakra chart (fig. 1.1, p. 15). The channeling protocol will follow the same basic structure as this earlier task, connecting to your partner and the energies while moving up through the chakras and energy body with your hands and consciousness.

Start by holding or connecting to the energy around your partner's feet. Connect to the earth or Kundalini energy as you did in the earlier hands-on protocol, making sure you are very grounded and connected to this vital energy source. Breathe, and bring the light of your consciousness up through all your chakras until you connect with the seventh chakra. Feel or sense this energy vortex at the crown of your head, drawing the light energy down from the heavens, through your whole body, into your arms and hands and into your partner. You will feel a sense of illumination and expansiveness. Channel this light and love into all of your partner's chakras one through seven, moving your hands in appropriate ways on the physical body or in the energy field. Don't stop until you sense your partner is filled with this beautiful high-vibration light and love from the heavens. You will see you partner's radiant aura (chakra eight) or sense the light and expansion of her or his energy through your touch or intuition.

While you are channeling this universal light and love, messages may come from Spirit at any time. The messages that come while you are working on a particular chakra will be related to the developmental issues or spiritual strengths the chakra embodies. The channeled material may come directly from Spirit or from spirit beings, guides, or energies. They may be expressed in words, sounds, or other images. With sensitivity, share these channeled messages or gifts with the partner you are working on. You can process with your partner what the meaning of these messages, if any, might be. Your partner may also have received messages while you were working. It is important for you both to share your messages with each other, see if they resonate, complement, or combine into a complete and powerful message.

My women clients in their fifties and sixties are very drawn to this hands-on energy and channeling work. One such client was experiencing some inflammation, manifesting as burning, pressure, and bloating in her stomach area. As I channeled the love energy, I could feel the rawness around her third chakra area. When I connected with her third chakra I saw an image of her as a teenager, coping with issues of asserting who she really was in spite of disapproval. This dynamic was occurring in the client's life in the present time with members of her immediate and extended family, as she was asserting her unpopular but valid views on an issue affecting the whole family. The discomfort may have been a result of or aggravated by this emotional situation.

I saw an image of Mary Magdalene who had a message for my client affirming her strength to assert herself and grow as her authentic self in spite of disapproval. Simultaneously, my client saw her grandmother who, though deceased, was a source of unwavering unconditional love. We shared our channeled images with each other. They complemented each other in energetic quality. Her grandmother's energy was soft and soothing for her inflammation, Mary Magdalene was firm and provided protective boundaries. My client breathed deeply, softened her belly, and received the energy from all sources. She felt much better after the channeling session.

▼

As we work with this chakra's energy we are channeling love, the most healing force in the universe. We channel it first to ourselves through the physical exercises, next to our ancestors through ancestral healing, and then to our friends (or if you are a professional healer, your clients). To love in this clear, powerful way, with wisdom and impact, is the path of the masters. If we could all consistently embrace and extend this heavenly energy, the world would shapeshift into complete beauty, embodying love itself. From this place of being centered in universal love, perhaps we can all be inspiring and powerful sources of change in the world.

8
Expanding Beyond Death
A Journey to Oneness

When I was eighteen and began my conscious journey with the work of Fritz Perls and his Gestalt psychotherapy, I was intrigued by a quotation of his. "To suffer one's death and to be reborn is not easy." I was drawn to this, knowing it contained a vital truth for me. It resonated with the deadness of depression I was feeling, and the promised rebirth was very compelling. But it was more than that. I knew there was profound life poetry in this statement. Growing up in New York, I had watched the seasons change for all the years of my life. This supported me in understanding cycles of birth and death. For shamans, death is a vital part of the healing process. We have to let our old dreams, nightmares, fantasies, dysfunctional ways of coping, and entire selves die, to be reborn again.

▼

Death is a vital part of the process of renewal and growth. In a shamanic context, death is an initiation allowing us to fully embrace our core selves and authenticity. In this death we surrender to Spirit, moving beyond the imagined safety of our roles and inner power struggles. Throughout this book we have been connecting to Spirit to gather what we need on a deep level while letting go of all that no longer serves us. We've been engaged in a sort of dismantling of the old self, chakra by chakra. In this chapter we will fully surrender this old self in all its pieces to Spirit. Like the horseshoe crab that must surrender its old shell to grow, so must we surrender our old selves to be reborn.

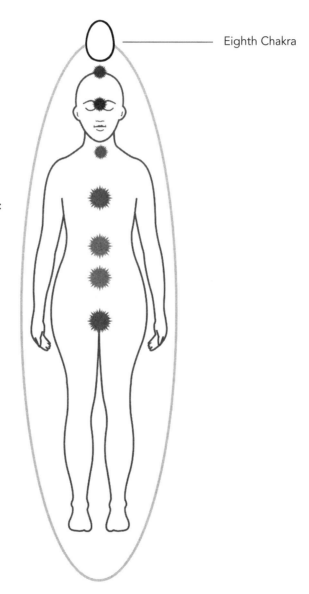

Eighth Chakra

Color: White Light

Element: Expansion

Developmental Age:
70+ years

Spiritual Strength:
Radiance

Developmental Crisis:
Expansion versus
Limiting Attachment

Fig. 8.1. Eighth Chakra

Rebirth provides us with the opportunity to put the pieces together in a whole new way, infusing and integrating them with life and spiritual energies. If you have performed all the previous tasks in this book, you may be ready to let yourself "die" so you may be reborn as a shaman. This involves surrendering your sense of separateness, and embracing the community of shamans and its mission of providing service to the greater good.

The previous exercises in this book have supported us in connecting to the spiritual forces in the universe and the spiritual strengths within ourselves. We are now capable of releasing into a total expansion of consciousness where we fully identify with the spirit and its eternal nature and have the courage to recognize the mortality of the body and ego. Now it becomes completely safe and necessary to release our attachment to the body and whatever has not already fallen away. We must let go of the troublesome or superfluous aspects of the ego so we can move on to this next stage of development. It is time to experience being pure essence, beyond the vehicles of expression for our spirit which are the body, emotions, mind, and soul.

The eighth chakra is often referred to as the human aura, or the energy field within and surrounding the physical body. It radiates out from the center of the body to an average of three feet or more around a healthy person. The energy that is generated from the spinning of all the chakras creates the aura, so the aura embodies all the colors of the spectrum. The aura is an energetic container for our wholeness. As we work on our issues and resolve what drains our energy needlessly, we receive energy from the universe, retain it, and expand.

The universe is expanding, and the more we align with this dynamic the better our lives can be. For us to transcend old patterns and to fully express lives of beauty, we must connect with the essential universal element or dynamic of expansion. Because we have worked through our energy consuming wounds, we now have the capacity to connect, hold, and dance with these infinite energies of the universe. The element of the eighth chakra, then, is infinite expansion. Paradoxically, infinite expansion is made possible by successfully completing the tasks in the preceding chakras, becoming powerfully grounded.

This chakra embodies the age of seventy plus, an age of uncompromising maturity and ability to move through the spiritual growth process with greater ease. The crisis of this time is full identification with Spirit versus identification with the ego and body. At this stage, we need to fully understand that we are Spirit as we express ourselves through the vehicles of the soul, mind, emotions, and body. It becomes important to identify with the self that is eternal, as death of the body and its return to the earth will come inevitably at the end of this stage. To know this self is a source of great power, and this knowledge can lead to acts of profound courage. The greatness of our spirits can expand well beyond the confines of the vehicles of expression (body, emotions, mind, soul), the limitations of our egos, and the structures of our lives.

We all will have an opportunity to experience this phenomenon at some point in this stage of life when we die, but we can achieve this expansion before through work with our "death layer." Here we allow ourselves to face our fear of death by surrendering our ego defenses. Energetically, we allow ourselves to know and experience how much our defenses contract our life energy even though they may also support or protect us. By dying in this sense we create a space for Spirit to support us in our deepest authenticity as we experience our greatest vulnerability. Through this dynamic we maximize our ability to expand and find our greatest strength. All the problems we create as humanity have to do with contracting or being less than we can be, rather than expanding.

Wonderful work can be done from this chakra when we have the courage to face our death layer. There is often a stuck place or impasse that exists between recognizing our old patterns and sensing our hurts, and feeling them very deeply so we can fully clean out our old wounds and move on to new life. Often, this impasse needs to be overcome with the support of a therapist or shaman. It is helpful in this process to know that we are Spirit moving through an evolving soul, and mental, emotional, and physical bodies.

CONNECTING TO DEATH

From the time I did my first Gestalt work at age eighteen with my therapist Hermene and truly let myself sob and fall into the pit of intense emotion in my belly, I have believed in this spiritual process of death and rebirth as the most essential healing dynamic. It truly allows the fibers and molecules of one's being to reconfigure. The doorway to death can open at any point, but it is best to be very connected with supportive energies, guides, and a sense of your own strength first.

I suggest connecting to death as an eighth-chakra task because it gives you plenty of time to develop the necessary supports and protections. At the right time, when one has adequate supports, allowing ourselves to "die" enables transitions that would not occur otherwise, such as the release of deeply entrenched life-squashing defenses. As I allowed myself to be skillfully led through the death layer, denial about the abusive dynamics of my family of origin lifted and I was able to get to deeper levels where healing was needed because I had the strength to face the truth.

In my shamanic and psychotherapy practices, I have taken many people on this journey to death, to their core, to find their life. It can be fierce and loud and painful, or it can be gentle. Like any process of death and birth, it can have many phases, many faces, and many variables. When you die and are reborn in the shamanic sense, you are the ancient one, the new baby, and the midwife.

The journey we will take during this task can be summed up by using a map of the layers of the personality (fig. 8.2), inspired by Fritz Perls and Gestalt psychotherapy. On this journey, we will spiral through the concentric circles on the left from the outside in, and the concentric circles on the right from the inside out. We begin by releasing our superficial selves and all the games we play (layer A). We will let go of the roles and defenses that keep us from expressing our authenticity (layer B). We will let go of our hurt child, whose wounds we have addressed in the previous tasks, and our inner victim and victimizer, who may still perpetuate these hurts (layer C).

Continuing to spiral inward, we come to the death layer (layer D). This is the place we fear surrendering to, because if we surrender to it, we are afraid we will die. Spiritually, the death layer is the place where we know we will leave our physical, emotional, and mental bodies one day at the end of this incarnation, as our soul and spirit continue on. Psychologically, it is usually a place of powerful emotions. As we acknowledge our own inevitable death and our spirit's eternal life, we recognize what is truly vital about our core selves. All that is superficial must fall away, leaving only the eternal and the essential. The essential is our spirit, our true life. In this journey, we surrender to death, allowing the implosion, explosion, and release to life in its greatest sense (layer E of the drawing on the left and layer 1 of the one on the right).

From this journey inward, we now begin to emerge. As we spiral outward we acquire healthy coping mechanisms (layer 2 on drawing at right), affirm our authenticity (layer 3), bring forth joyful expressions of Spirit (layer 4), and, finally, expand into connection with Spirit (layer 5). To fully shapeshift into expansion at this level beyond mastery, we

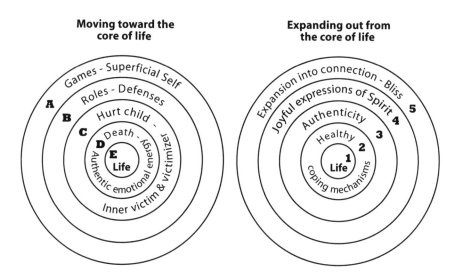

Fig. 8.2. Map of the Layers of the Personality

have to acknowledge ourselves as part of the collective energy of the universe—we all are one.

Once we recognize the immortal within us, we recognize that same spirit within all other beings. This immortal spirit is one spirit, our Spirit. When we recognize our true selves, we see that we and all other beings are actually Spirit. As our separateness dies, we are free to connect with the sacred hoops of knowledge of our collective wholeness and weave vital webs of consciousness within our human family.

One shamanic client of mine struggled with issues of abandonment. She was in a relationship with a partner she loved deeply, but who could not show up for her consistently, emotionally or physically, no matter how many hoops (of the lower or ego-mind variety) she jumped through. My client believed this partner was her soul mate. This client's parents were both very narcissistic and had totally abandoned her emotionally in her childhood and her adulthood. But they paid excessive attention to the externals in her life, such as her dramatic and musical talents and her role as the good daughter. She embraced these and other talents as her parents wished and became extremely successful manifesting them in the world despite the absence of any nurturing from her parents.

By allowing them to feel a part of her success but refusing to confront them about their total lack of emotional support, she was, in effect, parenting her parents. In her relationship with her partner, she was replicating her childhood experience, pretending her partner was more capable of a mature, loving relationship than this person actually was.

I encouraged her to "die" into her pain about the relationship. She saw the games she was playing to maintain the illusion about the relationship (fig. 8.2, layer A), and how she played the role of parent/dutiful daughter (layer B) to make up for her partner's failure to hold up her end of the relationship. She felt and moved through the layer of the hurt child, where she could see how her parents victimized her in the past and how she was revictimizing herself now (layer C). She let herself "die" into her death layer, her feelings of abandonment, while immersing herself in the reality that her parents were not there for her heart (layer D).

This was very hard for her to do and required exceptional courage. This client needed to let herself sob for hours while her guides and I held her. She felt as though she *were* dying as her heart was breaking.

A couple of months later, she was able to leave this relationship, fully connecting to her life energy (layers E and 1). This client was able to begin to feel she deserved more and could reach out to healthier people (layer 2). She has been able to have a couple of subsequent relationships in which her partners have been more present and consistent, providing an opportunity for her to relax her roles and defenses and express more of the authenticity she has become committed to (layer 3). She was able to expand gradually beyond her old patterns into greater satisfaction and joy (layer 4). She is now spending more time with her meditation practice and is more fully committed to connecting with her spirit guides, feeling their supportive presence (layer 5). This supports her in continuing to grow and to avoid reverting to old patterns.

▼

Over the course of many years, I have developed a relationship with Kali, the Hindu goddess of death, transformational rage, rebirth, dance, and blood. She will be the central presence in this journey to encounter our death. I first connected with her when I was twenty-three years old and needed to let the rage from my childhood and young adulthood move through my physical body so it could be fully released. She supported me in my death and birth into shamanism.

I encountered her more consciously when I was raped at age twenty-nine and did not know if I would live or die. As I endured being held captive that night, she held me in my terror, a compassionate mother. Feeling her presence, I understood that my world was shapeshifting, shrinking and then cracking open into new understandings and possibilities as I shivered in my sleeplessness. Time seemed suspended and endless. As the hours passed, the world expanded for me once again. I saw a need for the healing of humanity at large, the balance of the sacred feminine and masculine. So many dangers lurked beyond the scope of my self-empowerment. In some part of myself, I knew that if I could hang in there, I would be supported and guided in making a difference beyond the small circle of my own world.

We will now journey to the cave of Kali. Allow your spirit guide to journey with you. Through spiritual death and rebirth, this task will open you to knowledge of the element of this eighth chakra, the full expansion of your being. Though this shamanic task is a gentle one, it is very powerful.

❖ Task One: A Journey to Death

Start this journey in your sacred place. Connect to it fully and sensually; feel its nurturance. Connect to a power animal or spirit guide who will be your companion on this journey. Spend a little time really feeling centered in nonordinary reality. Be ready to let go of all that holds you back in any way. From working on all of the previous tasks, you probably have a very clear idea of what these things are.

Traveling through nonordinary reality, see the opening to Kali's cave. It is a sacred *yoni,* or vaginal opening, to Mother Earth. Enter, taking this invitation to return to the womb for healing and transformation. As you descend through rock, earth, roots, streams, and tunnels, you find a large open space with pits of molten lava and the smell of deep, inner heat. There are many fires burning, cauldrons bubbling.

You hear her laughter, a compelling cackling that embraces the ironies, the paradoxes of this dance of life and death, creation and destruction. You cannot help but move toward her, as you know she is the next portal to your growth. You feel the desire for transcendence with a passion surpassing what you have felt for your most compelling lover.

Then you see her. She is breathtakingly beautiful as she turns to you with her ravenous smile. You are captivated by the fire in her eyes. You move toward her, wanting your freedom, wanting with insatiable hunger to know your essence. She dances with the bloody flames of her cave and then becomes them as she devours you. She holds you and engulfs you and lovingly releases you as your ego and old dynamics vanish to the space between life and death that exists within all spirits and beings. All the games, roles, wounds, and scars are being incinerated. As you surrender to your death, allow yourself powerful sounds of release, screams, wails, sobs, moans. Then let the quiet engulf you. For moments, or for eternity, you are all that is. In this moment you may feel oneness with all of existence, released into the collective consciousness of being.

Soon, you find yourself in a pool of sacred water, an earth womb. You are floating, or swimming freely, accompanied in some way by your power animal or spirit guide. Breathe to support your rebirth, perhaps a connected ujjai breath, as you are born from this amniotic sea. Perhaps you will be born through a passageway to a beautiful river that flows with your life force. At some point, you become conscious of your self and your rebirth, free from old, unnecessary layers. Allow yourself to experience this liberation as you flow downstream, moving with your guide to your sacred place. Feel how you can handle all that is in your life from a place of power. Feel the pulse of your life force energy. Allow yourself to express joy regarding your rebirth through sound, whoops, laughter, and song. Feel yourself as a part of everything beautiful.

Integrate this experience in your sacred place. Review the experience of dying and being reborn with your guide and explore how it feels and what it has meant to you. Express your gratitude to Kali for the opportunity to die and to be reborn. Feel your resilience, essence, and freedom.

When you are ready, come back into ordinary reality. Feel the rebirth in your physical and energy body. Take the time to also experience your emotions and your mind. How did this journey facilitate the evolution of your soul? How are the parts of yourself coming together after this transformation to create a new, powerful whole? Know that you can experience your life energy fully as you embrace healthier coping mechanisms and authenticity. Fully ground yourself by breathing and feeling your connection to the earth. Feel your expanded, radiant energy and connection to Spirit.

We will now spend a little time feeling the auric field within and around the physical body. The aura can be differentiated into fields that correspond to the chakras. The first chakra corresponds to the physical body and its energy is contained there. The second chakra corresponds to the emotional body, which energetically radiates slightly out from the physical body. The third chakra corresponds to the mental body, which radiates out beyond the emotional body. The fourth chakra corresponds to the body of the soul, which radiates out beyond the mental body. The fifth, sixth, and seventh chakras correspond to your spirit and spirit body, which radiate out beyond the soul's body. The soul is the part of the self that has evolved in prior lifetimes and continues to evolve through this lifetime. Our spirit is the aspect of ourselves that is already evolved, illuminated, enlightened consciousness.

As the chakras do, this spirit body has aspects corresponding to expression (fifth chakra), wisdom (sixth chakra), and connection of the spirit as it relates to your embodied being and all beings and spirits everywhere (seventh chakra). The eighth chakra is the completeness or wholeness of the energy field. It expresses the integration of the spiraling light energy of the chakras into one complete radiance, connected to all the radiance of life and consciousness in the universe.

As the shaman, you may work with these bodies—the physical, emotional, mental, soul, and spirit bodies that comprise the aura or the eighth chakra—in supporting yourself and others in their healing. You can energize and balance these bodies, and work with images and guiding spirits that emerge from these bodies, very much as you worked with the chakras in the channeling exercise in chapter seven. You may be drawn to working with your hands and consciousness in the aura and bringing through healing images from your contact with this eighth chakra.

At this point in your journey through this book, I strongly recommend spending time each day performing one physical task for each of the chakras (perhaps mountain, wave, triangle, tree, bridge, yoga mudra, downward dog) while being aware of the deeper significance and impact of your movements. Then you will be ready to do the following integrative exercise in which you trace and feel the entirety of your aura. The yoga movement we will use in this task is called Sun Breath.

⟨⟩ Task Two: Experiencing the Auric Field

Start by standing with your feet hip-width apart and your hands in Prayer pose. As you inhale, reach up to the sun, palms facing forward, gathering the sun energy. You may squeeze your gluteal muscles to protect the lower back as you gently arch the upper back, heart, and upper belly gently reaching up toward the sky.

As you exhale, open the arms out to the sides to shoulder height and, hinging at the hips with the knees gently bent, "swan dive" down to the earth, bringing your arms down and forward. In this exercise, your arms trace a circle, your aura, around your body. When you reach the earth in a soft forward bending position the arms are hanging toward the ground.

Begin your inhale now as you roll up from the earth, hands coming into Prayer pose again as you straighten. Inhale fully, bringing the hands up through the midline of the body, up above the head again, gathering the sun energy. Exhale down, swan dive, tracing the aura around the body again, filling it with light energy from the heavens. Inhale up again, bringing rich magnetic energy from Mother Earth through the midline of the body. Repeat at least ten times, strengthening your aura.

When you are finished energizing and balancing your aura through this task, feel the energy within and all around you. Feel how you are grounded, centered, and expanded, connected to the kundalini and to prana, the light energy from the heavens. Feel your core of strength and your radiant aura.

From this place of wholeness, it is time to gather your inner council. The inner council is the energetic, conscious coming together of all your inner selves from each chakra, along with your guide or guides for each chakra, your power animals, and your sacred objects. Your inner council will help you to examine the challenges you face from a thorough, expanded perspective. You will only want to call a meeting of this council when you need to address the larger questions of life, as working with such a large group can be somewhat cumbersome for less weighty issues.

For some actions we need to take in life, it is vital to come from the fullest integrity possible. At these times it is good to feel our wholeness embodied in our sacred inner council. This council mirrors the fullness of our eighth chakra and its dynamic, expansive nature.

⊸⊱ Task Three: Connecting with Your Inner Council

Sit with a question that you are asking from the level of your soul or heart. This should be an important question, perhaps regarding a decision you have to make or an action you may have to take. Journal about this question with an intention to clarify as much as you can about the situation.

Get into a comfortable position and allow yourself to relax and journey to your sacred place. Experience it through your senses. Connect with the wisdom of your sacred place. Ask your sacred place to show you where you will have the meeting of your inner council. It may be part of your sacred place, or you may be led to another place. Sit in the council meeting area and ask your inner wisdom if this is indeed exactly the right spot for your inner council meeting. If it is, begin to invite the cast of characters.

For your sacred inner council meeting, you need to invite all aspects of yourself, including all of your developmental stages. Perhaps you will be able to visualize your physical form in its manifestation at particular developmental stages. You will have to use your imagination for stages you have not yet reached, but don't let that stop you from inviting these parts of you to the meeting. You will also want to invite all your power animals and spirit guides. Perhaps you have one for each of the chakras. It is also good to invite your sacred objects, as they may have wisdom to share.

Bring the important question to all your inner developmental selves and to all your guides and all your sacred objects. Allow everyone to feel supported by Mother Earth and Spirit as they think and feel.

Allow all the members of the council to share, each from her or his perspective. Some will share in words, some in images, some in energies. You may want to suggest that they pass a talking stick or other object if this creates the order necessary for you to listen to everyone's perspective.

At the end of the sharing, perhaps the council as a whole will have a message of collective guidance. If they do, it is wise to follow this guidance with respect to the question you have asked. If they don't, you may allow yourself to simply feel a greater sense of integration, as all parts of you have been allowed a voice. Collective messages may also come at a later time.

Express your gratitude to all aspects of yourself, your guides, your sacred objects, and Spirit. Spend some time in solitude and integration in your sacred place if that feels right. When you are ready, journey back to ordinary reality.

BECOMING A SHAMAN

Now it is time, from this place of infinite expansion of Spirit, to connect with the "spirit of the shaman." By "dying," being reborn, and reintegrating and identifying with our expansive nature, our eighth chakra or aura is open to connect with this shaman energy. This process has prepared us to become a shaman if that is what we choose. We will start by connecting to the shaman within.

❧ Task Four: Receiving a Name from Spirit

Start by going to your sacred place, fully experiencing it, as you have many times before. See what is new and evolving about your sacred place. In your sacred place, see the shaman version of yourself emerging, as if from a fog, and walking toward you. What do you look like? What is your physical body wearing? Are you holding anything? Do you carry sacred objects from your journey and tradition? What is your visceral sense of yourself as the shaman?

Watch yourself as this shaman, performing your healing ceremony in your sacred place, for your deep connection with the spirit of the shaman. In this ceremony, you may want to plant the seed you hold for fully actualizing yourself and your dream (chapter 5, task 5). Observe this ceremony so you can repeat as necessary in ordinary reality.

Now, allow yourself to become the shaman. Feel your observing self merge with the observed version of yourself as the shaman. Know that you have become the shaman through your willingness to walk the courageous road outlined in these pages and the pages of your life. How does your energy body feel as you merge with the spirit of the shaman that is you? Feel your true power. Ask what your mission is as the shaman. As you are planting your deepest seed and watching it grow, notice if what manifests is different than your previous understanding of your dream.

Does Spirit give you a name as the shaman? Listen for your true name of power. Hear all your guides and supportive beings call you by your true name.

When Don Jose, the Ecuadorian shaman, conducted a series of three private healing ceremonies for me, he strengthened my energetic connection to Mother Earth (Pachamama), the Creator God (God in Heaven), and the "spirit of the shaman," or lineage of healers and saints throughout time. Now we will journey to join that community of shamans. It is vital as a shaman to feel connected to a community of shamans; otherwise you can feel lonely. The support that healers have for one another can be wonderful, and group intentions and extensions of consciousness are infinitely more powerful than what we can do as individuals. As all cultures have their unique strengths, shamans from other cultures have wisdom to share from their perspective. As we join with them we are continuing to expand, gathering energy and wisdom to address the issues of collective humanity.

◈ Task Five: Joining the Community of Shamans

Again, allow yourself to journey to your sacred place, your home in nonordinary reality. Connect with your power animals and guides. Then, journey beyond your sacred place and find the meeting place for the community of shamans. Shamans throughout the world, the universe, and time will be present there. What is this spectacular meeting place like?

What is it like to meet with all of these great shamans? Perhaps a few of them are already your guides, whom you know quite well. Some of them are spirits you've heard of. And some are totally unfamiliar. They may include power animals, saints, people from sacred literature, your ancestors of great character, gods, goddesses, prophets, healers, artists, politicians with vision, and philosophers.

See the configuration of this meeting of shamans, including yourself. Do you meet in a great circle? A pyramid? Or a sacred lotus? Experience the lattice of these great beings. Who in this group compels you, touches your heart the most?

What is the mission of this larger group, this community of shamans? How are you a vital part of this collective mission? Take comfort in being a part of this sacred group while acknowledging the challenging journey of every individual participant. Feel the collective strength of energy, character, and heart. Really feel how the whole is greater than the sum of all its parts as you gather the strength to continue the mission.

When you are ready to come back to your sacred place and then ordinary reality, know that you are part of something much greater. Know that we dream this world of balance and beauty together.

We are now ready to begin our last task: healing the world family. This is an expanded version of the ancestral healing in the previous chapter. We will move beyond our individual, direct familial bloodline. This task focuses only on our human family, as other species and beings have not created and perpetuated the imbalances that we seek to address here.

Having performed all of the previous tasks in this book you are uniquely prepared to do this level of expansive dreaming. By dying and being reborn you have demonstrated your willingness and courage to release the old form of self, get in touch with your immortal spirit, and expand into new life. With this experience you are in a position to encourage other people to release the old forms and embrace Spirit so we can shapeshift humanity together. You now have the courage to invest, at the powerful energetic level, in a healthy world for generations of our grandchildren and their grandchildren, and to manifest your passion for this dream at the level of ordinary reality as well. Expansive dreaming must be followed by courageous acts.

◆ Task Six: Healing the Human Family

Start this journey in your sacred place. Feel the power there. Connect with the elements through your senses. Know that your intention is to bring healing to the world family. Contact all your spirit guides and feel their presence.

Allow your consciousness to expand beyond your sacred place to your world family's sacred place, Mother Earth. Expand to hold all of Mother Earth in your consciousness. Humble yourself so you can feel all of her. Know that you and all creatures and beings are made in her image. Feel your connection to the whole world family.

When you are ready, ask yourself the following questions and journey to receive the answers:

What groups are you a part of? (These include your nation, race, religion, ethnic heredity, class, gender, sexual preference, political and social ideologies, and so on.) Who has this group exploited or violated, and who has exploited or violated this group? What healing does this group need? How can you offer healing to this group? Imagine this group both making and receiving amends. Feel supported by the spirit of the shamans. Transitioning between nonordinary and ordinary reality, or perhaps beginning to sense how you can hold both states simultaneously, journal as you explore this process. Healing images may come to you. Allow their energy to radiate to balance humanity.

Be thorough with this task, addressing every group you are connected to. When you are finished you will feel a sense of completeness; there is no one in your web of life or energetic community who has been left untouched by your healing energy. Everyone will feel held in your expanded aura and taken care of in ways you hadn't imagined. It may take several sittings to complete this task. When you are finished with the spiritual healing aspect of the task, ask Spirit what you can do in ordinary reality to support your best wishes for our human family. It is good to have at least one task to perform each day, large or small, that supports this dreaming in ordinary reality.

Through completing the tasks in this book and expanding my consciousness, I have become acutely aware of how the collective human energy body is hurting. I hope to begin to heal our human family by centering on areas where I have had the greatest energetic connection in my lifetime.

I begin this task by looking at my socioeconomic perspective. It seems I have almost always lived on the upper end of lower class or the lower end of middle class. When I have allowed myself to really look, I have been struck by the heartbreak and preventable damage that certain types of economic deprivation can create. And I have been saddened and disgusted by the oblivious, self-centered, self-righteous excesses I see demonstrated by the classes "above" mine.

I dream a world where everyone has the health care they require and adequate, safe housing. I must dream a world where no babies remain hungry. I understand that much of the hunger and deprivation in this world are not because we cannot produce enough for all, but because some take much more than their fair share while others go without. I wish for everyone to understand that people are not born victims of poverty, hunger, or violence because they deserve to be.

I dream a world where everyone feels the love of Mother Earth and the divine paternal energy of Spirit dancing together in ecstasy, rather than being at odds with each other.

As expanded beings we must make amends for the harm we have done to others, because we come to understand energetically that the other is us—we are all one. As a European American, I have inherited group karma from ancestors who wiped out almost entire races of indigenous people from these lands and others, along with the species and beings that supported their way of life. We egregiously pollute the earth on this and other continents. I also have inherited the karma of people who built a country on the backs of slaves, extolling the virtues of self-determination while squeezing the lifeblood of freedom and dignity out of others. So as a European American, I clearly have amends and reparations to make. I have begun this journey of amends by stating this truth here.

I dream a world where European Americans step up to make these amends and reparations. We cannot evolve out of this dynamic other-wise. I dream a world where we feel our spiritual connections and do not take more from the earth than we need. We will not have to exploit, violate, and destroy others if we are not taking more than we need. If we feel our connection, spiritually and energetically, to Mother Earth and the light energy of the universe, we will not be afraid. And if we are not afraid, we will not be greedy. And if we are not greedy, we will not hurt other beings and spirits. There is an ecstasy in this simple connection that exceeds anything produced by our feeble, lethal human dramas.

Lastly, I am part of this group called women. Despite the fact that the United States has been in existence for more than two hundred years, women have had the right to vote for less than a hundred. As of this writing, we have never had a woman elected to lead the executive branch of the federal government. For centuries, my female ancestors were prohibited from acquiring and holding capital and property.

On the surface it might appear that these inequities are now a thing of the past, but a closer look reveals that the patriarchal streak in the institutions of marriage and the nuclear family is still thriving and protected in America. Women usually do most of the housework even though they work outside the home just as hard as men do, and children almost always take their father's names. When a couple gets divorced the woman almost always ends up poorer than her male counterpart. As recently as three decades ago, when I reported my stepfather's abuse the police supported him by refusing to interfere in family matters.

Women need healing. In so many ways, they have stepped into their power and created much social, political, and economic revolution, and it needs to continue. Women of all ages, nationalities, races, creeds, and classes need to know that they can step into their power and not be abused, raped, and exploited. I envision a world where this is universally true. I envision their power growing beyond the shame and confinement of traditional patriarchal religion as they reunite the split parts of their sexual energy, the virgin and the whore. I sense women holding and determining the expression of their sexuality in its full, grand sacredness. I dream that we unplug from the media and the propaganda that would have us forever disempowered in unhealthy thinness, surgically and pharmaceutically enhanced. I dream that all women come to know deeply that we are the earth and the ocean of life, and we can dream, speak, and act from a place of deep, expansive, authentic authority.

▼

As humans, we are made in the image of Mother Earth. The shamans and indigenous people have taught me that the very survival of humanity depends on honoring her in every moment, in every way, as she is bathed in the sacred, masculine light of consciousness from the heavens.

As we expand, grow old, and die, our children, grandchildren, and great-grandchildren are being born. I have tried to be fearless in unearthing my soul and its transformation in this book, bringing my dream for healing humanity into action. As we heal ourselves, the village of our culture, with its collective wisdom, can raise its children with greater integrity. I dream this with all my heart. The world of Spirit, of Pachamama, and of the universe holds us all, always, in our infinite humanity, her loving arms wrapped around us as we grow.

Bibliography

Al-Rawi, Rosina-Fawzia. *Grandmother's Secrets: The Ancient Rituals and Healing Power of Belly Dancing*. Brooklyn: Interlink Books, 1999.

Anand, Margot. *The Art of Everyday Ecstasy: The Seven Tantric Keys for Bringing Passion, Spirit, and Joy into Every Part of Your Life*. New York: Broadway Books, 1998.

Awiakta, Marilou. *Selu: Seeking the Corn Mother's Wisdom*. Golden, Colo.: Fulcrum Publishing, 1993.

Bruyere, Roslyn L. *Wheels of Light*. New York: Fireside, 1994.

Cowan, Tom. *Shamanism: As a Spiritual Practice for Daily Life*. Berkeley, Calif.: The Crossing Press, 1996.

Eagle, Brooke Medicine. *Buffalo Woman Comes Singing*. New York: Ballantine Books, 1991.

Ensler, Eve. *The Good Body*. New York: Villard Books, 2005.

———. *The Vagina Monologues*. New York: Villard Books, 2001.

Evans, Joel M., and Robin Aronson. *The Whole Pregnancy Handbook: An Obstetrician's Guide to Integrating Conventional and Alternative Medicine Before, During and After Pregnancy*. New York: Gotham Books, 2005.

Feiler, Bruce. *Abraham: A Journey to the Heart of Three Faiths*. New York: Perennial, 2004.

Goldstein, Eda G. *Ego Psychology and Social Work Practice*. New York: The Free Press, 1984.

Gregg, Susan. *The Toltec Way: A Guide to Personal Transformation.* Los Angeles: Renaissance Books, 2000.

Halifax, Joan. *Shamanic Voices: A Survey of Visionary Narratives.* New York: Penguin Group, 1979.

Harner, Michael. *The Way of the Shaman: A Guide to Power and Healing.* New York: Bantam Books, 1980.

Khalsa, Gurmukh Kaur. *The Eight Human Talents: The Yogic Way to Restore the Balance and Serenity Within You.* New York: HarperCollins, 2000.

King, Martin Luther, Jr. *I Have a Dream: Writings and Speeches That Changed the World.* New York: HarperSanFrancisco, 1992.

Leloup, Jean-Yves. *The Gospel of Mary Magdalene.* Rochester, Vt.: Inner Traditions, 2002.

Mandela, Nelson. *Long Walk to Freedom: The Autobiography of Nelson Mandela.* Boston: Back Bay Books, 1995.

Miller, Alice. *For Your Own Good: Hidden Cruelty in Child-Rearing and the Roots of Violence.* New York: Farrar, Straus & Giroux, 1984.

———. *Thou Shalt Not Be Aware: Society's Betrayal of the Child.* New York: Meridian, 1986.

Moore, Michael. *Dude, Where's My Country?* New York: Warner Books, Inc., 2003.

Narby, Jeremy. *The Cosmic Serpent: DNA and the Origins of Knowledge.* New York: Penguin Group, 1998.

The New American Bible. Compiled by the United States Conference of Catholic Bishops. Nashville: Catholic Bible Press, 1987.

Perkins, John. *Confessions of an Economic Hit Man.* San Francisco: Berrett-Koehler Publishers Inc., 2004.

———. *Shapeshifting: Techniques for Global and Personal Transformation.* Rochester, Vt.: Destiny Books, 1997.

———. *The World Is As You Dream It: Teachings from the Amazon and Andes.* Rochester, Vt.: Destiny Books, 1994.

Perls, Frederick, Ralph F. Hefferline, and Paul Goodman. *Ego, Hunger and Aggression: The Gestalt Therapy of Sensory Awakening through Spontaneous Personal Encounter, Fantasy and Contemplation.* New York: Vision Books, 1969.

———. *Gestalt Therapy: Excitement and Growth in the Human Personality.* New York: Bantam, 1951.

———. *Gestalt Therapy Verbatim*. New York: A Bantam Book, 1959.

Pritchard, Evan T. *No Word for Time: The Way of the Algonquin People*. San Francisco: Council Oak Books, 1997.

Sachs, Jeffrey D. *The End of Poverty: Economic Possibilities for Our Time*. New York: Penguin Books, 2005.

Sams, Jamie. *The 13 Original Clan Mothers: Your Sacred Path to Discovering the Gifts, Talents and Abilities of the Feminine Through the Ancient Teachings of the Sisterhood*. New York: HarperCollins, 1994.

Sanchez, Victor. *Toltecs of the New Millennium*. Santa Fe: Bear & Company, Inc., 1996.

Specht, Riva, and Grace J. Craig. *Human Development: A Social Work Perspective*. New Jersey: Prentice-Hall, Inc., 1987.

Steinem, Gloria. *Moving Beyond Words: Age, Rage, Sex, Power, Money, Muscles: Breaking Boundaries of Gender*. New York: Simon & Schuster, 1994.

———. *Outrageous Acts and Everyday Rebellions*. New York: Holt, Rinehart, and Winston, 1983.

———. *Revolution from Within: A Book of Self-Esteem*. Boston: Little, Brown, and Company, 1992.

Tiwari, Bri Maya. *The Path of Practice: A Woman's Book of Ayurvedic Healing*. New York: Ballantine Publishing Group, 2000.

Trattner, Walter I. *From Poor Law to Welfare State: A History of Social Welfare in America*. New York: The Free Press, 1989.

Villoldo, Alberto. *Shaman, Healer, Sage: How to Heal Yourself and Others with the Energy of Medicine of the Americas*. New York: Harmony Books, 2000.

Walker, Alice. *Sent by Earth: A Message from the Grandmother Spirit after the Bombing of the World Trade Center and the Pentagon*. New York: Seven Stories Press, 2002.

Walker, Barbara G. *The Woman's Encyclopedia of Myths and Secrets*. New York: Harper & Row, 1983.

List of Tasks and Exercises

Index